ORIGINS OF TERRORISM

Origins of terrorism

Psychologies, ideologies, theologies, states of mind

Edited by
WALTER REICH

Published by the
WOODROW WILSON CENTER PRESS
Washington, D.C.

Distributed by the
JOHNS HOPKINS UNIVERSITY PRESS
Baltimore and London

The Woodrow Wilson Center Press
Editorial Offices
One Woodrow Wilson Plaza
1300 Pennsylvania Avenue, N.W.
Washington, D.C. 20004 U.S.A.
telephone 202-691-4000

Distributed by
The Johns Hopkins University Press
P.O. Box 50370
Baltimore, Maryland 21211
order department telephone 1-800-537-5487

9 8

Library of Congress Cataloging-in-Publication Data

Origins of terrorism : psychologies, ideologies, theologies,
states of mind / edited by Walter Reich.
p.   cm.
Originally published: Washington, D.C. : Woodrow Wilson
International Center for Scholars;
Cambridge; New York : Cambridge University Press, 1990, in series:
Woodrow Wilson Center series.
With new foreword.
Includes bibliographical references and index.
ISBN 0-943875-89-7 (pbk. : alk. paper)
1. Terrorism—Psychological aspects. 2. Terrorists—Psychology.
I. Reich, Walter, 1943–
HV6431.O74   1998
303.6'25—dc21   98-24652
                                                      CIP

For my children,
Daniel, David, and Rebecca

WOODROW WILSON INTERNATIONAL CENTER FOR SCHOLARS

BOARD OF TRUSTEES

The Center is the living memorial of the United States of America to the nation's twenty-eighth president, Woodrow Wilson. The U.S. Congress established the Woodrow Wilson Center in 1968 as an international institute for advanced study, "symbolizing and strengthening the fruitful relationship between the world of learning and the world of public affairs." The Center opened in 1970 under its own board of trustees, which includes citizens appointed by the president of the United States, federal government officials who serve ex officio, and an additional representative named by the president from within the federal government.

In all its activities, the Woodrow Wilson Center is a nonprofit, nonpartisan organization, supported financially by annual appropriations from the U.S. Congress, and by the contributions of foundations, corporations, and individuals.

Woodrow Wilson Center Press

The Woodrow Wilson Center Press publishes books written in substantial part at the Center or otherwise prepared under its sponsorship by fellows, guest scholars, staff members, and other program participants. Conclusions or opinions expressed in Center publications and programs are those of the authors and speakers and do not necessarily reflect the views of the Center staff, fellows, trustees, advisory groups, or any individuals or organizations that provide financial support to the Center.

Contents

Part III. States of mind: How do terrorists think? Which psychological mechanisms enable them to do what they do?

Part IV. Responding to terrorism: Decision making and the pressures on leadership

Part V. The psychology of terrorism: What can we know? What must we learn?

Foreword

Since this collection of essays was first conceived, the subject matter has become of even greater importance than it originally was. There are few studies on the psychological sources of terrorism and this for obvious reasons. It is a most difficult topic to investigate and discuss; there are few guiding posts in this uncharted territory and a great many pitfalls.

The character of terrorism is undergoing changes in our age; as the old, "traditional" terrorist movements continue to operate, new ones have appeared, more now on the extreme right of the political spectrum than on the left, activist religious-sectarian groups have come into being and there has been violence even on the radical fringe of the ecological movement. The borderline between terrorism and some forms of organized crime and narco-terrorism has become far less clear than it used to be.

While some terrorist groups have thousands of members (such as the Algerian Islamists and the Tamil Tigers) others are exceedingly small, and apparently getting smaller. Modern technological developments give unprecedented access to weapons of mass destruction and it is precisely at this point that the psychological dimension of the study of terrorism acquires new importance. Economic, social, and ideological factors can account perhaps for the behavior of large groups of people, but seldom for the operations of a handful. Another important feature is the growing fanaticism (and consequent brutality), which while not entirely new for the student of terrorism, has been more prominent in recent years than during earlier periods. Political analysis per se can seldom account for violence, let alone extreme violence, and while psychology has no magic, all comprehensive formulas concerning such phenomena as aggression, the urge to destroy and the belief in the proximity of Armageddon, it is precisely in this direction that one should look for at least some clues to understand the coming threats.

WALTER LAQUEUR

ix

Preface

This book is a product of a project on the psychological dimensions of terrorism carried out by the Division of International Studies of the Woodrow Wilson International Center for Scholars. Jointly sponsored by the Woodrow Wilson Center and the National Institute of Mental Health, the project consisted of research done by scholars from several countries and many disciplines. Some of this research was done at the Center itself and some at universities and research institutes around the world. All of it was ultimately presented and discussed at a series of conferences and other meetings held at the Center.

This volume is based on this considerable research effort. Its chapters reflect not only the scholarship of their authors but also the comments and criticisms of the many other scholars and behavioral scientists who participated in this project. In the cases of several of the chapters, those comments and criticisms resulted in new research and extensive revisions of substance, language, approach, and perspective. In the cases of all of the chapters, they resulted in an enriched and clarified focus that was further shaped and informed by ongoing developments in the international arena.

None of this would have been possible without the participation of two institutions internationally known for their devotion to, and support of, scholarship and research.

I am indebted, first of all, to the Woodrow Wilson Center, which welcomed the project, embraced it, and gave it a rich and intellectually vibrant home. Located in Washington, D.C., and established by Congress as "a living institution expressing the ideals and concerns of Woodrow Wilson . . . symbolizing and strengthening the fruitful relationship between the world of learning and the world of public affairs," the Center's administrators and staff saw the project as an opportunity to generate new research and scholarship in the service of understanding, and contending with, vexing international challenges. The Center's Division of International Studies, long devoted to studies of international order and disorder, saw the threat posed by terrorism as a complex one requiring novel avenues of research.

Nor would the work have been possible without the support of the National Institute of Mental Health. Recognizing that the psychological dimensions of terrorism have been poorly understood and little studied, and that such study, to be effectively pursued, requires expertise in the social sciences and humanities as well as in the behavioral sciences, the NIMH, where I served as a senior research psychiatrist, generously permitted me to devote the time necessary to organize this research and edit this book at the Woodrow Wilson Center, which has a rich tradition of interdisciplinary study.

But persons have been no less vital to this project than institutions. In particular, I am indebted to James H. Billington, former director of the Woodrow Wilson Center, and Charles Blitzer, director emeritus; Samuel F. Wells, Jr., deputy director; Robert S. Litwak, the director of its Division of International Studies; Jon E. Yellin, former associate director; and many of the Center's other former and current staff members. Their trust, advice, and friendship, as well as their generous assistance, made the work an immensely satisfying and enriching experience. Special note should be made of the warm, unstinting, and very personal efforts by Sam Wells, Rob Litwak, and Jon Yellin to make all of the human and archival resources of the Center available to me and to the project.

Others whose efforts made this project possible include Shervert H. Frazier and Lewis L. Judd, former directors of the National Institute of Mental Health; Donald I. Macdonald and Frederick K. Goodwin, former administrators of the Alcohol, Drug Abuse, and Mental Health Administration; Robert L. Trachtenberg, that agency's former deputy administrator; C. Everett Koop, the former surgeon general of the United States; former Assistant Surgeon General John C. Duffy; Robert Raclin, formerly deputy undersecretary of the U.S. Department of Health and Human Services; and Seymour S. Kety, senior scientist at the NIMH.

Yet other officials, both elected and appointed, were also extremely helpful in participating in or encouraging the project. They include Ambassador Max M. Kampelman, former chair of the Woodrow Wilson Center's Board of Trustees; Senator Orrin G. Hatch; Congressman Henry A. Waxman; L. Paul Bremer III and Robert Oakley, former ambassadors-at-large for counterterrorism; Robert Friedlander and Carol Rae Hansen, formerly of the staff of the Senate Foreign Relations Committee; Richard Bloom; and Joseph V. Montville.

Several scholars, some of whom wrote chapters for this book, provided valuable advice on the development of this project. I owe especially much to Martha Crenshaw of Wesleyan University; Michel Wieviorka of the Ecole des Hautes Etudes en Sciences Sociales in Paris; Jerrold M. Post of the George Washington University; David C. Rapoport of UCLA; Harry C. Holloway of the Uniformed Services University of the Health Sciences; Walter Laqueur; Conor Cruise O'Brien; and Jo Groebel of the Erziehungswissenschaftliche Hochschule Rheinland-Pfalz in Germany.

Major funding for this effort was provided by the Robert Wood Johnson Jr. Charitable Trust and the Pew Charitable Trusts, with additional support provided by Donald M. Blinken, a former member of the Wilson Council, and Leonard Lauder of Estée Lauder, Inc.

Finally, and emphatically, I am indebted to my former research assistants, Laura Cooley, Eric L. Liebler, and Susan Pratt. Their organizational and editorial efforts, as well as their research skills, brought a welter of ideas, documents, books, words, and people into the kind of order without which neither the project nor this book would have been possible.

This long list hardly exhausts the wealth of human resources and support that helped bring this project to fruition. To those whose names were included above, as well as to those whose names were not included as a result of limitations of space or inexcusable flaws of memory, I am, and will always remain, deeply grateful. I only hope that this book is worthy of their devotion.

WALTER REICH

Introduction

WALTER REICH

This book's focus is on the psychology of terrorism, yet many of its chapters are not concerned primarily with traditional psychological explorations and were written neither by persons who have confined themselves to terrorism studies nor by behavioral scientists. But it is precisely this broadening of subject matter and authorship that this editor, in planning the book, and in choosing the authors of its chapters, hoped to accomplish.

What I hoped to accomplish—a study of terrorism's psychology, but a psychology broadly defined—was something at once risky and, I felt, necessary. Terrorism is a complex problem: Its origins are diverse; and those who engage in it, even more so. Any attempt to understand the motivations and actions of terrorist individuals and groups must obviously take into account that enormous diversity. But no single psychological theory, and no single field of scholarly study, can possibly do that.

Accordingly, I chose, in planning this book, to turn to scholars and researchers with expertise in the many realms that must be understood if terrorist behaviors, world views, and states of mind are to have any chance of being understood. After all, how can the psychology of terrorism be appreciated in even the simplest ways without a prior appreciation of, say, the particular conditions that have shaped the development of terrorism in various countries in Western Europe and the United States? How can the psychology of terrorism be appreciated without a prior appreciation of the rich and vexed religious circumstances and traditions that have contributed to the development of terrorism in the Middle East? And how, for that matter, can the psychology of terrorism be appreciated, particularly the psychological mechanisms that enable terrorists to

1

attack civilians unrelated to the cause in whose name those attacks are launched, without a prior appreciation of the basic psychological mechanisms that enable all human beings to carry out acts that contravene the deepest moral precepts that ordinarily constrain them?

Many of the authors of the chapters in this book are, therefore, distinguished scholars whose primary work has been not in terrorism studies but in other realms—history, for example, or political science, or Islam, or social psychology. But they are also scholars who recognize that knowledge of each of those realms can contribute significantly to an understanding of the ways in which terrorists see the world and behave in it. And, in writing the chapters assigned to them, these scholars drew deeply from that knowledge in order to advance that understanding.

But in carrying out their work they did more than draw on their separate fields. As part of the enterprise of conceptualizing and writing, they met with each other, including the several of them who *are* experts in the historical and psychological dimensions of terrorism, to present drafts of their work and to engage each other in examining and criticizing it. The results of these exchanges were provocative and often illuminating. For example, a specialist on one religion, hearing a social psychologist describe the psychological mechanisms that enable people to disengage themselves from the moral rules that ordinarily constrain their actions, appreciated, in a way he hadn't before, how particular religious explanations can facilitate such disengagements and, therefore, terrorist behavior; and the social psychologist, for his part, hearing others present their work, was able to use it to enrich his. The result, presented in this book, consists of research that is informed both by specialized realms of learning and by the cross-fertilization provided through the process of interdisciplinary study.

One danger that attends any effort to understand a complex phenomenon in psychological terms is the possibility that an attempt will be made to understand it *exclusively* in those terms. This seems an especially acute danger in dealing with the psychology of terrorism: The subject is so confounded by problems of diversity, complexity, and definition that any simplifying approach is bound to tempt one to use it beyond its valid limits. It is for this reason that this book begins, in Part I, with a debate on the ways in which terrorist actions and motivations can best be approached.

One way of approaching such actions and motivations is to assume that they are purely results of strategic choice—that is, logical thinking that is aimed at achieving rational, strategic ends. An alternative way of approaching them is to assume that they are, instead, purely results of psychological forces. Clearly, neither of these approaches offers an adequate explanation of all terrorist behaviors and motivations; and the purpose of the debate in Part I, in which Martha Crenshaw, an immensely accomplished student of terrorist history and strategy, marshals the arguments of the first approach and Jerrold M. Post, who has studied terrorist psychologies, does the same for the second, is to develop these two polar approaches in their purest forms and to enable the reader to recognize that *both* approaches—the analysis of strategy as well as the analysis of psychology—must be used in the attempt to account for most instances and forms of terrorist behavior.

The book then proceeds, in Part II, to examine the varieties of terrorist motivations—that is, the ways in which certain belief systems, particularly ideological and religious ones, contribute to world views that make terrorism attractive to some persons. Konrad Kellen, a specialist on terrorism in Germany; Franco Ferracuti, an Italian psychiatrist; Ehud Sprinzak, an American-educated Israeli political scientist; and Ted Robert Gurr, an expert on violent behaviors and movements, explore the psychological dimensions of ideologically oriented terrorist groups that have emerged within Western democracies; and David C. Rapoport, a historian and political scientist, and Martin Kramer, an expert on Islam, particularly Shi'ism, then focus on terrorist movements that have emerged in the Middle East, especially under the banner of Islam.

I should note that a focus on the Middle East, and especially on Islam, is offered here not because Islam is intrinsically linked to terrorism—it is probably not so linked any more than are, say, Christianity, Judaism, and Hinduism, within each of which, at some point, terrorist movements have arisen—but because terrorism emanating from the Middle East, including terrorism associated with regimes or groups professing allegiance to Islamic interests, has been especially prominent in recent years. It is that prominence that accounts for the scrutiny that is paid to such terrorism in this book.

Part III of the book explores the psychological mechanisms that enable terrorists to do what they do—in particular, to kill persons who are, by most criteria, not responsible for whatever wrong terrorists may be trying to right; and, too, it explores the question of suicidal terrorism. Albert

Bandura, a distinguished social psychologist, applies his rich expertise to the former issue, and Ariel Merari, a psychologist and student of terrorism, applies his to the latter.

Part IV turns from the psychology of terrorists to the psychology of governmental responses to terrorists. Clearly, the latter psychology is an important phenomenon to understand because, when mishandled, those responses, instead of easing terrorist incidents, may exacerbate them and even raise the level of tension between great powers. Margaret G. Hermann and Charles F. Hermann, the first a political psychologist and the second a political scientist, examine the challenge that hostage taking, and the stresses that it provokes, poses to a U.S. president; and Gary Sick explores the ways in which one hostage-taking incident, the one involving the U.S. embassy staff in Iran, did produce such stresses for President Carter, on whose National Security Council staff the author served at the time as the specialist on Iran.

Finally, Part V considers future research on the psychology of terrorism and the intrinsic limits of such research. In it Martha Crenshaw outlines the most important questions regarding the psychology of terrorism that should be addressed by scholars and scientists, and I end the book with a cautionary chapter on the opportunities, but also the limits, of such research.

This book on the psychology of terrorism has, appropriately, a psychology of its own. It is a psychology of explanation as well as limitation. It recognizes that the subject should be understood, but recognizes also that that understanding is both difficult and inevitably imperfect. The book is a beginning; there is no other, to my knowledge, that has the same goals or approach. I hope, as do my fellow authors of its chapters, that other books will follow and, in their explorations and findings, soon overtake it.

Part I

Strategy or psychology?:
Origins of terrorist behavior

1

The logic of terrorism: Terrorist behavior as a product of strategic choice

MARTHA CRENSHAW

[*Editor's note:* The purpose of this chapter is, in a way, contrapuntal. The main theme of this volume is a psychological one: In chapter after chapter, it explores the psychological underpinnings of terrorist motivations and behaviors. In focusing on this theme, it could well leave the impression that psychology more than any other factor—or, indeed, *instead of* any other factor—determines terrorist behavior. The author of this chapter agrees that psychology is indeed important in determining such behavior, but she has been asked by the editor, in order to balance the perspective of the book and to place its main theme within a realistic context, to identify the main nonpsychological—that is, the instrumental—bases of terrorist actions.

This chapter, then, and the succeeding one, by Jerrold Post, which lays out the main arguments for the psychological approach to terrorism, together identify the poles of the explanatory debate about terrorist motivations and actions—the strategic pole, at one end, and the psychological pole, at the other. In the opinion of the editor, as well as the authors of both this chapter and the next, both poles must be recognized as delimiting the boundaries of an explanatory landscape. This chapter focuses on one; the next, and much of the rest of the book, focuses on the other.]

This chapter examines the ways in which terrorism can be understood as an expression of political strategy. It attempts to show that terrorism may follow logical processes that can be discovered and explained. For the purpose of presenting this source of terrorist behavior, rather than the psychological one, it interprets the resort to violence as a willful choice

7

made by an organization for political and strategic reasons, rather than as the unintended outcome of psychological or social factors.[1]

In the terms of this analytical approach, terrorism is assumed to display a collective rationality. A radical political organization is seen as the central actor in the terrorist drama. The group possesses collective preferences or values and selects terrorism as a course of action from a range of perceived alternatives. Efficacy is the primary standard by which terrorism is compared with other methods of achieving political goals. Reasonably regularized decision-making procedures are employed to make an intentional choice, in conscious anticipation of the consequences of various courses of action or inaction. Organizations arrive at collective judgments about the relative effectiveness of different strategies of opposition on the basis of observation and experience, as much as on the basis of abstract strategic conceptions derived from ideological assumptions. This approach thus allows for the incorporation of theories of social learning.

Conventional rational-choice theories of individual participation in rebellion, extended to include terrorist activities, have usually been considered inappropriate because of the "free rider" problem. That is, the benefits of a successful terrorist campaign would presumably be shared by all individual supporters of the group's goals, regardless of the extent of their active participation. In this case, why should a rational person become a terrorist, given the high costs associated with violent resistance and the expectation that everyone who supports the cause will benefit, whether he or she participates or not? One answer is that the benefits of participation are psychological. Other chapters in this volume explore this possibility.

A different answer, however, supports a strategic analysis. On the basis of surveys conducted in New York and West Germany, political scientists suggest that individuals can be *collectively* rational.[2] People realize that their participation is important because group size and cohesion

---

[1] For a similar perspective (based on a different methodology) see James DeNardo, *Power in Numbers: The Political Strategy of Protest and Rebellion* (Princeton, N.J.: Princeton University Press, 1985). See also Harvey Waterman, "Insecure 'Ins' and Opportune 'Outs': Sources of Collective Political Activity," *Journal of Political and Military Sociology* 8 (1980): 107–12, and "Reasons and Reason: Collective Political Activity in Comparative and Historical Perspective," *World Politics* 33 (1981): 554–89. A useful review of rational choice theories is found in James G. March, "Theories of Choice and Making Decisions," *Society* 20 (1982): 29–39.

[2] Edward N. Muller and Karl-Dieter Opp, "Rational Choice and Rebellious Collective Action," *American Political Science Review* 80 (1986): 471–87.

matter. They are sensitive to the implications of free-riding and perceive their personal influence on the provision of public goods to be high. The authors argue that "average citizens may adopt a collectivist conception of rationality because they recognize that what is individually rational is collectively irrational."[3] Selective incentives are deemed largely irrelevant.

One of the advantages of approaching terrorism as a collectively rational strategic choice is that it permits the construction of a standard from which deviations can be measured. For example, the central question about the rationality of some terrorist organizations, such as the West German groups of the 1970s or the Weather Underground in the United States, is whether or not they had a sufficient grasp of reality—some approximation, to whatever degree imperfect—to calculate the likely consequences of the courses of action they chose. Perfect knowledge of available alternatives and the consequences of each is not possible, and miscalculations are inevitable. The Popular Front for the Liberation of Palestine (PFLP), for example, planned the hijacking of a TWA flight from Rome in August 1969 to coincide with a scheduled address by President Nixon to a meeting of the Zionist Organization of America, but he sent a letter instead.[4]

Yet not all errors of decision are miscalculations. There are varied degrees of limited rationality. Are some organizations so low on the scale of rationality as to be in a different category from more strategically minded groups? To what degree is strategic reasoning modified by psychological and other constraints? The strategic choice framework provides criteria on which to base these distinctions. It also leads one to ask what conditions promote or discourage rationality in violent underground organizations.

The use of this theoretical approach is also advantageous in that it suggests important questions about the preferences or goals of terrorist organizations. For example, is the decision to seize hostages in order to bargain with governments dictated by strategic considerations or by other, less instrumental motives?

[3] Ibid., 484. The authors also present another puzzling question that may be answered in terms of either psychology or collective rationality. People who expected their rebellious behavior to be punished were more likely to be potential rebels. This propensity could be explained either by a martyr syndrome (or an expectation of hostility from authority figures) or intensity of preference—the calculation that the regime was highly repressive and thus deserved all the more to be destroyed. See pp. 482 and 485.

[4] Leila Khaled, *My People Shall Live: The Autobiography of a Revolutionary* (London: Hodder and Stoughton, 1973), 128–31.

The strategic choice approach is also a useful interpretation of reality. Since the French Revolution, a strategy of terrorism has gradually evolved as a means of bringing about political change opposed by established governments. Analysis of the historical development of terrorism reveals similarities in calculation of ends and means. The strategy has changed over time to adapt to new circumstances that offer different possibilities for dissident action—for example, hostage taking. Yet terrorist activity considered in its entirety shows a fundamental unity of purpose and conception. Although this analysis remains largely on an abstract level, the historical evolution of the strategy of terrorism can be sketched in its terms.[5]

A last argument in support of this approach takes the form of a warning. The wide range of terrorist activity cannot be dismissed as "irrational" and thus pathological, unreasonable, or inexplicable. The resort to terrorism need not be an aberration. It may be a reasonable and calculated response to circumstances. To say that the reasoning that leads to the choice of terrorism may be logical is not an argument about moral justifiability. It does suggest, however, that the belief that terrorism is expedient is one means by which moral inhibitions are overcome, as Albert Bandura argues in Chapter 9 of this volume.

The conditions for terrorism

The central problem is to determine when extremist organizations find terrorism useful. Extremists seek either a radical change in the status quo, which would confer a new advantage, or the defense of privileges they perceive to be threatened. Their dissatisfaction with the policies of the government is extreme, and their demands usually involve the displacement of existing political elites.[6] Terrorism is not the only method of working toward radical goals, and thus it must be compared to the alternative strategies available to dissidents. Why is terrorism attractive to some opponents of the state, but unattractive to others?

The practitioners of terrorism often claim that they had no choice but terrorism, and it is indeed true that terrorism often follows the failure of other methods. In nineteenth-century Russia, for example, the failure of

[5] See Martha Crenshaw, "The Strategic Development of Terrorism," paper presented to the 1985 Annual Meeting of the American Political Science Association, New Orleans.
[6] William A. Gamson, *The Strategy of Social Protest* (Homewood, Illinois: Dorsey Press, 1975).

nonviolent movements contributed to the rise of terrorism. In Ireland, terrorism followed the failure of Parnell's constitutionalism. In the Palestinian-Israeli struggle, terrorism followed the failure of Arab efforts at conventional warfare against Israel. In general, the "nonstate" or "substate" users of terrorism—that is, groups in opposition to the government, as opposed to government itself—are constrained in their options by the lack of active mass support and by the superior power arrayed against them (an imbalance that has grown with the development of the modern centralized and bureaucratic nation-state). But these constraints have not prevented oppositions from considering and rejecting methods other than terrorism. Perhaps because groups are slow to recognize the extent of the limits to action, terrorism is often the last in a sequence of choices. It represents the outcome of a learning process. Experience in opposition provides radicals with information about the potential consequences of their choices. Terrorism is likely to be a reasonably informed choice among available alternatives, some tried unsuccessfully. Terrorists also learn from the experiences of others, usually communicated to them via the news media. Hence the existence of patterns of contagion in terrorist incidents.[7]

Thus the existence of extremism or rebellious potential is necessary to the resort to terrorism but does not in itself explain it, because many revolutionary and nationalist organizations have explicitly disavowed terrorism. The Russian Marxists argued for years against the use of terrorism.[8] Generally, small organizations resort to violence to compensate for what they lack in numbers.[9] The imbalance between the resources terrorists are able to mobilize and the power of the incumbent regime is a decisive consideration in their decision making.

More important than the observation that terrorism is the weapon of the weak, who lack numbers or conventional military power, is the explanation for weakness. Particularly, why does an organization lack the potential to attract enough followers to change government policy or overthrow it?

One possibility is that the majority of the population does not share

---

[7] Manus I. Midlarsky, Martha Crenshaw, and Fumihiko Yoshida, "Why Violence Spreads: The Contagion of International Terrorism," *International Studies Quarterly* 24 (1980): 262–98.

[8] See the study by David A. Newell, *The Russian Marxist Response to Terrorism: 1878–1917* (Ph.D. dissertation, Stanford University, University Microfilms, 1981).

[9] The tension between violence and numbers is a fundamental proposition in DeNardo's analysis; see *Power in Numbers*, chapters 9–11.

the ideological views of the resisters, who occupy a political position so extreme that their appeal is inherently limited. This incompatibility of preferences may be purely political, concerning, for example, whether or not one prefers socialism to capitalism. The majority of West Germans found the Red Army Faction's promises for the future not only excessively vague but distasteful. Nor did most Italians support aims of the neofascist groups that initiated the "strategy of tension" in 1969. Other extremist groups, such as the *Euzkadi ta Akatasuna* (ETA) in Spain or the Provisional Irish Republican Army (PIRA) in Northern Ireland, may appeal exclusively to ethnic, religious, or other minorities. In such cases, a potential constituency of like-minded and dedicated individuals exists, but its boundaries are fixed and limited. Despite the intensity of the preferences of a minority, its numbers will never be sufficient for success.

A second explanation for the weakness of the type of organization likely to turn to terrorism lies in a failure to mobilize support. Its members may be unwilling or unable to expend the time and effort required for mass organizational work. Activists may not possess the requisite skills or patience, or may not expect returns commensurate with their endeavors. No matter how acute or widespread popular dissatisfaction may be, the masses do not rise spontaneously; mobilization is required.[10] The organization's leaders, recognizing the advantages of numbers, may combine mass organization with conspiratorial activities. But resources are limited and organizational work is difficult and slow even under favorable circumstances. Moreover, rewards are not immediate. These difficulties are compounded in an authoritarian state, where the organization of independent opposition is sure to incur high costs. Combining violent provocation with nonviolent organizing efforts may only work to the detriment of the latter.

For example, the debate over whether to use an exclusively violent underground strategy that is isolated from the masses (as terrorism inevitably is) or to work with the people in propaganda and organizational efforts divided the Italian left-wing groups, with the Red Brigades choosing the clandestine path and Prima Linea preferring to maintain contact with the wider protest movement. In prerevolutionary Russia the Socialist-Revolutionary party combined the activities of a legal political

[10] The work of Charles Tilly emphasizes the political basis of collective violence. See Charles Tilly, Louise Tilly, and Richard Tilly, *The Rebellious Century 1830–1930* (Cambridge: Harvard University Press, 1975), and Charles Tilly, *From Mobilization to Revolution* (Reading, Mass.: Addison-Wesley, 1978).

party with the terrorist campaign of the secret Combat Organization. The IRA has a legal counterpart in Sinn Fein.

A third reason for the weakness of dissident organizations is specific to repressive states. It is important to remember that terrorism is by no means restricted to liberal democracies, although some authors refuse to define resistance to authoritarianism as terrorism.[11] People may not support a resistance organization because they are afraid of negative sanctions from the regime or because censorship of the press prevents them from learning of the possibility of rebellion. In this situation a radical organization may believe that supporters exist but cannot reveal themselves. The depth of this latent support cannot be measured or activists mobilized until the state is overthrown.

Such conditions are frustrating, because the likelihood of popular dissatisfaction grows as the likelihood of its active expression is diminished. Frustration may also encourage unrealistic expectations among the regime's challengers, who are not able to test their popularity. Rational expectations may be undermined by fantastic assumptions about the role of the masses. Yet such fantasies can also prevail among radical undergrounds in Western democracies. The misperception of conditions can lead to unrealistic expectations.

In addition to small numbers, time constraints contribute to the decision to use terrorism. Terrorists are impatient for action. This impatience may, of course, be due to external factors, such as psychological or organizational pressures. The personalities of leaders, demands from followers, or competition from rivals often constitute impediments to strategic thinking. But it is not necessary to explain the felt urgency of some radical organizations by citing reasons external to an instrumental framework. Impatience and eagerness for action can be rooted in calculations of ends and means. For example, the organization may perceive an immediate opportunity to compensate for its inferiority vis-à-vis the government. A change in the structure of the situation may temporarily alter the balance of resources available to the two sides, thus changing the ratio of strength between government and challenger.

Such a change in the radical organization's outlook—the combination of optimism and urgency—may occur when the regime suddenly appears vulnerable to challenge. This vulnerability may be of two sorts. First, the

[11] See Conor Cruise O'Brien, "Terrorism under Democratic Conditions: The Case of the IRA," in *Terrorism, Legitimacy, and Power: The Consequences of Political Violence*, edited by Martha Crenshaw (Middletown, Conn.: Wesleyan University Press, 1983).

regime's ability to respond effectively, its capacity for efficient repression of dissent, or its ability to protect its citizens and property may weaken. Its armed forces may be committed elsewhere, for example, as British forces were during World War I when the IRA first rose to challenge British rule, or its coercive resources may be otherwise overextended. Inadequate security at embassies, airports, or military installations may become obvious. The poorly protected U.S. Marine barracks in Beirut were, for example, a tempting target. Government strategy may be ill-adapted to responding to terrorism.

Second, the regime may make itself morally or politically vulnerable by increasing the likelihood that the terrorists will attract popular support. Government repressiveness is thought to have contradictory effects: it both deters dissent and provokes a moral backlash.[12] Perceptions of the regime as unjust motivate opposition. If government actions make average citizens willing to suffer punishment for supporting antigovernment causes, or lend credence to the claims of radical opponents, the extremist organization may be tempted to exploit this temporary upsurge of popular indignation. A groundswell of popular disapproval may make liberal governments less willing (as opposed to less able) to use coercion against violent dissent.

Political discomfort may also be internationally generated. If the climate of international opinion changes so as to reduce the legitimacy of a targeted regime, rebels may feel encouraged to risk a repression that they hope will be limited by outside disapproval. In such circumstances the regime's brutality may be expected to win supporters to the cause of its challengers. The current situation in South Africa furnishes an example. Thus a heightened sensitivity to injustice may be produced either by government actions or by changing public attitudes.

The other fundamental way in which the situation changes to the advantage of challengers is through acquiring new resources. New means of financial support are an obvious asset, which may accrue through a foreign alliance with a sympathetic government or another, richer revolutionary group, or through criminal means such as bank robberies or kidnapping for ransom. Although terrorism is an extremely economical method of violence, funds are essential for the support of full-time activists, weapons purchases, transportation, and logistics.

Technological advances in weapons, explosives, transportation, and

---

[12] For example, DeNardo, in *Power in Numbers,* argues that "the movement derives moral sympathy from the government's excesses" (p. 207).

communications also may enhance the disruptive potential of terrorism. The invention of dynamite was thought by nineteenth-century revolutionaries and anarchists to equalize the relationship between government and challenger, for example. In 1885, Johann Most published a pamphlet titled *Revolutionary War Science,* which explicitly advocated terrorism. According to Paul Avrich, the anarchists saw dynamite "as a great equalizing force, enabling ordinary workmen to stand up against armies, militias, and police, to say nothing of the hired gunmen of the employers."[13] In providing such a powerful but easily concealed weapon, science was thought to have given a decisive advantage to revolutionary forces.

Strategic innovation is another important way in which a challenging organization acquires new resources. The organization may borrow or adapt a technique in order to exploit a vulnerability ignored by the government. In August 1972, for example, the Provisional IRA introduced the effective tactic of the one-shot sniper. IRA Chief of Staff Sean MacStiofain claims to have originated the idea: "It seemed to me that prolonged sniping from a static position had no more in common with guerrilla theory than mass confrontations."[14] The best marksmen were trained to fire a single shot and escape before their position could be located. The creation of surprise is naturally one of the key advantages of an offensive strategy. So, too, is the willingness to violate social norms pertaining to restraints on violence. The history of terrorism reveals a series of innovations, as terrorists deliberately selected targets considered taboo and locales where violence was unexpected. These innovations were then rapidly diffused, especially in the modern era of instantaneous and global communications.

It is especially interesting that, in 1968, two of the most important terrorist tactics of the modern era appeared—diplomatic kidnappings in Latin America and hijackings in the Middle East. Both were significant innovations because they involved the use of extortion or blackmail. Although the nineteenth-century Fenians had talked about kidnapping the prince of Wales, the People's Will (Narodnaya Volya) in nineteenth-century Russia had offered to halt its terrorist campaign if a constitution were granted, and American marines were kidnapped by Castro forces in 1959, hostage taking as a systematic and lethal form of coercive bargaining was essentially new. This chapter later takes up the issue in more detail as an illustration of strategic analysis.

[13] Paul Avrich, *The Haymarket Tragedy* (Princeton: Princeton University Press, 1984), 166.
[14] Sean MacStiofain, *Memoirs of a Revolutionary* (N.p.: Gordon Cremonisi, 1975), 301.

Terrorism has so far been presented as the response by an opposition movement to an opportunity. This approach is compatible with the findings of Harvey Waterman, who sees collective political action as determined by the calculations of resources and opportunities.[15] Yet other theorists—James Q. Wilson, for example—argue that political organizations originate in response to a threat to a group's values.[16] Terrorism can certainly be defensive as well as opportunistic. It may be a response to a sudden downturn in a dissident organization's fortunes. The fear of appearing weak may provoke an underground organization into acting in order to show its strength. The PIRA used terrorism to offset an impression of weakness, even at the cost of alienating public opinion: in the 1970s periods of negotiations with the British were punctuated by outbursts of terrorism because the PIRA did want people to think that they were negotiating from strength.[17] Right-wing organizations frequently resort to violence in response to what they see as a threat to the status quo from the left. Beginning in 1969, for example, the right in Italy promoted a "strategy of tension," which involved urban bombings with high numbers of civilian casualties, in order to keep the Italian government and electorate from moving to the left.

Calculation of cost and benefit

An organization or a faction of an organization may choose terrorism because other methods are not expected to work or are considered too time-consuming, given the urgency of the situation and the government's superior resources. Why would an extremist organization expect that terrorism will be effective? What are the costs and benefits of such a choice, compared with other alternatives? What is the nature of the debate over terrorism? Whether or not to use terrorism is one of the most divisive issues resistance groups confront, and numerous revolutionary movements have split on the question of means even after agreeing on common political ends.[18]

THE COSTS OF TERRORISM. The costs of terrorism are high. As a domestic strategy, it invariably invites a punitive government reaction, although

[15] Waterman, "Insecure 'Ins' and Opportune 'Outs' " and "Reasons and Reason."
[16] *Political Organizations* (New York: Basic Books, 1973).
[17] Maria McGuire, *To Take Arms: My Year with the IRA Provisionals* (New York: Viking, 1973), 110–11, 118, 129–31, 115, and 161–62.
[18] DeNardo concurs; see *Power in Numbers,* chapter 11.

the organization may believe that the government reaction will not be efficient enough to pose a serious threat. This cost can be offset by the advance preparation of building a secure underground. *Sendero Luminoso* (Shining Path) in Peru, for example, spent ten years creating a clandestine organizational structure before launching a campaign of violence in 1980. Furthermore, radicals may look to the future and calculate that present sacrifice will not be in vain if it inspires future resistance. Conceptions of interest are thus long term.

Another potential cost of terrorism is loss of popular support. Unless terrorism is carefully controlled and discriminate, it claims innocent victims. In a liberal state, indiscriminate violence may appear excessive and unjustified and alienate a citizenry predisposed to loyalty to the government. If it provokes generalized government repression, fear may diminish enthusiasm for resistance. This potential cost of popular alienation is probably least in ethnically divided societies, where victims can be clearly identified as the enemy and where the government of the majority appears illegal to the minority. Terrorists try to compensate by justifying their actions as the result of the absence of choice or the need to respond to government violence. In addition, they may make their strategy highly discriminate, attacking only unpopular targets.

Terrorism may be unattractive because it is elitist. Although relying only on terrorism may spare the general population from costly involvement in the struggle for freedom, such isolation may violate the ideological beliefs of revolutionaries who insist that the people must participate in their liberation. The few who choose terrorism are willing to forgo or postpone the participation of the many, but revolutionaries who oppose terrorism insist that it prevents the people from taking responsibility for their own destiny. The possibility of vicarious popular identification with symbolic acts of terrorism may satisfy some revolutionaries, but others will find terrorism a harmful substitute for mass participation.

THE ADVANTAGES OF TERRORISM. Terrorism has an extremely useful agenda-setting function. If the reasons behind violence are skillfully articulated, terrorism can put the issue of political change on the public agenda. By attracting attention it makes the claims of the resistance a salient issue in the public mind. The government can reject but not ignore an opposition's demands. In 1974 the Palestinian Black September organization, for example, was willing to sacrifice a base in Khartoum, alienate the Sudanese government, and create ambivalence in the Arab world by seizing the Saudi Arabian embassy and killing American and Belgian diplomats. These costs were apparently weighed against the message to the world "to take us seriously." Mainstream Fatah leader Salah Khalef (Abu Iyad) explained: "We are planting the seed. Others will harvest it. . . . It is enough for us now to learn, for example, in reading the Jerusalem Post, that Mrs. Meir had to make her will before visiting Paris, or that Mr. Abba Eban had to travel with a false passport."[19] George Habash of the PFLP noted in 1970 that "we force people to ask what is going on."[20] In these statements, contemporary extremists echo the nineteenth-century anarchists, who coined the idea of propaganda of the deed, a term used as early as 1877 to refer to an act of insurrection as "a powerful means of arousing popular conscience" and the materialization of an idea through actions.[21]

Terrorism may be intended to create revolutionary conditions. It can prepare the ground for active mass revolt by undermining the government's authority and demoralizing its administrative cadres—its courts, police, and military. By spreading insecurity—at the extreme, making the country ungovernable—the organization hopes to pressure the regime into concessions or relaxation of coercive controls. With the rule of law disrupted, the people will be free to join the opposition. Spectacular humiliation of the government demonstrates strength and will and maintains the morale and enthusiasm of adherents and sympathizers. The first wave of Russian revolutionaries claimed that the aims of terrorism were to exhaust the enemy, render the government's position untenable, and wound the government's prestige by delivering a moral, not a physical, blow. Terrorists hoped to paralyze the government by their presence merely by showing signs of life from time to time. The hesitation, irresolution, and tension they would produce would undermine the processes of government and make the Czar a prisoner in his own palace.[22] As Brazilian revolutionary Carlos Marighela explained: "Revolutionary terrorism's great weapon is initiative, which guarantees its survival and continued

[19] See Jim Hoagland, "A Community of Terror," *Washington Post*, 15 March 1973, pp. 1 and 13; also *New York Times*, 4 March 1973, p. 28. Black September is widely regarded as a subsidiary of Fatah, the major Palestinian organization headed by Yasir Arafat.

[20] John Amos, *Palestinian Resistance: Organization of a Nationalist Movement* (New York: Pergamon, 1980), 193; quoting George Habash, interviewed in *Life Magazine*, 12 June 1970, 33.

[21] Jean Maitron, *Histoire du mouvement anarchiste en France (1880–1914)*, 2d ed. (Paris: Société universitaire d'éditions et de librairie, 1955), 74–5.

[22] "Stepniak" (pseud. for Sergei Kravshinsky), *Underground Russia: Revolutionary Profiles and Sketches from Life* (London: Smith, Elder, 1883), 278–80.

activity. The more committed terrorists and revolutionaries devoted to anti-dictatorship terrorism and sabotage there are, the more military power will be worn down, the more time it will lose following false trails, and the more fear and tension it will suffer through not knowing where the next attack will be launched and what the next target will be."[23]

These statements illustrate a corollary advantage to terrorism in what might be called its excitational function: it inspires resistance by example. As propaganda of the deed, terrorism demonstrates that the regime can be challenged and that illegal opposition is possible. It acts as a catalyst, not a substitute, for mass revolt. All the tedious and time-consuming organizational work of mobilizing the people can be avoided. Terrorism is a shortcut to revolution. As the Russian revolutionary Vera Figner described its purpose, terrorism was "a means of agitation to draw people from their torpor," not a sign of loss of belief in the people.[24]

A more problematic benefit lies in provoking government repression. Terrorists often think that by provoking indiscriminate repression against the population, terrorism will heighten popular disaffection, demonstrate the justice of terrorist claims, and enhance the attractiveness of the political alternative the terrorists represent. Thus, the West German Red Army Faction sought (in vain) to make fascism "visible" in West Germany.[25] In Brazil, Marighela unsuccessfully aimed to "transform the country's political situation into a military one. Then discontent will spread to all social groups and the military will be held exclusively responsible for failures."[26]

But profiting from government repression depends on the lengths to which the government is willing to go in order to contain disorder, and on the population's tolerance for both insecurity and repression. A liberal state may be limited in its capacity for quelling violence, but at the same time it may be difficult to provoke to excess. However, the government's reaction to terrorism may reinforce the symbolic value of violence even if it avoids repression. Extensive security precautions, for example, may only make the terrorists appear powerful.

SUMMARY. To summarize, the choice of terrorism involves considerations of timing and of the popular contribution to revolt, as well as of

---

[23] Carlos Marighela, *For the Liberation of Brazil* (Harmondsworth: Penguin, 1971), 113.

[24] Vera Figner, *Mémoires d'une révolutionnaire* (Paris: Gallimard, 1930), 206.

[25] *Textes des prisonniers de la "fraction armée rouge" et dernières lettres d'Ulrike Meinhof* (Paris: Maspéro, 1977), 64.

[26] Marighela, *For the Liberation of Brazil*, 46.

the relationship between government and opponents. Radicals choose terrorism when they want immediate action, think that only violence can build organizations and mobilize supporters, and accept the risks of challenging the government in a particularly provocative way. Challengers who think that organizational infrastructure must precede action, that rebellion without the masses is misguided, and that premature conflict with the regime can only lead to disaster favor gradualist strategies. They prefer methods such as rural guerrilla warfare, because terrorism can jeopardize painfully achieved gains or preclude eventual compromise with the government.

The resistance organization has before it a set of alternatives defined by the situation and by the objectives and resources of the group. The reasoning behind terrorism takes into account the balance of power between challengers and authorities, a balance that depends on the amount of popular support the resistance can mobilize. The proponents of terrorism understand this constraint and possess reasonable expectations about the likely results of action or inaction. They may be wrong about the alternatives that are open to them, or miscalculate the consequences of their actions, but their decisions are based on logical processes. Furthermore, organizations learn from their mistakes and from those of others, resulting in strategic continuity and progress toward the development of more efficient and sophisticated tactics. Future choices are modified by the consequences of present actions.

Hostage taking as bargaining

Hostage taking can be analyzed as a form of coercive bargaining. More than twenty years ago, Thomas Schelling wrote that "hostages represent the power to hurt in its purest form."[27] From this perspective, terrorists choose to take hostages because in bargaining situations the government's greater strength and resources are not an advantage. The extensive resort to this form of terrorism after 1968, a year that marks the major advent of diplomatic kidnappings and airline hijackings, was a predictable response to the growth of state power. Kidnappings, hijackings, and barricade-type seizures of embassies or public buildings are attempts to manipulate a government's political decisions.

Strategic analysis of bargaining terrorism is based on the assumption

[27] Schelling, *Arms and Influence* (New Haven, Conn.: Yale University Press, 1966), 6.

that hostage takers genuinely seek the concessions they demand. It assumes that they prefer government compliance to resistance. This analysis does not allow for deception or for the possibility that seizing hostages may be an end in itself because it yields the benefit of publicity. Because these limiting assumptions may reduce the utility of the theory, it is important to recognize them.

Terrorist bargaining is essentially a form of blackmail or extortion.[28] Terrorists seize hostages in order to affect a government's choices, which are controlled both by expectations of outcome (what the terrorists are likely to do, given the government reaction) and preferences (such as humanitarian values). The outcome threatened by the terrorist—the death of the hostages—must be worse for the government than compliance with terrorist demands. The terrorist has two options, neither of which necessarily excludes the other: to make the threat both more horrible and more credible or to reward compliance, a factor that strategic theorists often ignore.[29] That is, the cost to the government of complying with the terrorists' demands may be lowered or the cost of resisting raised.

The threat to kill the hostages must be believable and painful to the government. Here hostage takers are faced with a paradox. How can the credibility of this threat be assured when hostage takers recognize that governments know that the terrorists' control over the situation depends on live hostages? One way of establishing credibility is to divide the threat, making it sequential by killing one hostage at a time. Such tactics also aid terrorists in the process of incurring and demonstrating a commitment to carrying out their threat. Once the terrorists have murdered, though, their incentive to surrender voluntarily is substantially reduced. The terrorists have increased their own costs of yielding in order to persuade the government that their intention to kill all the hostages is real.

Another important way of binding oneself in a terrorist strategy is to undertake a barricade rather than a kidnapping operation. Terrorists who are trapped with the hostages find it more difficult to back down (because the government controls the escape routes) and, by virtue of this commitment, influence the government's choices. When terrorists join the hostages in a barricade situation, they create the visible and irrevocable

---

[28] Daniel Ellsburg, *The Theory and Practice of Blackmail* (Santa Monica: Rand Corporation, 1968).

[29] David A. Baldwin, "Bargaining with Airline Hijackers," in *The 50% Solution*, edited by William I. Zartman, 404–29 (Garden City, N.Y.: Doubleday, 1976), argues that promises have not been sufficiently stressed. Analysts tend to emphasize threats instead, surely because of the latent violence implicit in hostage taking regardless of outcome.

commitment that Schelling sees as a necessary bond in bargaining. The government must expect desperate behavior, because the terrorists have increased their potential loss in order to demonstrate the firmness of their intentions. Furthermore, barricades are technically easier than kidnappings.

The terrorists also attempt to force the "last clear chance" of avoiding disaster onto the government, which must accept the responsibility for noncompliance that leads to the deaths of hostages. The seizure of hostages is the first move in the game, leaving the next move—which determines the fate of the hostages—completely up to the government. Uncertain communications may facilitate this strategy.[30] The terrorists can pretend not to receive government messages that might affect their demonstrated commitment. Hostage takers can also bind themselves by insisting that they are merely agents, empowered to ask only for the most extreme demands. Terrorists may deliberately appear irrational, either through inconsistent and erratic behavior or unrealistic expectations and preferences, in order to convince the government that they will carry out a threat that entails self-destruction.

Hostage seizures are a type of iterated game, which explains some aspects of terrorist behavior that otherwise seem to violate strategic principles. In terms of a single episode, terrorists can be expected to find killing hostages painful, because they will not achieve their demands and the government's desire to punish will be intensified. However, from a long-range perspective, killing hostages reinforces the credibility of the threat in the next terrorist incident, even if the killers then cannot escape. Each terrorist episode is actually a round in a series of games between government and terrorists.

Hostage takers may influence the government's decision by promising rewards for compliance. Recalling that terrorism represents an iterative game, the release of hostages unharmed when ransom is paid underwrites a promise in the future. Sequential release of selected hostages makes promises credible. Maintaining secrecy about a government's concessions is an additional reward for compliance. France, for example, can if necessary deny making concessions to Lebanese kidnappers because the details of arrangements have not been publicized.

Terrorists may try to make their demands appear legitimate so that governments may seem to satisfy popular grievances rather than the whims

[30] See Roberta Wohlstetter's case study of Castro's seizure of American marines in Cuba: "Kidnapping to Win Friends and Influence People," *Survey* 20 (1974): 1–40.

of terrorists. Thus, terrorists may ask that food be distributed to the poor. Such demands were a favored tactic of the *Ejercito Revolucionario del Pueblo* (ERP) in Argentina in the 1970s.

A problem for hostage takers is that rewarding compliance is not easy to reconcile with making threats credible. For example, if terrorists use publicity to emphasize their threat to kill hostages (which they frequently do), they may also increase the costs of compliance for the government because of the attention drawn to the incident.

In any calculation of the payoffs for each side, the costs associated with the bargaining process must be taken into account.[31] Prolonging the hostage crisis increases the costs to both sides. The question is who loses most and thus is more likely to concede. Each party presumably wishes to make the delay more costly to the other. Seizing multiple hostages appears to be advantageous to terrorists, who are thus in a position to make threats credible by killing hostages individually. Conversely, the greater the number of hostages, the greater the cost of holding them. In hijacking or barricade situations, stress and fatigue for the captors increase waiting costs for them as well. Kidnapping poses fewer such costs. Yet the terrorists can reasonably expect that the costs to governments in terms of public or international pressures may be higher when developments are visible. Furthermore, kidnappers can maintain suspense and interest by publishing communications from their victims.

Identifying the obstacles to effective bargaining in hostage seizures is critical. Most important, bargaining depends on the existence of a common interest between two parties. It is unclear whether the lives of hostages are a sufficient common interest to ensure a compromise outcome that is preferable to no agreement for both sides. Furthermore, most theories of bargaining assume that the preferences of each side remain stable during negotiations. In reality, the nature and intensity of preferences may change during a hostage-taking episode. For example, embarrassment over the Iran-*contra* scandal may have reduced the American interest in securing the release of hostages in Lebanon.

Bargaining theory is also predicated on the assumption that the game is two-party. When terrorists seize the nationals of one government in order to influence the choices of a third, the situation is seriously complicated. The hostages themselves may sometimes become intermediaries and participants. In Lebanon, Terry Waite, formerly an intermediary and

---

[31] Scott E. Atkinson, Todd Sandler, and John Tschirhart, "Terrorism in a Bargaining Framework," *Journal of Law and Economics* 30 (1987): 1–21.

negotiator, became a hostage. Such developments are not anticipated by bargaining theories based on normal political relationships. Furthermore, bargaining is not possible if a government is willing to accept the maximum cost the terrorists can bring to bear rather than concede. And the government's options are not restricted to resistance or compliance; armed rescue attempts represent an attempt to break the bargaining stalemate. In attempting to make their threats credible—for example, by sequential killing of hostages—terrorists may provoke military intervention. There may be limits, then, to the pain terrorists can inflict and still remain in the game.

Conclusions

This essay has attempted to demonstrate that even the most extreme and unusual forms of political behavior can follow an internal, strategic logic. If there are consistent patterns in terrorist behavior, rather than random idiosyncrasies, a strategic analysis may reveal them. Prediction of future terrorism can only be based on theories that explain past patterns.

Terrorism can be considered a reasonable way of pursuing extreme interests in the political arena. It is one among the many alternatives that radical organizations can choose. Strategic conceptions, based on ideas of how best to take advantage of the possibilities of a given situation, are an important determinant of oppositional terrorism, as they are of the government response. However, no single explanation for terrorist behavior is satisfactory. Strategic calculation is only one factor in the decision-making process leading to terrorism. But it is critical to include strategic reasoning as a possible motivation, at a minimum as an antidote to stereotypes of "terrorists" as irrational fanatics. Such stereotypes are a dangerous underestimation of the capabilities of extremist groups. Nor does stereotyping serve to educate the public—or, indeed, specialists—about the complexities of terrorist motivations and behaviors.

2

Terrorist psycho-logic: Terrorist behavior as a product of psychological forces

JERROLD M. POST

In the preceding chapter, Martha Crenshaw examines the proposition that terrorist reasoning follows logical processes. This chapter on terrorist psychology takes no issue with the proposition that terrorists reason logically. On the contrary, it argues for a special logic that characterizes terrorists' reasoning processes, a logic from which this chapter draws its title—"terrorist psycho-logic." The chapter does take significant issue, however, with the propositions that terrorists resort to violence as a *willful* choice and that terrorism as a course of action is an *intentional* choice selected from a range of perceived alternatives. Rather, it argues that *political terrorists are driven to commit acts of violence as a consequence of psychological forces*, and that their special psycho-logic is constructed to rationalize *acts they are psychologically compelled to commit*. Thus the principal argument of this essay is that *individuals are drawn to the path of terrorism in order to commit acts of violence*, and their special logic, which is grounded in their psychology and reflected in their rhetoric, becomes the justification for their violent acts.

Considering the diversity of causes to which terrorists are committed, the uniformity of their rhetoric is striking. Polarizing and absolutist, it is a rhetoric of "us versus them." It is a rhetoric without nuance, without shades of gray. "They," the establishment, are the source of all evil, in vivid contrast to "us," the freedom fighters, consumed by righteous rage. And if "they" are the source of our problems, it follows ineluctably, in the special psycho-logic of the terrorist, that "they" must be destroyed. It is the only just and moral thing to do. Once the basic premises are accepted, the logical reasoning is flawless. Shall we then conclude, because their reasoning is so logical, that terrorists are psychologically well balanced and that terrorist campaigns are the product of a rationally derived strategic choice?

There is, of course, no necessary relationship between emotional health and logic. Some delightfully happy and psychologically well-balanced persons are utterly unable to track their way through a syllogism. And the tight, logical structure of the well-organized paranoid is a marvel to behold. In a jewel of a treatise, the mathematical psychologist E. von Domarus[1] delineated the logical structure of delusions, a logic he named "paleologic." The fixed delusional conclusion of the paranoid schizophrenic woman that "I am the Virgin Mary" is drawn from a paleological syllogism: "I am a virgin. Mary was a virgin. Therefore I am the Virgin Mary." Hers is a conclusion in search of evidence, driven by her anguished search for meaning, by the lonely torment within. Similarly, the balance of this chapter will attempt to demonstrate that the fixed logical conclusion of the terrorist that the establishment must be destroyed is driven by the terrorist's search for identity, and that, as he strikes out against the establishment, he is attempting to destroy the enemy within.

If we dismiss the notion of a terror network with a central staff providing propaganda guidance, what accounts for the uniformity of the terrorists' polarizing absolutist rhetoric? The author's own comparative research[2] on the psychology of terrorists does not reveal major psychopathology, and is in substantial agreement with the finding of Crenshaw[3] that "the outstanding common characteristic of terrorists is their normality." Her studies of the National Liberation Front (FLN) in Algeria in the 1950s found the members to be basically normal. Nor did Heskin[4] find members of the Irish Republican Army (IRA) to be emotionally disturbed. In a review of the social psychology of terrorist groups, McCauley and Segal[5] conclude that "the best documented generalization is negative; terrorists do not show any striking psychopathology."

[1] E. von Domarus, "The Specific Laws of Logic in Schizophrenia," in *Language and Thought in Schizophrenia: Collected Papers*, edited by J. S. Kasanin (Berkeley: University of California Press, 1944).

[2] J. Post, "Notes on a Psychodynamic Theory of Terrorist Behavior," *Terrorism* 7, no. 3 (1984): 241–56.

[3] M. Crenshaw, "The Causes of Terrorism," *Comparative Politics* 13 (1981): 379–99.

[4] K. Heskin, "The Psychology of Terrorism in Ireland," in *Terrorism in Ireland*, edited by Y. Alexander and A. O'Day (New York: St. Martin's Press, 1984).

[5] C. R. McCauley and M. E. Segal, "Social Psychology of Terrorist Groups," in *Group Processes and Intergroup Relations*, vol. 9 of *Annual Review of Social and Personality Psychology*, edited by C. Hendrick (Beverly Hills: Sage, 1987).

Nor does a comparative study reveal a particular psychological type, a particular personality constellation, a uniform terrorist mind. But although diverse personalities are attracted to the path of terrorism, an examination of memoirs, court records, and rare interviews suggests that people with particular personality traits and tendencies are drawn disproportionately to terrorist careers.

What are these traits, these personality characteristics? Several authors[6,7] have characterized terrorists as action-oriented, aggressive people who are stimulus-hungry and seek excitement. Particularly striking is the reliance placed on the psychological mechanisms of "externalization" and "splitting," psychological mechanisms found in individuals with narcissistic and borderline personality disturbances.[8] It is not my intent to suggest that all terrorists suffer from borderline or narcissistic personality disorders or that the psychological mechanisms of externalization and splitting are used by every terrorist. It is my distinct impression, however, that these mechanisms are found with extremely high frequency in the population of terrorists, and contribute significantly to the uniformity of terrorists' rhetorical style and their special psycho-logic.

In this regard, it is particularly important to understand the mechanism of "splitting." This is believed to be characteristic of people whose personality development is shaped by a particular type of psychological damage during childhood which produces what clinicians have characterized as narcissistic wounds. This leads to the development of what Kohut[9] has termed "the injured self."

Individuals with a damaged self-concept have never fully integrated the good and bad parts of the self. These aspects of the self are "split" into the "me" and the "not me." An individual with this personality constellation idealizes his grandiose self and *splits out* and *projects* onto others all the hated and devalued weakness within. Individuals who place high reliance on the mechanisms of splitting and externalization look outward for the source of difficulties. They need an outside enemy to blame. This is a dominant mechanism of the destructive charismatic,[10] such as Hitler, who projects the devalued part of himself onto the interpersonal environment and then attacks and scapegoats the enemy with-

---

[6] W. Laqueur, *The Age of Terrorism* (Boston: Little, Brown, 1987).

[7] See L. Süllwold, in *Analysen Zum Terrorismus 2: Lebenslauf-Analysen,* edited by H. Jäger, G. Schmidtchen, and L. Süllwold (Darmstadt: Westdeutscher Verlag, 1981).

[8] O. Kernberg, *Borderline Conditions and Pathological Narcissism* (New York: Jacob Aronson, 1975).

[9] H. Kohut, *The Analysis of the Self* (New York: International University Press, 1983).

[10] J. Post, "Narcissism and the Charismatic Leader-Follower Relationship," *Political Psychology* 7, no. 5 (1986): 675–88.

out. Unable to face his own inadequacies, the individual with this personality style needs a target to blame and attack for his own inner weakness
and inadequacies. Such people find the polarizing absolutist rhetoric of
terrorism extremely attractive. The statement, "It's not us—it's them;
they are the cause of our problems," provides a psychologically satisfying
explanation for what has gone wrong in their lives.

And a great deal has gone wrong in the lives of people who are drawn
to the path of terrorism. Research in the field of political terrorism—if
field it is—continues to suffer from a paucity of data to satisfy even the
minimal requirements of social scientists. Perhaps the most rigorous and
broad-based investigation of the social background and psychology of
terrorists was conducted by a consortium of West German social scientists under the sponsorship of the Ministry of the Interior.[11] Published in
four volumes, the two volumes of particular value for our attempts to
understand the psychological foundations of terrorism are the second,[12]
which is concerned with a social-psychological examination of the life
course of terrorists, and the third,[13] which addresses terrorist group processes.

The social scientists examined the life course of 250 West German
terrorists, 227 left-wing and 23 right-wing. Their analysis of the data
from their study of the left-wing terrorists from the Red Army Faction
and the 2 June Movement is particularly interesting. They found a high
incidence of fragmented families. Some 25 percent of the leftist terrorists
had lost one or both parents by the age of fourteen; loss of the father was
found to be especially disruptive. Seventy-nine percent reported severe
conflict, especially with the parents (33 percent), and they described the
father, when present, in hostile terms. One in three had been convicted
in juvenile court. In general, it was the authors' conclusion that the group
of terrorists whose lives they had studied demonstrated a pattern of failure both educationally and vocationally. Viewing the terrorists as "advancement oriented and failure prone," they characterized the terrorist
career as "the terminal point of a series of abortive adaptation attempts."

Although the study is interdisciplinary and comprehensive, it is subject
to criticism because of the lack of a control group, and it is not clear to

[11] Ministry of the Interior, Federal Republic of Germany, *Analysen Zum Terrorismus 1–4*,
(Darmstadt: Deutscher Verlag, 1981, 1982, 1983, 1984).
[12] H. Jäger, G. Schmidtchen, and L. Süllwold, eds., *Analysen Zum Terrorismus 2: Lebens-
laufanalysen* (Darmstadt: Deutscher Verlag, 1981).
[13] W. von Baeyer-Kaette, D. Classens, H. Feger, and F. Neidhardt, eds., *Analysen Zum
Terrorismus 3: Gruppenprozesse* (Darmstadt: Deutscher Verlag, 1982).

what degree the statistics cited are found in the West German population at large. However, the findings from clinical interviews and memoirs do tend to confirm the sociological impressions just cited. In his psychoanalytically oriented interviews of incarcerated Red Army Faction terrorists, Bollinger[14] found developmental histories characterized by narcissistic wounds and a predominant reliance on the psychological mechanisms of splitting and externalization.

To be sure, each terrorist group is unique and must be studied in the context of its own national culture and history. It would be extremely unwise to generalize to other terrorist groups from the observed characteristics of West German left-wing terrorists. Attempting to remedy the control problem just identified, Ferracuti[15] has conducted a similar study with Red Brigade terrorists in Italy, using politically active youth as controls. Although his results are not yet fully available, preliminary impressions are that the family backgrounds of terrorists do not differ strikingly from the backgrounds of their politically active counterparts. He, too, found an absence of gross psychopathology, but did observe the personality characteristics described earlier.

Clark's studies[16] of the social backgrounds of the Basque separatist terrorists ETA (*Euzkadi Ta Askatasuna,* or the Basque Fatherland and Liberty Movement) are revealing. The Basque region of Spain is extremely homogeneous. Only 8 percent of the families are of mixed Basque-Spanish origin, and the offspring of these families are treated as half-breeds and reviled. But his studies of ETA members reveal that a much higher percentage—more than 40 percent—come from such mixed Basque-Spanish parentage, suggesting they are sociologically marginal. These outcasts may be attempting to "out-Basque the Basques" to demonstrate through their acts of terrorism their authenticity.

The social dynamics of the "anarchic-ideologues," such as the Red Army Faction in West Germany, differ strikingly from the dynamics of the "nationalist-separatists,"[17] such as ETA of the Basques or the Armenian Secret Army for the Liberation of Armenia (ASALA), as is depicted in Figure 2.1. The upper left-hand cell signifies that persons who are loyal

[14] See L. Bollinger, in *Analysen Zum Terrorismus 3: Gruppenprozesse* (Darmstadt: Deutscher Verlag, 1982).

[15] F. Ferracuti, "Psychiatric Aspects of Italian Left Wing and Right Wing Terrorism," paper presented to VIIth World Congress of Psychiatry, Vienna, Austria, July 1983.

[16] R. Clark, "Patterns in the Lives of ETA Members," *Terrorism* 6, no. 3 (1983): 423–54.

[17] J. Post, " 'Hostilité,' 'Conformité,' 'Fraternité': The Group Dynamics of Terrorist Behavior," *International Journal of Group Psychotherapy* 36, no. 2 (1986): 211–24.

PARENTS' ATTITUDE TOWARD REGIME

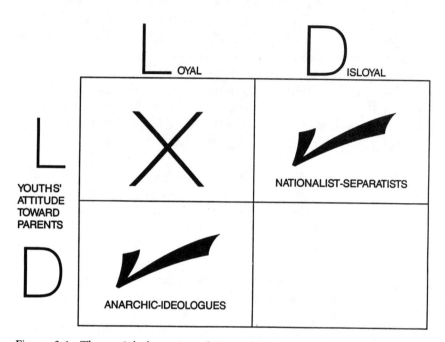

Figure 2.1. The social dynamics of "anarchic-ideologues" and "nationalist-separatists."

to parents who are loyal to the regime do not become terrorists. The upper right-hand cell signifies that "nationalist-separatist" terrorists are loyal to parents who are disloyal to their regime; they are carrying on the mission of their parents, who were wounded by the establishment. In the lower left-hand cell, in contrast, the "anarchic-ideologues" are disloyal to their parents' generation, which is identified with the establishment. Through acts of terrorism these anarchic-ideologues are striking out at the generation of their parents, seeking to heal their inner wounds by attacking the outside enemy. (The lower right-hand cell does not necessarily represent a subset of terrorists per se. Although it could be argued to represent fundamentalist youth who have turned from the path of modernizing parents, it could also be said to represent the dynamics of children of antiregime liberals who in their own politics have turned to hard-line conservatism.)

Although the social-psychological provenance and dynamics of the anarchic-ideologues and nationalist-separatists are quite different, in both cases the act of joining the terrorist group represents an attempt to consolidate a fragmented psychological identity, to resolve a split and be at one with oneself and with society, and, most important, to belong. Comparable data are not available for Shi'ite and Palestinian terrorists, but specialists who have closely followed Middle Eastern terrorist groups share the impression that many of their members come from the margins of society and that belonging to these fundamentalist or nationalist groups powerfully contributes to consolidating psychosocial identity at a time of great societal instability and flux.

In summary, most terrorists do not demonstrate serious psychopathology. Although there is no single personality type, it appears that people who are aggressive and action-oriented, and who place greater-than-normal reliance on the psychological mechanisms of externalization and splitting, are disproportionately represented among terrorists. Data indicate that many terrorists have not been successful in their personal, educational, and vocational lives. The combination of the personal feelings of inadequacy with the reliance on the psychological mechanisms of externalization and splitting leads them to find especially attractive a group of like-minded individuals whose credo is, "It's not us—it's them; they are the cause of our problems."

The power of the group

Although not all the people who find their way into a terrorist group share the characteristics just described, to the degree that many in the group do, the group takes on a particular coloration. For many, belonging to the terrorist group may be the first time they truly belonged, the first time they felt truly significant, the first time they felt that what they did counted. As Bion[18] has persuasively demonstrated, when individuals function in a group setting, their individual judgment and behavior are strongly influenced by the powerful forces of group dynamics.[19] This is true of psychologically healthy people, including successful business executives and educators. Bion's constructs are particularly useful in understanding the group dynamics of terrorist behavior.

In every group, according to Bion, there are two opposing forces—what Bion calls "the *work group*" and "the *basic assumption group*." The work group is that aspect of the group that acts in a goal-directed

[18] W. Bion, *Experiences in Groups* (London: Tavistock, 1961).
[19] M. Rioch, "The Work of Wilfred Bion on Groups," *Psychiatry* 33 (1978): 55–66.

manner to accomplish its stated purposes. But as anyone who has ever worked on a committee or task force will ruefully testify, the occasions when a group proceeds to work in a fully cooperative manner to accomplish its goals in a conflict-free manner are rare indeed. Rather, groups, in their functioning, often sabotage their stated goals. They act, to use Bion's words, as if they are operating under "basic assumptions," in what Bion calls the basic assumption group. He has identified three such psychological symptoms: the *"fight-flight"* group, the *"dependency"* group, and the *"pairing"* group:

1. The *fight-flight* group defines itself in relation to the outside world, which both threatens and justifies its existence. It acts as if the only way it can preserve itself is by fighting against or fleeing from the perceived enemy.
2. The *dependency* group turns to an omnipotent leader for direction. Members who fall into this state subordinate their own independent judgment to that of the leader and act as if they do not have minds of their own.
3. The *pairing* group acts as if the group will bring forth a messiah who will rescue them and create a better world.

If these states characterize the healthiest of groups, it should hardly be surprising that, when the group contains a disproportionate number of members who have fragmented psychosocial identities as well as a strong need to strike out against the cause of their failure, there should be an especially strong tendency to fall into these psychological postures, with extremely powerful group forces emerging. In my judgment, the terrorist group is the apotheosis of the "basic assumption" group, and regularly manifests all three "basic assumption" states.

In any assessment of the dynamics of the terrorist group it is important to differentiate among terrorisms. Both structure and social origin are of consequence. Identification of the locus of power and decision-making authority is particularly important to structural analysis.[20] In the autonomous terrorist cell, the leader is within the cell, and all warts are visible. These cells tend to be emotional hothouses, rife with tension. In contrast, in the well-differentiated organization, such as the Red Brigades, the action cells are organized within columns, and policy decisions are developed outside the cells, although details of implementation are left to the cells.

The differences between the social origins and psychosocial dynamics of nationalist-separatist terrorists and anarchic-ideologues have already been described. Their group dynamics also differ significantly. The

---

[20] J. Post, "Group and Organizational Dynamics of International Terrorism: Implications for Counterterrorist Policy," in *Contemporary Research in Terrorism*, edited by P. Wilkinson and A. M. Stewart (Aberdeen: Aberdeen University Press, 1987).

nationalist-separatist terrorists are often known in their communities and maintain relationships with friends and family outside the group. They can move into and out of the community with relative ease. In contrast, for the anarchic-ideologues the decision to cross the boundary and enter the underground illegal group is an irrevocable one, what the German scholars call "Der Sprung" (the leap). Group pressures are especially magnified for the underground group, so that the group is the only source of information, the only source of confirmation, and, in the face of external danger and pursuit, the only source of security.

The resultant group pressure cooker produces extremely powerful forces. In particular, there are pressures to conform and pressures to commit acts of violence.

PRESSURES TO CONFORM. Given the intensity of the need to belong, the strength of the affiliative needs, and, for many members, the as-yet incomplete sense of individual identity, terrorists have a tendency to submerge their own identities into the group, so that a kind of "group mind" emerges.[21] The group cohesion that emerges is magnified by the external danger, which tends to reduce internal divisiveness in unity against the outside enemy. "The group was born under the pressure of pursuit" according to members of the Red Army Faction,[22] and group solidarity was "compelled exclusively by the illegal situation, fashioned into a common destiny." Another Red Army Faction member went so far as to consider this pressure "the sole link holding the group together."[23]

Doubts concerning the legitimacy of the goals and actions of the group are intolerable to such a group. The person who questions a group decision risks the wrath of the group and possible expulsion. Indeed, the fear is even more profound, for, as Baumann[24] has stated, withdrawal was impossible "except by way of the graveyard." *The way to get rid of doubt is to get rid of the doubters.* Extreme pressure to conform has been reported by all who have discussed the atmosphere within the group. Baeyer-Kaette[25] has described the first meeting of a new recruit to the Heidelberg cell of the Red Army Faction. The group, which previously had targeted only identified representatives of the establishment such as

[21] Post, "'Hostilité,' 'Conformité,' 'Fraternité.'"
[22] B. Sturm, *Der Spiegel* 7 (1972): 57.
[23] V. Spietel, *Der Spiegel* 33 (1980): 35.
[24] See Baumann, in Baeyer-Kaette et al., *Analysen Zum Terrorismus.*
[25] W. Baeyer-Kaette, "A Left-Wing Terrorist Indoctrination Group," paper presented to the 6th Annual Meeting of the International Society of Political Psychology, Oxford, England, July 1983.

magistrates and policemen, was discussing a plan to firebomb a major department store. Horrified, the new recruit blurted out, "But that will lead to loss of innocent lives!" A chill fell over the room, and the new recruit quickly realized that to question the group consensus was to risk losing his membership in the group. What an interesting paradox, that these groups, whose ideology is intensely against the dominance of authority, should be so authoritarian and should so insist on conformity and unquestioning obedience.

The group ideology plays an important role in supporting this conformity-inducing group environment. When questions are raised, the absolutist ideology becomes the intellectual justification. Indeed, the ideology becomes, in effect, the scripture for the group's morality. In the incident just described, the leader of the cell patiently explained to the new recruit that anyone who would shop in such an opulent store was no innocent victim, but was indeed a capitalist consumer.

Questions have often been raised as to how people socialized to a particular moral code could commit such violent antisocial acts. Insofar as an individual submerges his own identity into the group, the group's moral code becomes each individual's moral code. As Crenshaw[26] has observed, "The group, as selector and interpreter of ideology, is central." What the group, through its interpretation of its ideology, defines as moral becomes moral—and becomes the authority for the compliant members. And if the ideology indicates that "they are responsible for our problems," to destroy "them" is not only viewed as justified but can be seen to be a moral imperative.

The studies of charismatic religious cults by Galanter et al.[27,28,29] contribute usefully to our understanding of the dynamics of the terrorist group. These researchers found that the more isolated and unaffiliated the new members, the more likely they were to hold assiduously—and unquestioningly—to their group membership, because it provided the members' sole definition of themselves, their sole source of support.

[26] M. Crenshaw, "An (Organizational Approach to the Analysis of Political Terrorism," *Orbis* 29 (1985): 465–89.

[27] M. Galanter, R. Rabkin, J. Rabkin, and A. Deutsch, "The 'Moonies': A Psychological Study of Conversion and Membership in a Contemporary Religious Sect," *American Journal of Psychiatry* 136 (1979): 165–70.

[28] M. Galanter, "Psychological Induction into the Large Group: Findings from a Modern Religious Sect," *American Journal of Psychiatry* 137 (1980): 1574–79.

[29] M. Galanter, "Engaged Members of the Unification Church: Impact of a Charismatic Large Group on Adaptation and Behavior," *Archives of General Psychiatry* 40, no. 11 (November 1983): 1197–202.

Moreover—and this is particularly important for the question of the capacity of terrorists to commit antisocial acts—these researchers found that the greater the relief the new cult recruits felt on joining, the greater the likelihood they would engage in acts that violated the mores to which they had been socialized. Galanter and associates studied the willingness of 1,410 members of the Unification Church to accept the Reverend Moon's choice of marital partner, assigned in a bizarre mass engagement ceremony in Madison Square Garden. Those who depended entirely on the cult for their sense of emotional well-being accepted the Reverend Moon's selection without question.

PRESSURES TO COMMIT ACTS OF VIOLENCE. In attempting to clarify whether acts of political violence are chosen as a willful strategy or are products of psychological forces, it is of central importance to evaluate the goal of the act of violence. The rationalist school, as explicated by Crenshaw in the previous chapter, would aver that in an unequal political struggle, acts of political terrorism become an equalizer. These acts of political violence call forceful attention to the group's legitimate grievances and are designed to have an impact on a much wider audience than the immediate target of the violence. (Schmid[30] has observed that it is very important to differentiate between the target of the violence and the target of influence; what distinguishes terrorism from other forms of political violence is the differentiation of the target of violence, that is, the innocent victim or noncombatant, from the target of influence, that is, the broader public or elite decision makers.) But implicit in this line of reasoning is an assumption that the political violence is instrumental, a tactic to achieve the group's political goals, to help it achieve its cause.

The position argued in this essay—that political violence is driven by psychological forces—follows a different line of reasoning. It does not view political violence as instrumental, but as the end itself. *The cause is not the cause.* The cause, as codified in the group's ideology, according to this line of reasoning, becomes the rationale for acts the terrorists are driven to commit. Indeed, the central argument of this position is that *individuals become terrorists in order to join terrorist groups and commit acts of terrorism.*

That is surely an extreme statement, but since we are discussing political extremism, perhaps that excess can be forgiven.

[30] A. P. Schmid, *Political Terrorism: A Research Guide to Concepts, Theories, Data Bases, and Literature* (Amsterdam: North-Holland, 1983).

Consider a youth seeking an external target to attack. Before joining the group, he was alone, not particularly successful. Now he is engaged in a life-and-death struggle with the establishment, his picture on the "most wanted" posters. He sees his leaders as internationally prominent media personalities. Within certain circles, he is lionized as a hero. He travels first class, and his family is provided for should his acts of heroism lead to his death as a martyr to the cause. Heady stuff that; surely this is the good life, a role and position not easily relinquished.

Now if authenticity is defined as "revolutionary heroism," then this definition has important implications for the outcomes of debates and personal rivalries within the group. A leader who advocates prudence and moderation is likely to lose his position quickly to a bolder person committed to the continuation of the struggle. Indeed, on the basis of his observations of underground resistance groups during World War II, Zawodny[31] has concluded that the primary determinant of underground group decision making is not the external reality but the psychological climate within the group. He has described the unbearable tension that builds when a resistance group is compelled to go underground. For these action-oriented people, forced inaction is extremely stressful. What, after all, are freedom fighters if they do not fight? *A terrorist group needs to commit acts of terrorism in order to justify its existence.* The wise leader, sensing the building tension, will plan an action so that the group's members can reaffirm their identity and discharge their aggressive energy. Better to have the group attack the outside enemy, no matter how high the risk, than turn on itself—and him.

This suggests a dynamic within the group pressing for the perpetuation of violence and leading toward ever-riskier decisions. Indeed, the terrorist group displays, in extreme degree, the characteristics of "groupthink" as described by Janis.[32] Among the characteristics he ascribes to groups demonstrating "groupthink" are the following:

1. Illusions of invulnerability leading to excessive optimism and excessive risk taking
2. Presumptions of the group's morality
3. One-dimensional perceptions of the enemy as evil
4. Intolerance of challenges by a group member to shared key beliefs.

---

[31] J. K. Zawodny, "Internal Organizational Problems and the Sources of Tensions of Terrorist Movements as Catalysts of Violence," *Terrorism* 1, no. 3/4 (1978): 277–85.
[32] I. Janis, *Victims of Groupthink* (Boston: Houghton-Mifflin, 1972).

This research on "groupthink" relates to another important body of research bearing on risky decision making by groups. Using U.S. military officers as subjects, Semel and Minix[33] found that groups regularly opted for riskier choices than those that would have been preferred by individuals.

This momentum toward ever-riskier choices has important implications for mass-casualty terrorism. Analysis conducted for the International Task Force for the Prevention of Nuclear Terrorism[34] leads me to conclude that the internal constraints against the unthinkable prospect of nuclear terrorism are weakening, that although it is still in the realm of "low probability-high consequences," the prospects are increasing, and a major contribution to that increase are the risk-increasing group dynamics of the terrorist group.

The threat of success

If the cause were indeed the cause, should not its achievement lead to the dissolution of the terrorist groups committing violent acts in its name? Consider the Basque separatists. Many would say that they have achieved a significant proportion of their goals. While they are not a separate nation, to be sure, the degree of autonomy they have achieved is remarkable. Why does ETA not clap its collective hands in satisfaction, declare victory, dissolve the organization, and go back to work in the region's factories? ETA roars on. Its goals are absolutist, and nothing less than total victory will suffice, say its leaders, although many Basque politicians feel their actions are now counterproductive.

On a number of occasions Yasir Arafat, by divesting himself of the radical left wing of the Palestine Liberation Organization (PLO) and pursuing a political course, accepting United Nations Resolution No. 242 and acknowledging Israel's right to exist, would have placed major pressure on Israel and might well have achieved the beginnings of a partial territorial solution to the Palestinian problem. But on each of these occasions, when push came to shove, he opted to be leader of the unified Palestinian resistance movement, yielding to the radical left, who were

[33] See A. K. Semel and D. A. Minix, in *Psychological Models and International Politics*, edited by L. S. Falkowski (Boulder, Colo.: Westview Press, 1979).

[34] J. Post, "Prospects for Nuclear Terrorism: Psychological Motivations and Constraints," in *Preventing Nuclear Terrorism*, edited by P. Leventhal and Y. Alexander (Lexington, Mass.: Lexington Books, 1987).

committed to winning their struggle through violence. The espoused cause—a Palestinian homeland—did not seem to be the PLO's primary goal. Similarly, on how many occasions in Northern Ireland, on the threshold of a move to conciliation, did the proponents of violence so act as to perpetuate the cycle of violence?

For any group or organization, the highest priority is survival. This is especially true for the terrorist group. *To succeed in achieving its espoused cause would threaten the goal of survival.* This fact suggests a position of cybernetic balance for the group. It must be successful enough in its terrorist acts and rhetoric of legitimation to attract members and perpetuate itself, but it must not be so successful that it will succeed itself out of business. As can be seen in the case of Basque separatist terrorism, the absolutist quality of the ideology, and its associated rhetoric, guarantees that the terrorist group can always find plausible justifications for continuing its struggle. However great the degree of autonomy granted to the Basques by the Spanish central government, ETA's absolutist demands will not be fully satisfied until ETA forces the central government to grant the Basque people their total independence as a separate nation, something Madrid is not about to do.

Policy implications

If the foregoing conclusions concerning the individual, group, and organizational psychology of political terrorism are valid, what are the implications for antiterrorist policy?

Terrorists whose only sense of significance comes from being terrorists cannot be forced to give up terrorism, for to do so would be to lose their very reason for being. Indeed, for such persons, violent societal counterreactions reaffirm their core belief that "it's us against them and they are out to destroy us."

Because terrorisms differ in their structure and dynamics, policies should be tailored to the specific group, which must be understood in its historical, cultural, and political context. As a general rule, the smaller and more autonomous the group, the more counterproductive is external force. When the autonomous cell comes under external threat, the external danger has the consequence of reducing internal divisiveness and uniting the group against the outside enemy. The survival of the group is paramount because of the sense of identity the group provides. Violent societal counterreactions can transform a tiny band of insignificant persons into a major opponent of society, making their "fantasy war," to use Ferracu-ti's apt term, a reality. One can indeed make the case that, left to their own devices, these inherently unstable groups will self-destruct.

Similarly, for the terrorist organization for which violence is defined as the only legitimate tactic for achieving its espoused goals, outside threat and a policy of reactive retaliation cannot intimidate the organizational leaders into giving up their acts of political violence. To do so would be, in effect, to commit organizational suicide.

For complex organizations in which an illegal terrorist wing operates in parallel with a legal political wing as elements of a larger, loosely integrated organization, the dynamics—and the policy implications—are again different. (The Basque separatist movement is a good example.) In such circumstances, if the overall organizational goals are threatened by societal reactions to terrorism, it can be argued that internal organiza-tional pressures can operate to constrain the terrorist wing. However, insofar as the terrorist group is not fully under political control, this is a matter of influence and partial constraint, for, as has been noted earlier, ETA has its own internal dynamics and continues to thrive, despite the significant degree of separatism already achieved.

For state-supported and state-directed terrorist groups, the group is, in effect, a paramilitary unit under government control. Terrorism is being employed as an equalizing tactic in an undeclared war. In this situation, the individual, group, and organizational psychological considerations just discussed are not especially relevant. The target of the antiterrorist policy in this circumstance should not be the group per se but the chief of state and the government of the sponsoring state. Because the survival of the state and of national interests are the primary values for that state, there is a rational case to be made that retaliatory policies can have a deterring effect, at least in the short term. In the long run, however, youthful witnesses to retaliatory violence may themselves later join the terrorists' ranks.

Just as political terrorism is the product of generational forces, so, too, it is here for generations to come. *There is no short-range solution to the problem of terrorism.* Once an individual is in the pressure cooker of the terrorist group, it is extremely difficult to influence him. In the long run, the most effective antiterrorist policy is one that inhibits potential re-cruits from joining in the first place.

Political terrorism is not simply a *product* of psychological forces; its central *strategy* is psychological, for *political terrorism, is, at base, a par-*

ticularly vicious species of psychological warfare. Until now, the terrorists have had a virtual monopoly on the weapon of the television camera, as they manipulate their target audiences through the media. Terrorists perpetuate their organizations by shaping the perceptions of future generations of terrorists. Manipulating a reactive media, they demonstrate their power and significance and define the legitimacy of their cause. Countering the terrorists' highly effective media-oriented strategy through more effective dissemination of information and public education—deromanticizing the terrorists and portraying them for what they are—must be key elements of a proactive policy.

As important as it is to inhibit potential terrorists from joining terrorist groups, it is equally important to facilitate their leaving those groups. The powerful hold of the group has been detailed. By creating pathways out of terrorism, we can loosen that grip. Amnesty programs modeled after the highly effective program of the Italian government can contribute to that goal. Reducing support for the group—both in its immediate societal surroundings and in the nation at large—are further long-range programs worth fostering. In the long run, the most effective way of countering terrorism is to reduce external support, to facilitate pathways out of terrorism, and, most important, to reduce the attractiveness of the terrorist path for alienated youth.

Part II

Varieties of terrorism:
Ideological and religious motivations

3

Ideology and rebellion: Terrorism in West Germany

KONRAD KELLEN

It is both easy and difficult to examine the theme of ideologically based rebellion in the context of contemporary West German terrorism. It is easy because so much can be said about it, and it is difficult because so much has already been said about terrorism and rebellion in general. But it is also difficult because the analyst hopes that by contributing something new to the understanding of the phenomenon he can contribute something new to our capacity for dealing effectively with the phenomenon. And that is hard indeed, because terrorists, West German or otherwise, to the extent that we understand their psychology, are not in the habit of consulting us about their troubles or being otherwise susceptible to our force or our reason.

This is unfortunate because West German terrorists, like many—but by no means all—terrorists, suffer from a psychological trauma that does two things: First, it makes them see the world, including their own actions and the expected effects of those actions, in a grossly unrealistic light. Second, it motivates them to use violence against individuals in its most extreme form—cold-blooded murder. Thus the old cliché that portrays terrorists as madmen who engage in irrational and futile acts of violence has some roundabout and perhaps unexpected truth in it, certainly as far as the West German terrorists are concerned: Most of them suffer from a deep psychological trauma and act out what that trauma whispers into their conscious minds.

How do we know this? First, we have some autobiographies of ex-terrorists who, to this day, live in hiding—both from their former comrades, who would kill them as traitors, and from legitimate society, which would incarcerate them for many years. These terrorists have written and spoken of their early years from their hiding places. Second, we have interviews with terrorists who were caught, some of which I myself conducted. Third, we have reams of statements made in court by West German terrorists. Fourth, we have knowledge of their behavior, which includes, in the case of the leaders of the Red Army Faction, no fewer than five suicides committed in prison.

In the main, despite these instances of suicide—which suggest, at least in those cases, significantly compromised psychological health—the West German terrorists show strong ties to reality. They operate extremely efficiently in their own terms and have been able to get away with their crimes rather easily, despite the efforts of the biggest and most effective antiterrorist police machinery ever created. Certainly they are not simply madmen; indeed, they have a considerable grasp on some segments of reality, as well as an impressive ability to manipulate certain portions of it.

But are they effective? Only persons not aware of the true nature and purposes (I use the plural advisedly) of terrorism can scoff at the assassination of German industrialists Ernst Zimmermann in 1985 and Kurt Beckurts in 1986, or Foreign Service official Gerold von Braunmuehl, also in 1986, as ineffective. To be sure, such assassinations do not bring the establishment down. Like everyone else, these victims were easily replaceable. But the terrorists are psychological operatives—they aim to terrorize. Can there be any doubt that their actions have, at times, thrown a gnawing, even paralyzing fear into the West German establishment? This effect has been achieved even by the failed operations of the terrorists, such as the unsuccessful assassination attempts on generals Haig and Kroesen several years ago. Although these two men were unscathed in those attempts, the ingenious attempts on their lives spread great fear among the American representatives, officials, and dependents in Germany. Certainly, West German terrorists have not overthrown the state: they have not made the Americans go home, and they have not deterred people from going about their business in the accustomed fashion, including West German research on the Strategic Defense Initiative (SDI). But in other ways they have been vastly successful, and it is worth focusing a bit more on their success before returning to consider them as individuals working together in small groups.

The effects of terrorist successes in West Germany

The considerable successes of West German terrorists can be divided into three categories. The first has to do with the terror they have instilled into almost every West German heart—from the statesman to the common air traveler, from the business executive, especially one with foreign responsibilities, to the military commander who, if he does not tremble for himself, does so for his personnel and for West German military bases. Thus the first successful effect is the feeling of insecurity created by the terrorists, or what the Germans call a general *Verunsicherung*.

The second major effect of West German terrorism has been the almost incomprehensibly vast sum of money, effort, and brain power that has been devoted to fight, anticipate, and defend against it, from armored limousines for practically everybody who can carry a briefcase, to special guards and official police, to computer-based surveillance efforts. The measures dictated by the terrorists are growing. In the wake of the Braunmuehl killing in Bonn, the number of security guards and armored cars assigned to officials was doubled overnight, and no doubt the same obtains for private industry.

The third major effect of terrorism has been on the intellectual community. In West Germany perhaps even more than in the United States, all sorts of intellectuals (social scientists in particular) have thrown themselves into the problem of terrorism and have studied it now for more than twenty years. The collection of available books and treatises, meetings and symposia, political speeches and counterspeeches dealing with terrorism is a constantly swelling river, or more precisely an ocean, whose breadth and depth illustrate the fact that all those eager analysts are not really getting anywhere. The West German Ministry of the Interior itself conducted and published a thorough, five-volume study by social scientists from various disciplines and political outlooks that examines the nature of West German terrorism and the soul of West German terrorists. Certainly in West Germany, at least, the analysts studying the terrorists apparently far outnumber the terrorists.

The findings of terrorism scholars

What have all these students of terrorism and terrorists—of which I am, I admit, one—found? First, the more sensible among us have found that there are essential differences among types of terrorists. The Palestinian terrorists are different from the Irish terrorists, and the West German terrorists are "more different" yet, with their own special features, some of which are discussed later in this paper. This is very controversial territory politically because of its relation to the German past, which people in Europe and the United States, as well as in West Germany, conveniently insist on forgetting and relegating to history. However, that past is alive and has contributed, both directly and indirectly, to the spawning of West German terrorism. In the face of psychopathic behavior connected with more or less clearly evident traumata, some psychiatrists may say that nothing in the real world creates the ideas and behaviors of psychopaths—that they are merely the psychopaths' own perceptions and assessments. This may often be so, but the German case is unique.

Even today, four decades after the end of World War II, nothing in West Germany can be understood that is not viewed in light of the Nazi experience, activity, or derangement. The Western world talks a lot about the horrible crimes that were committed by the German nation—not the Gestapo or SS officials, who were seen as just the executors of the national consensus. Nevertheless, the victorious Allies tolerated—in fact, they promoted—the new rise to wealth and power of 90 percent of those most responsible for what was done. Even twenty years after Hitler's defeat, 75 percent of all West German judges were men who had been Nazi party members and had brutally carried out Nazi law. The number has subsequently declined, but only because quite a few have died; what Germans inelegantly call "the biological solution" has taken care of them.

In industry and business the situation was truly abysmal. As a result of the Marshall Plan, thousands of the very men who had driven millions to death under Hitler were given back their wealth, comfort, and the prestige of their Mercedes cars and villas, while true opponents of the Nazi regime could not rebuild a decent existence, having been deprived of it by the Nazis and then by the new/old bosses. Still more frustrating was the fact that these past opponents of the Hitler regime could not gain currency for their political ideas and desires in a Germany run by men who shared the guilt but were vociferously unrepentant. At the same time, these beneficiaries both of the Hitler regime and of the largess offered by the Allies created a climate in which only physical reconstruction was permitted. Political ideologies that might be called social or progressive were given no room to express themselves.

Some West Germans, especially the youth, took exception to that.

Among them were many whose parents may have disapproved of some feature of the Nazi state but had gone along because of fear or for opportunistic reasons. Many of the young people said, "Let's not be like them, like our parents. When we see evil, we must rebel immediately." And many did rebel. Disappointed by the purely materialistic and hedonistic course of the postwar decades in West Germany, many were further shocked by the Vietnam War, which disillusioned them about the United States. The resulting student rebellions, first sparked by a visit of the shah of Iran to Berlin, gave rise to widespread rebellion. Since then, most of the youth of West Germany have become as tame as the youth in the United States, even though South Africa, Chernobyl, and a few other events on the political scene have produced a mild stir. However, some of the "radicals" of the day remained just that; when there was no substantial response to their political drives among either the elite or the masses, their ideology turned them into terrorists. Thus, the rebellious West German youth of the 1960s had motivations quite different from the motivations of youth in the United States, and the West Germans' rebellion was in some ways more justified. Eventually, the terrorists grew out of that vast cauldron of dissatisfaction, and their terrorism assumed a life and momentum of its own.

Am I an apologist for the West German terrorists? Am I one of those so-called sympathizers, of whom the West German police still count up to two thousand and keep careful track in their computers? Do I approve of terrorists' taking armed action against a state or individuals, even if they are associated with the greatest crimes ever committed, and now follow a course regarded by many as "imperialist" and "aggressive" under the aegis of the United States? No, I do not approve. I only try to understand, and I do not support the French saying, *Tout comprendre c'est tout pardonner.* Besides, the situation in postwar West Germany is only half the reason why terrorists are what they are.

Most West German terrorists cite the need to take immediate and violent action against such malefactors of yore (and their American friends) as only one of the justifications for their actions. The other reason they give is that they are fighting against the "imperialism" of NATO and "its plans to make war" and for the "oppressed and exploited" in metropolitan areas of the West and of the third world. Anyone who wants to gain some understanding of these terrorists should listen carefully to what the terrorists themselves say about their actions and motivations, no matter how criminal or absurd these seem. In fact, one reason why we really do

not know much about West German or, in fact, most terrorists is that we
do not take the trouble of listening carefully to them. We study their
actions in the minutest detail, their affiliations, financial support, weapons, and travels, but we pay relatively little attention to what they say
and think. Like politicians who know no better and must impress their
electorates by dismissing everything terrorists say as rubbish, we do not
listen to the terrorists as carefully as psychiatrists listen to their patients.

There are several reasons why we do not listen, some of them perhaps
justified. The first is that we believe we really cannot do anything about
the terrorists except, if we are lucky, to catch and incapacitate them.
Psychiatrists listen to their patients in order to better understand them
and for the specific purpose of treating the patients effectively. So long as
we are unable to apply psychotherapy to terrorists—either because they
are not in our grasp or because if they were, they probably would not
seek therapy—we cannot see the use of trying.

A second reason we do not listen to terrorists as carefully as we might
is that even the most politically respectable of us may not want to appear
"too objective" (if I may coin this intrinsically illogical term) when dealing with them; we believe we must condemn anything they do or say as
being entirely unacceptable. And a third reason is that we may indeed be
too shocked by what they do to muster the requisite curiosity. When we
see innocent victims dead or wounded in an airport after a terrorist raid,
we cannot listen easily to what the terrorists may have to say, or ponder
what they may think or feel. We react instinctively with anger and loath-
ing, which is hardly a scientific approach. Even though this reaction is
understandable and even excusable, it hinders our quest.

What motivates the West German terrorists?

If we do listen to the West German terrorists and we use every means at
our disposal to learn about them, what can we conclude about their ideas,
motivations, and impulses—in short, their psychologies? And what can
we conclude about past attempts to study these questions?

Some analysis has been done on terrorists' wants, thoughts, and perceptions of the world and their role in it, but, at least as far as the West
German terrorists are concerned, the results are not impressive.[1] It must
be admitted that even if we had the materials to delve more effectively

[1] See H. Jäger, G. Schmidtchen, and L. Süllwold, *Analysen zum Terrorismus*, vol. 2: *Lebenslauf-Analysen* (Opladen: Westdeutscher Verlag, 1981).

into their psyches, the question remains as to what we would do with the findings. Would we try to respond to terrorists' needs? We certainly would never think of giving in to, say, kidnapping or some other coercive terrorist action, just because we understood its motivation. In general, even if we found some psychological remedy that might appease their rage, we would not use it: nobody would dismiss a single one of those old Nazi judges or industrialists simply to accommodate the terrorists who shoot one of them once in a while.

(Interestingly enough, not everybody in West Germany seems to feel that way. West Germany is the only West European country in which a considerable percentage of the population—a full 5 percent, which translates into about 2 million people—think that the terrorists were bred by society, whereas all the populations of other Western societies, especially American society, firmly and overwhelmingly refuse to believe that the ideology or rebellion of any terrorist has anything to do with the surrounding conditions. In other words, these 5 percent of the West German population accord to the terrorists in their midst some justification for not merely opposing the existing order but for opposing it by bloody means.)

Even the most ingenious theories of terrorism have not been very useful until now, because they have tended to get stuck in an analysis of violent people in general, and most violent people are not terrorists. What characterizes the terrorists is the political, or pseudopolitical, component of their motivations, which ordinary violent people lack. Terrorists— especially terrorists of the millenarian type, as in West Germany—have a comparatively rare personality combination of the intellectual (albeit usually not brilliant ones) and the physically violent person in the extreme. This combination, and not just the violent nature of their actions or the radicalism of their politics, makes the terrorists unique. Most of our theories do not cover such people.

What, in fact, do West German terrorists—in particular, members of the Red Army Faction—want? Dr. Günter Rohrmoser, a well-known political philosopher who participated in the aforementioned monumental study of West German terrorists conducted at the behest of West Germany's Ministry of the Interior in the early 1980s, summed up what he had learned about the terrorists in these striking words:

What do the terrorists want? They want The Revolution, a total transformation of all existing conditions, a new form of human existence, an entirely new relationship of people to each other, and also of people to nature. They want the total and radical breach with all that is, and with all historical continuity. Without a doubt they are utopians. The source of their (self-provided) legitimacy is the utopia which they want to make real, and it is the same utopia that makes them regard all historical and ideological factors as illusions. Inside their world, or outside their world, there is no voice that could call them back to reason. For them, there is no connection between the vision that drives them and the existing reality that, they feel, keeps them in chains; therefore destruction is the only form of freedom they can accept. In light of their own utopia, the existing system appears to them as hell, as a system which exploits, suppresses and destroys human beings and in which to dwell means living death. In their view, the decision to become revolutionaries is the beginning of becoming human (a form of rebirth); to act in a revolutionary fashion means to them the establishment of their own selves, the step from the realm of disaster and damnation into the realm of freedom and light. They are fascinated by the magic of the extremes, the hard and uncompromising either/or, life or death, salvation or perdition, "pig" or man—with nothing in between. They recognize only one principle: unconditional consistency. Any compromise they do not even regard as weakness, but as treason. They are driven by their pitiless hatred for those they look upon as their enemies, a hatred fed by a disgust with what they regard as a morbid, decadent society of sly and immoral practices and mendacious hypocrisy. They pretend to serve "the people," but the people exist only in their imagination. And they are interested in Marxist or Leninist theory only to the extent that they hope to find in it some effective methods of revolutionary action.[2]

Clearly, Rohrmoser regarded millenarianism as the most important characteristic of the thinking of the young men and women he studied, and what I have learned about them in my own years of study coincides with Rohrmoser's conclusion.

But some other, related conclusions can also be reached from interviews with terrorists and studies of their writings. One conclusion is that such people, so long as they hold on to their convictions, cannot be appeased by anyone or anything; nor can they be satisfied by any change in conditions—they will fight until they are killed or caught. Another conclusion is that their very manifest radicalism, taken to its ultimate extreme, is of a sort that holds a certain appeal, indeed a fascination, for a significant number of young people who proclaim their intense disgust at "dirty compromises," by which they mean all run-of-the-mill politics and bourgeois ways.

This radical rejection of all forms of compromise, at least intellectually, has always been a trait that is probably more easily found among German youth than elsewhere. It may be related to an intellectual and moral attitude that detests politics and politicians—an attitude that has

[2] Günter Rohrmoser, in *Analysen zum Terrorismus,* vol. 2, 87.

a long tradition in Germany. It is also evidence, I think, that the West German terrorists are ideologically by far the most radical terrorists in the world, just as before them, the German fascists were the most radical of all fascists the world has ever known. To be sure, this radicalism is not shared by a majority of youths in present-day West Germany. But there have been enough such people to provide a sizable circle of sympathizers to aid and abet the bloody deeds of the Red Army Faction—sympathizers without whom the Red Army Faction never could have functioned so effectively.

Rohrmoser's analysis, done in the early 1980s, addressed the terrorists of the 1970s. Are they still the same? I see one great difference: their targets have changed. Whereas they were once bent on overturning all West German society, they now are primarily concerned with the destruction of NATO or, more precisely, with a reduction or cessation of the West German role in it and a retreat of American forces back to the United States. Thus, even if it is highly improbable that they will succeed, their activities and objectives are no longer altogether unrealistic, because a dissolution of NATO, or a reduction of the American presence in Europe, is at least more thinkable than a millenarian transformation of West German society. There are, moreover, large numbers of people both in the United States and in West Germany who would like to see a reduction of emphasis on military activities in general. These antimilitaristic people, in the peace movements and elsewhere, may not like the methods of the terrorists, which of late consist of targeted assassinations of men they regard as linchpins in the process. But, in some vague sense, they are sympathizers with at least some of the aims of the Red Army Faction as they are now formulated.

The relationship between terrorists and society

One shortcoming of almost every analysis of terrorists is that they are studied as if they were goldfish in a bowl, without regard to the fact that they are highly responsive to what *we* do, how *we* react, what *we* say, what *we* seem to think. In that respect, the analysis of terrorism is very similar to Sovietology: We always ask the so-called experts what the Kremlin will do next, without first acknowledging that the Soviets' action depends largely on what *we* do or say, or seem to think and plan. Contrary to legend, terrorists are not rigid but quite flexible—not in their ideology or aims, of course, but in their methods, modus operandi, target selection, treatment of hostages. Like everybody else, they respond to perceived successes and failures, and to enemy actions and intentions.

In fact, West German terrorists, like other terrorists and like everyone else, do not operate in a vacuum; they coexist actively with various societies in the world, but primarily with the democratic societies, in a highly reciprocal relationship. They coexist in a highly reciprocal relationship not only with the West German society, but also with society in the United States, where any action of theirs or of their counterparts in other countries receives enormous media attention. In that sense, the United States is the terrorists' greatest booster, not only because it gives them so much media attention, but even more so because U.S. leaders make thunderous declarations to the effect that they will destroy the terrorists root and branch, thereby paying them high tribute. Naturally, because the United States neither roots them out nor prevents their acts, the terrorists gain great publicity leverage. As a result, "the terrorists" are now principal players in all global situations and events. When there are Olympic games, every person asks eagerly, "What will the terrorists do?" much as one might ask whether the crowned heads of Europe will be in attendance. This can only energize them.

Perhaps the greatest beneficiaries of this publicity and overblown opprobrium have been the members of the West German Red Army Faction. These people—probably much more than, say, Irish or Arab terrorists—seem to be plagued by feelings of impotence and insignificance, and such great boosts as are accorded to the terrorist fraternity in general throughout the world are likely to help them in particular.

The characteristics of West German terrorists

The personal and historical characteristics of individual West German terrorists are also worth noting. One such characteristic is educational level. It has been observed that West German terrorists are "intellectuals." To be sure, many of them have been students, in particular social science students. But—and this point seems important to me—they were not very successful students. Except for Horst Mahler, the cofounder of the Red Army Faction and long a renegade and "useful member" of society, few terrorists have ever even attained a university degree. None of them has ever published anything of note, except in the form of memoirs of failed terrorists; and none of them has ever developed a social or political theory.

Second, most Red Army Faction members came from middle-class surroundings. Such a background often induces a certain stability and self-confidence in people. But the West German terrorists were not in harmony with their early surroundings. Some came from homes where the father was a clergyman who may have caused his children to rebel by repressive attitudes. Other parents beat their children. Many of these young people never belonged anywhere and had no success, no money, and no power until suddenly they became players on the world stage, dealing with prime ministers and commanding headlines. The unhappy childhoods characteristic of most West German terrorists may have turned them into angry, contrary, and frustrated people. This seems to be particularly true, from the sketchy materials we have, of those who come from the highly restricted, often intolerably rigid backgrounds so typical of the German bourgeoisie, with its many compulsions and pretensions. Apparently, the terrorists are quite aware of their—to them—pernicious and shameful petit bourgeois background, so much so that the Red Army Faction, in its early stages, went out of its way to recruit a young man they regarded as "a real worker" of whom they felt they had to have at least one in their midst, to justify their revolutionary fervor. Ironically, the "real" proletarian worker turned out to be a police stool pigeon through whom the German police had infiltrated the group.

The unease most Red Army Faction members feel about themselves because of their emotional past is also attested to by Michael Baumann,[3] who was a specialist in explosives for the group but eventually defected and is still in hiding after some dozen years. He managed to publish an autobiography, in which he reports on the contrast between himself—a young man from the working section of Berlin, and one of the few true nonbourgeois persons in the group—and his Red Army Faction colleagues. When speaking about music, for example, he says, "A worker definitely has more of a relation to rock music than an intellectual has. With him, it's more physical, you're only tuned into the body, not the mind, and dancing and stuff is more your thing because somehow you're closer to earth." In other words, he observed that most of the group were not "close to earth" and were too much led by their intellect. Conversely, Baumann relates that when robbing a bank, for example, "I would operate much more by feel than intuition and reason." Needless to say,

[3] Strictly speaking, Baumann was not a member of the Red Army Faction but of the 2 June Movement, a related organization which was eventually absorbed into the Red Army Faction.

Baumann was not a fervent ideologue, yet he was not without his political ideas, all of which ran contrary to the established order.

About his first day on the job at a construction site, Baumann remembers that "riding on the tram to the construction site, it suddenly hit me—you're gonna be doing this for fifty years, there's no escaping it. The terror of that hit my bones. I had to look for ways to get out." To be sure, Baumann's disapproval—indeed, revulsion—of ordinary society dates from earlier experiences: "Actually," he reports, "with me it all began with rock music and long hair. . . . In my case, in Berlin, it was like this [in the 1960s]: if you let your hair grow long you suddenly were in the position the blacks are in the United States. Do you understand? They threw us out of bars, they cursed us and chased after us . . . all you had was trouble. You got fired from your job or you could not even find one, or you got only the worst kind of job. And you had constant hassles with complete strangers in the street."

For Baumann, long hair seems to have been an article of faith, especially in the aggressively narrow-minded surroundings of the German bourgeoisie. He makes a remarkable statement in his own defense: "I was a completely normal person. With me it was like this: I suddenly saw a connection between my long hair and the problems that exist in America, like the problems of the blacks. And suddenly because of my long hair I was like a black or Jew or leper. In any event, with long hair you were pushed into the position of an outcast. . . . For me it was clear from the outset—I liked long hair. With long hair you get a different relationship with yourself, a new identity—at least that is what happened to me. You develop a really healthy narcissism which you need simply to survive. After some early youthful confusion, you become more conscious and begin to like yourself."[4]

These passages are interesting primarily for the following reason: Baumann, like most terrorists in the world, seems to feel on the defensive rather than the offensive; he feels coerced rather than being a coercer; he feels justified in what he is doing, and in no way guilty. In fact, probably all terrorists, whether of the religious, ethnic, nationalist, or political/social variety, believe that their targets, individually and collectively, are not only guilty because of what they do and represent, but because they oppress and mistreat the terrorists. It seems to be extremely difficult for

[4] Michael Baumann, *Terror or Love: Bommi Baumann's Own Story of His Life as a West German Urban Guerrilla* (New York: Grove Press, 1979), 19–24.

Western observers to see and accept that terrorists, whom society regards as the ultimate aggressors, believe that they themselves act out of self-defense. How can that be in West Germany? Very simply, from the beginning, West German terrorists have regarded themselves as the innocent victims of an aggressive, intrusive, repressive West German state ready to use violence—structural violence, they call it—to keep itself in power and to repress them and other "rightminded people."

Most people and their leaders in the Western democracies refuse to accept this psychological phenomenon. In fact, it seems they are no more aware of it than they realize that the Soviet Union is honestly afraid of the West and generally acts from that impulse. Psychologically, however, by far the most important key to understanding terrorists is that they feel they are defending themselves against an aggressive, evil, intrusive, and murderous world.

Ideology and rebellion among the West German terrorists

It would be useful, at this point, to return to the themes of ideology and rebellion in West German terrorism. It is assumed nowadays that all radicals, and most other people who are not in full harmony with the existing order, have an "ideology." But the ideology of the West German terrorists is hardly consistent and cohesive. They are bent on the destruction of the current Western system, in West Germany and if possible beyond the West German borders, but they are not really interested in what should come after that destruction.

This was not always the case. In its earliest days, when Andreas Baader and Ulrike Meinhof organized themselves loosely into what came to be called the Baader-Meinhof Gang, much standard leftist ideology animated the group. Baader, a bad boy who was adept at stealing cars and, later, at planning and leading terrorist assaults and who displayed a great fascination for the female members of the gang, was a rather nonideological fellow, at least in the beginning; terrorism was his way of life. He was also a "weapons nut" who was fascinated by guns and their use. In contrast, Meinhof, a journalist moving easily in the fashionably intellectual circles in various parts of West Germany, was dedicated to a leftist, nonviolent, vaguely socialist ideology. Ultimately, Meinhof abandoned her nonviolent beliefs and became ready to incite the group to murder—as when, speaking about policemen, she said, "Of course they can be shot" (even though she apparently never touched a gun herself, let alone pulled the trigger).[5]

Meinhof, a profoundly unhappy person with a profoundly frustrating personal life, became more apocalyptic as time went by. Worse for her even than the problems she had with an arrogant and philandering husband was the fact that, after her participation in her first terrorist act, she had to go underground, which meant she could no longer maintain contact with her two young children. Then, during the late 1960s, Meinhof's partner, Andreas Baader, with whom she never had a romantic relationship, started a superromance with a new member. The woman, a clergyman's daughter named Gudrun Ensslin, hated Meinhof and made life miserable for her until, in prison, Meinhof took her own life. On the road to that suicide, her attitudes toward surrounding society became ever more harsh. This does not mean that she became more ideologically committed to some form of social or national program or ideal. On the contrary, it became increasingly unclear what, if anything, she visualized as the proper order of things.

Once Meinhof was gone (her influence in the group had waned long before her suicide, both for practical and ideological reasons) and the group came under the direction of Baader, Ensslin, and a man named Raspe, it had even less of an ideological orientation, despite the violent hatred of these three for the existing regime. Raspe had been in the West German army and was an expert in explosives. Baader, as already stated, enjoyed his nonbourgeois existence and the occasional terror raids. And Ensslin only breathed her violent hatred on West German society and its establishment leaders, but was unconcerned about what would come after the West German state had come crashing down, as the group confidently expected it would. On 19 January 1976, when Ensslin was coleader of the Red Army Faction, she stated:

The canard that we have moved away from Marxism is nonsense. We have applied the Marxist analysis and method to the contemporary scene—not transformed it but actually applied it. Only an idiot can seriously believe that the Marxist analysis of capitalism and the Marxist concepts are obsolete. They will only become obsolete when the capitalist system has been abolished.[6]

---

[5] See "The Role and Motivation of Women in the Red Army Faction," *Der Spiegel*, 11 May 1981.

[6] *RAF Texte*, p. 435. *RAF Texte* is an underground publication published in Malmö, Sweden, containing a collection of written and spoken statements made by Red Army Faction members over the years.

But Ensslin also said, shortly thereafter, "As for the state of the future, the time after victory, that is not our concern. . . . We build the revolution, not the socialist model."[7]

These two statements are indeed contradictory, but they are not of equal import. The latter carries more weight than the former, in that it was voiced more frequently by members and—more important—formed, and still forms, the basic message of the "communiqués" the Red Army Faction generally leaves behind after assassinating a victim. Here are excerpts from a recent such communiqué, issued after the killing of Bonn diplomat Braunmuehl. (Except where entire passages are capitalized for emphasis, the Red Army Faction never capitalizes any letters, a practice that is even more striking in German than in English, because many more German words have initial capital letters.)

Today, the Commando Ingrid Schubert[8] has shot to death the practitioner of secret diplomacy, braunmuehl, one of the central figures in the formation of the west european policy in the overall system of imperialism. . . .

braunmuehl had been meeting with french representatives on a regular basis set up to institutionalize german-french cooperation, and also with officials of the american, british, and french foreign offices, for the purpose of integrating the policies of the strongest powers of the imperialist chain under american leadership, and to make the whole system capable of action, despite the conflicts that threaten the system on all levels. braunmuehl represented west germany in the "committee for european cooperation," the most important organ in west europe for coordinating policy.

THE WEST EUROPEAN FORWARD FRONT IN THE POLICIES OF THE OVERALL SYSTEM AND THE DEPLOYMENT OF ECONOMIC MEANS OF THE WEST GERMAN STATES AND LARGE CORPORATIONS IS DESIGNED TO BLOCK THE REVOLUTIONARY PROCESS AND PREVENT FURTHER LOSS OF THEIR POWER, UNTIL THEY HAVE THE CAPABILITY FOR A GLOBAL MILITARY OFFENSIVE.

the pentagon and nato strategists have failed to break the nuclear balance with the help of the pershings and at the same time to win their offensive against the liberation efforts of young national states. the international capital, under u.s. leadership, has been unable to win against revolutionary forces. . . .

Again, this communiqué shows two things: it says nothing about a political structure or program favored by the Red Army Faction, and it reveals a stance that is defensive against NATO and the "Western imperialists who suppress the masses in the metropolitan centers and prepare

---

[7] Ibid., p. 346.
[8] One of the original members of the Red Army Faction, now dead.

for imperialist war" (but are in too much disarray to reach their nefarious aims).

This absence of a positive program is not surprising if we look at what Hans Joachim Klein, a defector from terrorism, experienced as a boy. Klein was a small, weak boy treated brutally and irrationally by his "little man" of a father who beat him constantly with or without provocation. The boy received his worst beating when, at a very young age, he let his father's canary escape because he felt sorry for the caged bird. When Klein was in his teens, a girlfriend gave him a small chain to wear around his neck; the father ripped the chain off and beat him once again. Suddenly, however, young Klein rebelled and slapped his father's face, expecting to be killed a moment later for his transgression. But the old man treated his son with courtesy and respect from that moment on![9]

The lesson for the younger Klein was probably that force and the infliction of pain can do the trick. The bully who had been impervious to all else was transformed after the son had committed the ultimate sin of rebelling against him, whereas before that he had committed no sins at all. Presumably Klein concluded, at some level, that if he could do this to his father, he could do it to the state as well. But this did not give Klein an ideology; it gave him only rebellion.

In the end, as important as the penchants for ideology and rebellion are in provoking and shaping terrorist behavior, they are not all-important. At least as significant are the realities that infringe upon, and affect, the world that the terrorist experiences. And among the most affecting of these is the rhetoric that governments articulate in response to the terrorists' acts. Bombastic threats followed by abject cave-ins do more to sustain the terrorists than does any id or ego—or, for that matter, any ideology or rebellion.

[9] Hans Joachim Klein, *Rueckkehr in die Menschlichkeit* (Hamburg: Rowohlt, 1979), 32–9.

4

Ideology and repentance:
Terrorism in Italy

FRANCO FERRACUTI

Terrorism in Italy appears to have been defeated. Between 1969 and 1986, a total of 14,569 attacks by left-wing and right-wing terrorists—and international terrorists—occurred in Italy, resulting in 415 deaths and 1,181 injuries. But the attacks peaked at 2,513 in 1979 and fell to 30 in 1986.

In this chapter, which focuses on the psychological and motivational dimensions of terrorism in Italy, as well as on the ways in which terrorists can be induced or encouraged to leave a life of terrorism, I deal primarily with terrorists of the ideological left. The reason is that leftist terrorists tend to draw their motivations from common sources and to share similar goals; in contrast, rightist terrorists, and terrorists such as Palestinians who carry out terrorist acts on Italian soil for the purpose of achieving aims unrelated to the Italian political arena, are diverse, have a variety of motivations, ideologies, and goals, and cannot be considered, for the purposes of psychological understanding, in the same examination.

Ideological terrorism in general, and leftist terrorism in particular, must be distinguished from terrorism of the nationalist sort. To be sure, most ethnic or separatist groups attempt, at some point, to acquire a political identity (most frequently of a leftist orientation) in order to strengthen their international ties and enlarge their political base. Their main goal, however, tends to remain the achievement of freedom from a "foreign" or "alien" oppressor, whether perceived or real. The Basque ETA movement is a good example of this. Its Marxist character is rendered questionable, to at least some extent, by the support it has received from the church and by the, at best, vague Marxist thinking contained in its official pronouncements.

The Italian government has great difficulty in satisfying the demands of, and in finding a common ground for negotiation with, the Italian left-wing terrorists, who usually have a utopian ideology and tend to predict "inevitable" victory. Some of the roots for this ideology are Hegelian,[1] whereas others are nihilistic.[2] Psychiatric studies have not identified any psychopathological characteristics common to the Italian left-wing terrorists whose histories have been studied or who have themselves been accessible to direct examination.[3] The same holds true for the West German terrorists, most of them left-wing, studied as part of the monumental project conducted by the West German Ministry of the Interior.[4]

In many respects, Italian leftist terrorists satisfy the picture we usually have of the fanatic. The total commitment to an ideology and focus on a single purpose, which are typical of many ideologically inspired terrorists, bring to mind the portrait of the revolutionary drawn over a century ago by Nechayev:

The revolutionary is a man committed. He has neither personal interests nor sentiments, attachments, property, nor even a name. Everything in him is subordinated to a single exclusive interest, a single thought, a single passion: the revolution. . . .

All the soft and tender affection arising from kinship, friendship, love [and] gratitude must be obliterated in him by the singleminded and cold passion for the work of the revolution. . . . Night and day, he must have a single thought, a single goal—implacable destruction. Pursuing this goal coldly and relentlessly, he must be prepared to perish himself and to cause to perish, with his own hands, all those who would prevent him from achieving his goal.[5]

Among the many who have observed the terrorists of the ideological left, Kaplan has formulated an interesting psychodynamic hypothesis of the terrorist as a young man in search of absolute goals and moved by basic insecurity.[6] Bruno, for his part, has described terrorism as a "fan-

---

[1] H. Marcuse, *Ragione e rivoluzione. Hegel e il sorgere della "teoria sociale"* (Bologna: Il Mulino, 1965); and A. Negri, *Il comunismo e la guerra* (Milan: Feltrinelli, 1980).

[2] V. Verra, "Nichilismo," in *Enciclopedia del Novecento,* vol. 4 (Rome: Istituto dell' Enciclopedia Italiana, 1979), 778–90.

[3] F. Ferracuti and F. Bruno, "Psychiatric Aspects of Terrorism in Italy," in *The Mad, the Bad, and the Different,* edited by I. L. Barak-Galantz and C. R. Huff (Lexington, Mass.: Lexington Books, 1981), 199–213.

[4] H. Jäger, G. Schmidtchen, and L. Süllwold, eds., *Lebenslauf-Analyzen [Biographical Analysis],* vol. 2 of *Analyzen zum Terrorismus [Analysis of Terrorism]* (Opladen: Westdeutscher Verlag, 1981).

[5] A. Haynal, M. Molnar, and G. de Ruymege, *Fanaticism: A Historical and Psychoanalytical Study* (New York: Schocken Books, 1983).

[6] A. Kaplan, "The Psychodynamics of Terrorism," *Terrorism* 1, no. 3/4 (1978): 237–54.

tasy war"—that is, a process in which the terrorists believe themselves to be soldiers in a war against society, and in which the struggle to obtain a utopian world fulfills needs the terrorists cannot satisfy through the usual channels of socialization.[7] Jäger, Schmidtchen, and Süllwold, in their studies of German terrorists, have noted the frequency of extroversion and narcissism in their subjects.[8] And Clark, in an analysis of Basque terrorists, has described their search for identity and the indeterminate, conflict-producing status of Basque youth, who are members of a minority that is no longer oppressed in post-Franco Spain but has not yet entered the Spanish mainstream.[9]

Many of the characteristics of terrorist groups described by various authors appear to be true of leftist terrorist groups in Italy. For example, the process described by Post, in which individuals identify with the terrorist group as a means of resolving their own intrapsychic conflicts and as a means of adopting a ready-made set of values, is common among Italian groups.[10]

In general, belonging to a group and remaining isolated from society at large reinforces the terrorists' ideology and strengthens their motivations. Deviants tend to group together and to cut their ties with society—which is seen as the alien and hostile enemy—and to engage in a "fantasy war" with it—a war whose reality seems enhanced when that society engages in repressive actions. Such actions reinforce the terrorists' deviance and make it difficult for such people to make an exit from the life of terrorism.

Is there anything the state can do to help the terrorists make such an exit? Is there, in fact, a way out? A separatist, such as a Basque, can escape the problem of choosing an identity—Basque or Spanish—by emigrating to Canada, say, or Latin America. For ideological terrorists, however, the enemy tends to be the state—any state. Society is seen as corrupt, inadequate, and oppressive; the terrorists are at war with it, and, once caught, have lost that war. For them, the dream of change is over. Friends have died, are imprisoned, or, worse, have defected. The masses

---

[7] F. Bruno, 1983. See also V. Verra, "Utopia," in *Enciclopedia del Novecento*, vol. 7 (Roma: Instituto dell' Enciclopedia Italiana, 1984), 988–1066.

[8] Jäger, Schmidtchen, and Süllwold, *Lebenslauf-Analyzen*.

[9] R. Clark, "Patterns in the Lives of ETA Members," *Terrorism* 6, no. 3 (1983): 423–54.

[10] J. M. Post, "Note on a Psychodynamic Theory of Terrorist Behavior," *Terrorism* 7, no. 3 (1984): 241–56; and " 'Hostilité,' 'Conformité,' 'Fraternité': The Group Dynamics of Terrorism," *International Journal of Group Psychotherapy* 36, no. 2 (April 1986): 211–24.

have not risen, and in many cases have turned against the terrorists and applauded their capture. The terrorists have, it seems to them, only three choices of action:

1. Submitting to insanity or self-destruction
2. Acknowledging error and defeat and abandoning their value system
3. Joining the enemy and attempting to undo past actions by helping the establishment

Because it is impossible to eliminate all terrorists, it is in the interest of every country to make it easy for terrorists to terminate their connection with terrorism—that is, to exit the life of terrorism. In order to encourage dissent within the terrorist group and then defection from it, the state must provide a way out. The best solution to political terrorism is to provide a place, within the country's political system, for persons with dissenting, and even radical, views. Thus, in exchange for a renunciation of terrorism, the terrorists find a place, perhaps radical but at least legitimate, in society itself.

Early in its recent struggle against terrorism, the Italian government recognized the need for a flexible judicial instrument that could facilitate an exit from terrorism. Two laws were enacted with this aim in mind. They promise substantial leniency if terrorists collaborate with the police and judicial authorities, and a lesser degree of leniency if they only separate themselves from the terrorist group.[11] Collaboration most frequently takes the form of denouncing former comrades and providing evidence against them. The reduction of penalty is related to the amount of "substantial" aid given to the police, and it can be as significant as a reduction of a life sentence to twelve years, or even the granting of freedom.

The frequency of terrorist events has fallen off sharply, and a number of observers attribute this decrease to the salutary effects of these "repentance" laws. Repentant and "dissociated" terrorists are estimated to make up at least 40 percent of the *official* total of 2,000 terrorists currently serving time or awaiting trial in Italian prisons. Requests for a general amnesty for terrorist activities have been put forward by several sources, but public opinion is divided on this matter. From the safety of asylum in Paris, a leading terrorist has aptly stated that terrorism has lost the war, but a war is only really over when the war prisoners go home.[12] This has been restated recently by former leaders of the Red Brigades.[13]

[11] N. 625, 15 December 1979, *Legge Cossiga;* n. 304, 29 May 1982, *Legge sui pentiti.*
[12] F. Cuomo, "Ma la guerra non é ancora finita?" *Fiera* 24 (1984): 26–8, 88.
[13] "The country has rejected the revolution, but war prisoners go home." D. Sacchettoni, "La gente non vuole la guerra civile," *Il Messaggero* (2 March 1987): 15.

One problem related to the laws encouraging "repentance" has been the confusion frequently provoked by that word. "Repentance" suggests, to some, a total rejection of past beliefs. In general, however, the laws encourage change, not the rejection of former ideals—an abandonment of terrorism, not of the beliefs about society that preceded it. Neither of the two types of repentance recognized by Italian law—simple dissociation from the terrorist group or active collaboration with the police—necessarily implies repentance in a moral or psychological sense. For example, dissociation may be an acknowledgment of defeat, a recognition that the revolutionary project has failed or that the killings and terror have alienated the masses and have not destroyed the establishment. In this sense, it may express political realism rather than moral internal change. Collaboration, for its part, may result from a cold calculation of possible benefits that would accrue if this course of action is taken. This action, too, does not require a rejection of past ideas—although collaborators who label themselves as such can never return to the terrorist life.

What happens in the minds of terrorists who decide to abandon terrorism is not known. The material available consists of a few interviews and autobiographies in which real motives lie hidden beneath rationalizations and self-serving reinterpretations of reality. Preliminary data from my research suggest that repentant terrorists are less stable and less well-adjusted than unrepentant ones. The earlier, hard-core "founding fathers" seldom repented. Cacciari, a leading Italian philosopher, has stated that the early terrorists (the "founding fathers" of the 1970s), given the total nature of their moral commitment to terrorism, could not repent. By contrast, the younger terrorists—those who entered a life of terrorism after 1977—chose terrorism in order to search for opportunities that they believed had been taken from them by society. Once terrorism failed, they could repent and betray.[14] The message from hard-core, unrepentant terrorists is, We are not repentant, we are tired.[15]

Clearly, there is a need for comparative studies related to these issues. One interesting study, conducted by A. J. Nassi in the United States, examined, fifteen years after the event, a large group of activists of the Free Speech Movement who were arrested at the Sproul Hall sit-in at Berkeley in 1964. The study compared them with student government members and with subjects from the general Berkeley student popula-

[14] P. Franchi, "Uno, cento, mille pentiti," *Panorama* (12 March 1984): 91–117.
[15] P. V. Buffa and F. Giustolisi, "Non sono un pentito, sono stanco," *L'Espresso* (8 April 1984): 16–19.

tion. The activists appeared not to have abandoned their radical political philosophy, but they were less politically active and they accepted the fact that changes can happen within the political system. They endorsed leftist politics, and they held social service or creative jobs. They showed moral commitment and principled moral judgment. Keniston, quoted by Nassi, says that one of the dilemmas facing a radical is to have to remain committed while at least formally becoming part of the system. The career choices of the former activists reflect both their political ideology and the search for a channel for their energies.[16]

In citing these findings I do not mean to imply that exiting a life of terrorism can be accomplished simply by, say, entering an ecology group or getting a job at the Environmental Protection Agency. Terrorists are more extreme than the kinds of political activists who sat in at Berkeley, and their return to legitimate, nonviolent roles in a democratic society is inevitably wrenching and difficult. Still, such a return is possible and must be encouraged in every way available to the society as a whole and, in particular, to its legal system. Without such an option, society has terrorists on its hands, either in hiding or in prison. With it, society could benefit from a cohort of persons who refrain from violent action and contribute usefully to its welfare.

[16] A. J. Nassi, "Survivors of the Sixties," *American Psychologist* 36, no. 7 (July 1981): 753–61.

5

The psychopolitical formation of extreme left terrorism in a democracy: The case of the Weathermen

EHUD SPRINZAK

Bringing the war home

On 7 October 1969, a blast destroyed a police monument in Chicago. Two days later, leaflets were circulated in that city by a small radical organization, the Weatherman, announcing four days of "national action" against the war in Vietnam. This action, the citizens of Chicago were told, would include a mass rally, an attack on the Chicago Armed Forces Induction Center by the "Women's Militia," demonstrations at high schools, a "move on the courts," and a massive march through Chicago's Loop.[1] The leaflets proclaimed:

We move with the people of the world to seize power from those who now rule. We . . . expect their pig lackeys to come down on us. We've got to be ready for that. This is a war we can't resist. We've got to actively fight. We're going to bring the war home to the mother country of imperialism. AMERIKA: THE FINAL FRONT.[2]

From the beginning, the hundreds of "Weathermen" and "Weatherwomen" who arrived that Wednesday in Chicago behaved differently from any previous white demonstrators in America. As soon as they arrived, they organized themselves in military fashion. No one was allowed to participate in the gathering who did not belong to the Weatherman organization, not even the photographers and correspondents of the "un-

[1] For a description of the "Days of Rage," see Tom Thomas, "The Second Battle of Chicago," in *Weatherman*, edited by Harold Jacobs (Berkeley: Ramparts Press, 1970), 196–226.
[2] Ibid., 197.

derground" media. In the meetings themselves, briefings were given by
the "Weather Bureau," the national leadership of the Weatherman. "Affinity Groups" of five or six members, who were to be the basic fighting
units in the forthcoming battle with the police, were formed by local
leaders. Surprised New Left members and veterans of previous confrontations with the police could not quite understand what was happening.
When they tried to approach the Weatherman's members to find out,
they were told:

You can't talk about the Movement because we have to crush the Movement to
build the revolution. . . . We start to build a Red Army by fighting in the streets
now. We're going to knock the pig on his ass in those streets. Sure there's going
to be pigs hitting people like before, but this time there's going to be people
hitting pigs. . . . The focal point is here in Chicago. We've got to show people
that white kids are willing to fight on the side of black people and on the side of
revolution around the world. If you're not going to fight, then you're not part of
us. It's as simple as that.[3]

Violence occurred as soon as the march began. Weathermen first attacked the North Federal Savings and Loan Building, breaking its large
plate-glass windows with rocks. As they moved down Clark Street they
started to run, systematically smashing windows of buildings and parked
cars on both sides of the street. People trying to protect their cars were
beaten and left bleeding on the streets. The police, caught by surprise,
did not interfere. Later, when a police line formed, the demonstrators
charged into it and the line was broken.

   Assessing the first evening of what became known in the history of the
American protest movement as the "Days of Rage," Stephen Zicher, a
Chicago assistant corporation counsel, said, "We never expected this kind
of violent demonstration. There always has been a big difference between
what they say and what they do."[4] And Tom Hayden, a central figure in
the protest movement of the 1960s, later said of the Weatherman action:

We never did what the government accused us of in 1968 [at the Democratic
National Convention in Chicago], but the Weathermen did it in 1969. What we
did in 1968 prefigured Weathermen; a few karate and snake dance exercises,
some disruption, a lot of running in the streets, and at the end of Convention
Week, a prediction that a fighting force would be created which would bring the
war in Vietnam home. It remained for the government to develop this seed into
a paranoid image of crazy, unruly, drug-ruined, club-carrying, Communist-
inspired mobs rampaging in the Loop, and for Weathermen to fulfill the image
one year later. Many Weathermen leaders were shaped by the events of Chicago

[3] Ibid., 199.   [4] Ibid., 204.

'68. When our legal protest was clubbed down they became outlaws. When our pitiful attempts at peaceful confrontation were overwhelmed, they adopted the tactic of offensive guerrilla violence.[5]

As on other occasions, Tom Hayden was not attempting to make a detached and theoretical observation about the behavior of radicals in a time of national crisis, but in his acute and peculiar way he managed to do so. What he observed and described was the development of a crisis of legitimacy in a democracy.[6] Like Zicher, Hayden noticed that rhetoric and symbols expressing an attitude of delegitimation vis-à-vis the regime were now being matched by overt and intentional illegal behavior, and that this second generation of radicals was ready to challenge not only the elected authorities but also their agencies of physical coercion. American observers of the student protest movement had witnessed worse scenes of student violence. But the violence in those previous scenes had not been planned; it was shaped primarily by the unintended interaction of committed activists, uncommitted observers, and the appearance of the police. The violence in Chicago, in 1969, was planned.

Soon after the "Days of Rage," the Weatherman leaders, at that time in command of the national headquarters of the Students for a Democratic Society (SDS) in Chicago, closed the offices of that organization and entrusted its massive archives to the State Historical Society of Wisconsin in Madison. Their new mood was reflected well in a headline in the Weatherman's journal, *Fire:* "DURING THE 1960S THE AMERICAN GOVERNMENT WAS ON TRIAL FOR CRIMES AGAINST THE PEOPLE OF THE WORLD. WE NOW FIND THE GOVERNMENT GUILTY AND SENTENCE IT TO DEATH ON THE STREETS."[7]

In a three-day "war council" in Flint, Michigan, the Weathermen came to the conclusion that they now had to become real revolutionaries. Bernardine Dohrn, the most determined leader of the organization, made it clear that "white kids," unlike their black counterparts, were not risking themselves sufficiently. Real revolution meant violence and terrorism, and this had to be the Weatherman's course. Suzan Stern, a participant at the "war council," reported on the themes that dominated the discussion:

[5] Tom Hayden, *Trial* (New York: Holt, Rinehart and Winston, 1970), 91–2.
[6] For an earlier analysis of this phenomenon see Ehud Sprinzak, "The Revolt Against the Open Society and the Phenomenon of Delegitimation: The Case of the American New Left," in *The Open Society in Theory and Practice,* Dante Germino and Klaus von Beime, eds. (The Hague: Martinus Neijhof, 1974). See also Jurgen Habermas, *Legitimation Crisis* (Portsmouth, N.H.: Heinemann, 1976).
[7] See Larry Grathwohl, *Bringing Down America* (New Rochelle, N.Y.: Arlington House Publishers, 1976), 84.

There was a history for us to follow. The Algerian guerrilla terrorists did play a big role in freeing Algeria from the French tyranny; [Viet Cong] terrorists, the Huks in the Philippines, the Tupamaros in Uruguay . . . the Palestinian Liberation Front. The topic was not approached lightly; it was a deadly serious meeting. Everyone knew the implications of even *talking* about terrorism. And we were discussing what would be necessary to actually do it.[8]

By the end of 1969 the course was set. The Weatherman, whose members already lived in very closed "collectives," went underground; it declared war on the government of the United States and announced its intention to build a Leninist vanguard and a "red army."[9] Splitting itself into small, secret, action-oriented "affinity groups" that were subject to the hierarchical command of the "Weather Bureau," it armed itself heavily and enforced strict rules of secrecy upon its members.[10] Through anonymous telephone calls and letters to the underground press, it claimed responsibility for otherwise unsolved cases of bombing and subversive operations.[11]

The new "barbarism"

The political transformation of the large SDS into the small and self-selected Weather organization, and of the "Weather People" into self-conscious terrorists, was not the only transformation these young people went through. Shreds of information surfacing from the American underground have suggested a remarkable story of personal-psychological transformation. Based on memoirs of former Weathermen, it is possible to reconstruct some of these transformations. The Weathermen appear to have developed antinomian norms of behavior. Out of their outrage and desperation they came to reject every rule and value they had known and had been socialized to respect. The whole symbolic framework within which they now operated was elaborated in Flint, Michigan, by the concept of "barbarism": "A new Weatherman catchword was 'barbarism.' The Weathermen see themselves as playing a role familiar to that of the barbaric tribes such as the Vandals and the Visigoths, who invaded and

[8] Suzan Stern, *With the Weatherman* (Garden City, N.Y.: Doubleday, 1975), 204.
[9] Karin Ashley, Bill Ayers, Bernardine Dohrn, John Jacobs, Jeff Jones, Gerry Long, Howie Machtinger, Jim Mellen, Terry Robbins, Mark Rudd, and Steve Tappis, "You Don't Need a Weatherman to Know Which Way the Wind Blows," in Jacobs, *Weatherman*, 87–90.
[10] See Harold Jacobs, "Inside the Weather Machine: Introduction," in Jacobs, *Weatherman*, 302–3.
[11] Ibid., 345.

destroyed the decadent, corrupt Rome. (Some Weathermen even suggested changing their name to the Vandals.)"[12]

This "barbaric" dehumanization of the existing social structure was not only ideological, it pertained to culture and morality as well. In addition to their previous involvement with the counterculture of drugs and free love, the members of the Weatherman assumed, as a group, a "negative identity," and challenged the normative order of the bourgeois society.[13] They created a new and all-inclusive *Weltanschauung* of their own. Young couples living in "Weather collectives" were required to "smash monogamy" and to reject natural parenthood. The "Weather Bureau" ordered that all female revolutionaries sleep with all male revolutionaries, and vice versa.[14] Women were also to make love to each other. Private relations of love and affection were declared counterrevolutionary, because they represented bourgeois habits.

"Weather" mothers who were suspected of devoting too much time to their babies (born in the course of the "revolution") were told to give the revolution first priority.[15] There were cases in which they were even ordered to give their babies to other, less committed, members of the organization, so that they could devote all of their energies to the cause. Public sessions of self-criticism and collective criticism were frequently held. Persons who could not conform fully to the rigid authoritarian line dictated by the "Bureau" were scolded by the whole group; they were forced to confess and to admit to their mistakes, and were frequently tested for their sincerity. The ordeals of these "deviants" were not stopped even in cases of nervous breakdown.[16] If a terror campaign against the outside world was to start soon, there could be no room for human compassion or exaggerated sensitivity. Everyone had to conform to the "groupthink" and to be ready for the revolution.[17]

[12] Stern, *With the Weatherman*, 114–15.
[13] I find Knutson's concept of "negative identity," which she uses to denote the psychology of the would-be terrorist, extremely useful for the portrayal of the group psychology of the would-be terrorists. See Jeanne N. Knutson, "Social and Psychodynamic Pressures Towards a Negative Identity: The Case of An American Revolutionary Terrorist" in *Behavioral and Quantitative Perspectives on Terrorism*, edited by Yona Alexander and John M. Gleason (New York: Pergamon Press, 1981), chapter 7. See also Martha Crenshaw, "The Psychology of Political Terrorism" in *Political Psychology*, edited by Margaret G. Hermann (San Francisco: Jossey-Bass, 1986), 393.
[14] Larry Grathwol, *Bringing Down America*, 149–50.
[15] Stern, *With the Weatherman*, 187–90.
[16] Ibid., 204.
[17] See Jerrold M. Post (following Janis), "Group and Organizational Dynamics of Political

Perhaps the most bizarre and antinomian act of the Weathermen was the applause they gave to the murder of movie actress Sharon Tate and her friends by Charles Manson and his "family," who tortured their victims and desecrated their bodies. Their slogan, "Helter-Skelter," and their "fork" sign, which were left behind, terrified and haunted the country. But the Weathermen celebrated the event as an act of liberation of utmost significance. The brutal murder fit their new *Weltanschauung* perfectly. "Almost everybody in the Bureau," wrote Suzan Stern, "ran around saluting people with the fork sign. . . . There was a picture of Sharon Tate on the wall."[18] And in Flint, Michigan, the final assessment of the murder, and the crowning of the new morality of dehumanization, was voiced by Bernardine Dohrn: "Dig it, first they killed those pigs then they ate dinner in the same room with them, then they even shoved a fork in the victim's stomach! Wild!"[19]

The radicalization of the SDS

What is so intriguing about the activities of the Weatherman, from a historical and theoretical perspective, is not so much the group's antinomian delegitimation of the entire American value system in 1969 but the fact that it was the direct offspring of a student organization, the Students for a Democratic Society (SDS), which in 1962 had constituted itself as a liberal and democratic movement in order to promote the value of a "democracy of individual participation."[20]

It is true that, in its founding manifesto, the Port Huron Statement, the SDS severely criticized the Democratic and Republican parties for being equally insensitive to the cold war, the third world, and racial discrimination at home.[21] But the conclusion of this critique was neither a call for antidemocratic revolution nor a quest for a political system guided by a Leninist party representing the proletariat. Rather, it projected a system of "Two genuine parties, centered around issues and essential

Terrorism: Implications for Counter Terrorist Policy," paper prepared for the International Conference on Terrorism Research, University of Aberdeen, Scotland, 21–23 April 1986, p. 12; and Jeanne N. Knutson, "The Terrorists' Dilemmas: Some Implicit Rules of the Game," *Terrorism: An International Journal* 4 (1980): 211–12.

[18] Stern, *With the Weatherman*, 191.

[19] Jacobs, ed., *Weatherman*, 347.

[20] "SDS: Port Huron Statement," in *The New Left: A Documentary History,* edited by Massimo Teodori (New York: Bobbs-Merrill, 1969), 167. (References to the complete text of the Port Huron Statement are made only when the texts referred to are omitted by Teodori.)

[21] Ibid., 170.

values . . . with sufficient party disagreement to dramatize major issues, yet sufficient party overlap to guarantee stable transition from administration to administration."[22] Indeed, the SDS saw itself as a spearhead of a "New Left" concentrated on the American campus. Yet this New Left was very peaceful and nonviolent. It did not try to "outrevolutionize" the Old Left, but to "underrevolutionize" it. Commenting on Marx, Tom Hayden, the cofounder of the SDS, maintained that although "Marx, the humanist, has much to tell us . . . his conceptual tools are outmoded and his final vision implausible."[23] He was equally unhappy with the "non-ideological" thinking of revolutionary leaders of the rising nations such as Che Guevara.[24] Not only did the SDS of the early 1960s reject the traditional solutions of the extreme left of the pre–World War II era, it also refused to grant membership to members of Communist and, in general, "totalitarian" organizations. The SDS constitution declared: "SDS is an organization of democrats. It is civil libertarian in its treatment of those with whom it disagrees, but clear in its opposition to any totalitarian principle as a basis for government or social organization. Advocates or apologists for such a principle are not eligible for membership."[25]

Reflecting the impact of another student organization—the black Student Nonviolent Coordinating Committee (SNCC), an organization that fought for civil rights in the South and thereby became to the SDS a subject of great admiration and respect—the Port Huron Statement insisted on a basic commitment to a philosophy of nonviolence:

We find violence to be abhorrent because it requires generally the transformation of the target, be it a human being or a community of people, into a depersonalized object of hate. It is imperative that the means of violence be abolished and the institutions—local, national, international—that encourage nonviolence as a condition of conflict be developed.[26]

The SDS conceived commitment to nonviolence not as a useful tactical means to be applied temporarily against a resourceful and powerful rival but as a normative ethical principle. Violence as a political means was to be abolished because it was basically a dehumanizing pattern of behavior. Politics could do well without violence, and institutions encouraging nonviolence had to be devised. The SDS's commitment to nonviolence was thus fully congruent with its idealistic vision of the desired perfor-

[22] *The Port Huron Statement* (New York: SDS Pamphlet, 1964), 46–7.
[23] Thomas Hayden, "A Letter to the New (Young) Left," in *The New Student Left*, edited by M. Cohen and D. Hale (Boston: Beacon Press, 1968), 3.
[24] Ibid.
[25] "SDS Constitution" (mimeographed pamphlet, 1963).
[26] "SDS: Port Huron Statement," in Teodori, *The New Left*, 168.

mance of liberal democracy as well as with its criticism of the actual performance of this system in the United States.

What happened in the seven years between the creation of the SDS and the rise of the Weatherman was the development of a process of group radicalization in which the SDS first grew into a radical mass movement and then split and shrank. The young, liberal critics of 1962 were swept up by the events of their stormy decade to an extent that neither they nor others thought possible. And in 1969 they themselves were left behind by a second generation of radicals that they had helped socialize into the politics of protest. A retrospective examination of two dimensions of this process of radicalization, the acts and practices of the radicals, on the one hand, and their symbolic behavior and rhetoric, on the other, is highly revealing.[27] It illustrates the collective psychopolitical process that turns some young, educated, sensitive human beings into tough revolutionaries and brutal killers.

As early as 1963, the young theoreticians of the New Left started to refer to their activities as "insurgent politics" and to refer to themselves as "new insurgents."[28] Recalling methods used by the civil rights and peace movements—sit-ins, protests, and demonstrations—they tried to identify types of political action that would defy the rules of the prevailing American game without being illegal. At the same time, these New Left theoreticians started to refer to the system against which they were protesting as "corporate liberalism."[29] They frequently repeated the phrase introduced by President Eisenhower and used in the Port Huron Statement, "the military-industrial complex."[30] In addition, as a result of their bitter experiences with the most brutal representatives of American authority—particularly the sheriffs of the South—the activists of the New Left started to see "participatory democracy" as an alternative type of democracy, thereby rejecting party and interest group politics.[31] This tendency greatly deepened in the summer of 1964, when young radicals

[27] The methodological justification for the emphasis on these two behavioral dimensions as indexes of delegitimation cannot be developed here in greater detail. It can be found in E. Sprinzak, "Democracy and Illegitimacy: A Study of the American and the French Student Protest Movements and Some Theoretical Implications" (Ph.D. dissertation, Yale University, 1972).

[28] "SDS: America and New Era," in Teodori, ed., *The New Left*, 180–2.

[29] This image was coined by the editorial board of *Studies On the Left*, a New Left journal. See James P. O'Brien, "The Development of a New Left in the United States 1960–1965" (Ph.D. dissertation, University of Wisconsin, 1971), 237.

[30] *The Port Huron Statement*, 17.

[31] See Staughton Lynd, "The New Radicals and Participatory Democracy," *Dissent* (Summer 1965).

failed to unseat the official Mississippi delegation to the Democratic National Convention held in Atlantic City. Having demonstrated the discriminatory practices of the official Democratic party of Mississippi, they came to the convention with the duly elected Mississippi Freedom and Democratic party (MFDP) as an alternative delegation; but the new party was rejected by the convention.[32]

Soon after, in February 1965, the United States began bombing North Vietnam. The SDS, already a radical organization, was discovered by many disenchanted students. It quickly tripled its membership and became the most vocal opponent of the war and the spearhead of the emerging antiwar movement. It was at this time of intense protest that the language and mentality of delegitimation first entered the vocabulary of the New Left, making its appearance in a discussion of the meaning of revolution in an article by Staughton Lynd, a historian and self-styled ideologue of the New Left:

So long as a revolution is pictured as a violent insurrection, it seems to me both distasteful and unreal. The traditional alternative, the social Democratic vision of electing more and more radical legislators until power passes peacefully to the left, seems equally illusory. However, the events of the past year—the creation of the MFDP and the protest against the war in Vietnam—suggest a third strategy. One can now begin to envision a series of nonviolent protests which would, from the beginning, question the legitimacy of the Administration's authority where it has gone beyond constitutional and moral limits and might, if this insane foreign policy continues, culminate in the decisions of hundreds of thousands of people to recognize the authority of alternative institutions of their own making.[33]

Although Lynd cautiously avoided a comprehensive presentation of the system as illegitimate and did not attack democracy in principle, he went beyond the charge that the government was acting unconstitutionally. He argued that it was immoral and insane and suggested that the charges of unconstitutionality and immorality could be first steps in questioning the legitimacy of the administration's authority. These first steps could then lead to the recognition of alternative (legitimate) institutions. What Lynd did, apart from his explicit argument, was to introduce the terminology and imagery of delegitimation into the "groupthink" of the New Left.

[32] The MFDP was offered by the Credentials Committee of the Democratic Party two "delegates-at-large," an offer that was bluntly rejected. The story of the conflict regarding the MFDP can be found in *Black Power: the Politics of Liberation in America*, edited by Stokely Carmichael and Charles V. Hamilton (New York: Random House, 1967), 86–97.

[33] Staughton Lynd, "Coalition Politics or Nonviolent Revolution," in Teodori, ed., *The New Left*, 199.

Tom Hayden, former president of the SDS, presented the case for alternative institutions in even stronger terms:

The Movement is a community of insurgents sharing the same radical values and identity, seeking an independent base of power wherever they are. It aims at a transformation of society led by the most excluded and unqualified people. Primarily, this means building institutions outside the established order which seek to become the genuine institutions of the total society: community unions, freedom schools, experimental universities, community-formed policy review boards, people's own antipoverty organizations fighting the federal money. . . . Ultimately, this movement might lead to a continental congress called by all the people who feel excluded from the higher circles of decision making in the country.[34]

The New Left was a movement motivated and directed by students, and these students' growing sense that the prevailing political authorities lacked legitimacy inevitably affected their attitude toward academic authorities, whom they came to view as part of the same system against which they were protesting.[35] In the fall of 1964, student activists of the Free Speech Movement (FSM) at Berkeley, many of whom had participated in earlier civil rights actions in the South, sent shock waves through the American academic world when they took over the administration building at their university. Mario Savio, one of the leaders of the FSM, stated clearly that what was happening in Mississippi was closely connected with what was going on at Berkeley:

In Mississippi an autocratic and powerful minority rules, through organized violence, to suppress the vast, virtually powerless, majority. In California, the privileged minority manipulates the university bureaucracy to suppress the students' political expression. That "respectable" bureaucracy masks the financial plutocrats; that impersonal bureaucracy is the efficient enemy in a "Brave New World."[36]

The SDS soon issued a demand for "student power."[37] This demand signaled a growing split with the academic authorities in the universities and reflected another process of radicalization taking place in the United States, a process experienced by the black liberation movement. The SNCC had also become radicalized. In 1966 it had dropped its previous liberal identity and its commitment to nonviolence in order to become a militant antigovernment organization. It now adopted "black power" as its slo-

---

[34] Tom Hayden, "The Politics of the Movement," *Dissent* (January–February 1966): 87.
[35] For a good analysis of the emergence of the student movement, see Michael Miles, *The Radical Probe* (New York: Atheneum, 1971), 88–108.
[36] Mario Savio, "An End to History," in *The Berkeley Student Revolt,* edited by S. M. Lipset and S. S. Wolin (New York: Doubleday, 1965), 216.
[37] Karl Davidson, "Toward Student Syndicalism," *New Left Notes,* 9 September 1966.

gan and developed an ideology of national liberation.[38] The government of the United States was presented as an illegitimate "colonial" ruler, necessitating an "anticolonial struggle" of the "black colonies."

At its 1965 national convention, the SDS dropped from its constitution the "exclusionist" clause that had denied eligibility for membership to "advocates or apologists" of "totalitarian principle." It did so because of its growing conflict with the political system responsible for the intervention in Vietnam and because of its need to join forces with those who shared with it the psychology of resistance.[39] Members of the Maoist Progressive Labor party (PLP) were now eligible for SDS membership. They streamed in, formally accepting the idea of "participatory democracy" but intending to take control of the SDS and bend it in their direction. The Maoists soon started a "Marxization" of the organization. Many SDS veterans were aware of the PLP's takeover intentions and were highly resentful of the whole process. They could not, however, resist the growing pressure from the local branches of their loose organization to implement these changes.[40] They were especially helpless against the delegitimating magic of the Marxist ideological categories, which were now so appealing. Convinced that the system was structurally corrupt, these veterans themselves searched independently for a new, symbolic frame of reference that would express their sense of delegitimation toward the regime without succumbing to the growing pressures of the PLP.

Early in 1967, an influential group within the SDS published a paper titled "Towards a Theory of Social Change in America," in which a theory of the "new working class" was formulated.[41] Gregory Calvert, the president of SDS, elaborated this new theory in a speech at Princeton University. He suggested that students were themselves part of a "new working class," created and exploited by "this super-technological capitalism."[42] The former image of "corporate liberalism" was replaced by "corporate capitalism." ("American corporate capitalism is an incredibly

---

[38] *Black Power, SNCC Speaks for Itself: A Collection of Statements and Interviews* (Boston: New England Free Press, 1966).

[39] On the issue of nonexclusionism, see Alan Haber, "Nonexclusionism: The New Left and the Democratic Left," in Teodori, ed., *The New Left,* 218–28.

[40] For an analysis of the struggles within SDS, see Andrew Kopkind, "The Real SDS Stands Up," in Jacobs, ed., *Weatherman,* 15–28.

[41] David Gilbert, Robert Gottlieb, and Gerry Tenny, "Toward a Theory of Social Change," *New Left Notes,* 23 January 1967.

[42] Gregory Calvert, "In White America: Radical Consciousness and Social Change," in Teodori, ed., *The New Left,* 417.

brutal and dehumanizing system whether at home or abroad.") The system was challenged not by "new insurgents" and "alternative institutions" but by the working class heading toward revolution. At the core of the new theory was the idea that modern society had created a new proletariat composed of middle-class and professional workers. This "new working class" was presented as a class not because of its relation to the means of production but because of conditions of "unfreedom" in society, conditions affecting deprived minorities, high-salaried, middle-class professionals, and students living in "factory-like multiversities."[43]

The new theory, and especially its conceptualization of a "new working class," had little relation to classical Marxism and no empirical support. How could one seriously create a class out of such diverse groups and believe that such a class could carry out a revolution? To be sure, Marxist concepts were, as Tom Hayden had noted in 1962, "outmoded" for diagnosing the American social, economic, and political realities. But in 1967 and 1968, the New Left did not need an analytically valid and reliable social theory. It needed, instead, a cultural system of symbols expressing its deep psychopolitical rejection of the established order. It was in the right mental state to adopt a new ideological master-key that would sanction a moral disengagement from the entire American way of life. In the late 1960s, Marxism had become such a master-key. It provided a framework for a rebellious "groupthink."[44] When, in the summer of 1969, the SDS split into three factions—each adhering to a different tactical and strategic perspective—they all had one thing in common: they presented their case in militant Marxist language directed at a discredited and illegitimate political system.[45]

The Marxization of many segments within the New Left betokened a principled delegitimation of liberal democracy. But this symbolic transformation was not used to justify illegal behavior and violence. Draft card burning, for example, was presented in the courts as a constitutional act falling within the First Amendment.[46] The practices of confrontation with public authorities and the police, extolled by the SDS and other radical groups after 1967, also were not clear cases of illegal action. They

---

[43] Ibid., 415.

[44] See Ehud Sprinzak, "Marxism As a Symbolic Action," in *Varieties of Marxism*, edited by Shlomo Avineri (The Hague: Martinus Neijhof, 1977). See also Edward E. Ericson, Jr., *Radicals in the University* (Stanford: Hoover Institution Press, 1975), 28–34.

[45] See *Debate Within SDS* (Detroit: Radical Education Project pamphlet, Summer 1969).

[46] Lawrence R. Velvel, "Freedom of Speech and the Draft Card Burning Cases," *Kansas Law Review* 16 (1968).

were an extreme application of earlier tactics of direct action.[47] If intensive violence occurred—and it did occur increasingly after 1967—it was usually not planned in advance but was a result of the interaction between impatient police and passionate demonstrators.

But the experience of low-grade violence, and the intensive use of symbols of delegitimation, have their own logic of incremental development.[48] The tactics of confrontation were soon supplemented by the bombings of induction centers. The radical Black Panthers, who armed themselves heavily and fought the police fiercely, provided an attractive model to follow. They also produced an immense sense of guilt in the hearts of the young radicals, who believed in the same cause but did not get the same brutal treatment from the authorities. Also important was the "urban guerrilla" model provided by the Tupamaros in Uruguay.[49] It remained for the Weatherman leaders, the second generation of the SDS who were politically socialized by the violent confrontations of the previous three years, to bring the process to its peak. This process—a psychopolitical crisis of legitimacy—was marked by a syndrome consisting of four components: (1) a political language of delegitimation of the regime, (2) rhetoric and symbols of depersonalization and dehumanization of individuals belonging to the system, (3) intended and planned violence, and (4) terrorism.

As a terror underground the Weatherman was a failure. It did not succeed, as the Red Army Faction did in West Germany, to shock an entire country. It was unable, as the Italian Red Brigades were able, to hold up a modern society at gun point. In fact, it never recruited more than four hundred members and followers, and most of the time its inexperienced leaders and recruits worried not about the revolution but about their hideouts, survival logistics, and internal group relations. Although the organization was responsible for dozens of bombings in 1970— and scored some spectacular successes, such as the explosions that took place in the Capitol, the Pentagon, and New York police headquarters— its greatest damage was self-inflicted: three leaders of the organization blew themselves up in a New York townhouse while manufacturing a bomb.[50] Despite the Weatherman's high-revolutionary rhetoric, its young

[47] See J. H. Skolnick, *The Politics of Protest* (New York: Ballantine Books, 1969), 106–9.

[48] See Albert Bandura, "Social Learning Theory of Aggression," in *The Control of Aggression: Implications from Basic Research,* edited by John F. Knutson (New York: Hawthorn, 1973).

[49] Stuart Daniels, "The Weatherman," *Government and Opposition* 9 (1974): 449–51.

[50] See *The Weather Underground: Report of the Subcommittee to Investigate the Adminis-*

leaders never recovered from this loss; the accident greatly diminished their enthusiasm for terrorism.[51] In their last public document, *Prairie Fire*, published in 1974, Weatherman leaders restated their revolutionary commitment to armed struggle and took credit for twenty explosions and other operations initiated over the previous years.[52] But they admitted, at the same time, that very little had been achieved in the United States and that a long and protracted world struggle was still ahead. Nothing of significance has been heard from them since.

The formation of ideological terrorism: Some general conclusions

What is the theoretical lesson to be drawn from this developmental analysis of the Weatherman? What can be learned from a comparative observation of similar New Left terror organizations in Europe and Japan that emerged in the 1960s and operated mainly in the 1970s? Is it possible to identify some universal behavior patterns that govern the rich historical context of ideological terrorism in a democracy? Can we make some general sense of the political psychology of ideological terrorism?

All these questions can be answered constructively if the two most significant observations emerging from fifteen years of terrorism research are taken into consideration:

1. Terrorism is neither a sui generis plague that comes from nowhere, nor an inexplicable, random strike against humanity.
2. Terrorism is not the product of mentally deranged persons.

Terrorism, and ideological terrorism in particular, is a political phenomenon par excellence and is therefore explicable in political terms. It is an extension of opposition politics in democracy, a special case of an ideological conflict of authority. It is, furthermore, the behavioral product of a prolonged process of delegitimation of the established society or the regime—a process whose beginning is, almost always, nonviolent and nonterroristic. In the main, the process does *not* involve isolated individuals who become terrorists on their own because their psyche is split or they suffer from low esteem and need extravagant compensation.[53] Rather,

---

tration of the Internal Security Act and Other Internal Security Laws of the Committee on the Judiciary, United States Senate, January 1975, 133.
[51] Daniels, "The Weatherman," 445.
[52] *Prairie Fire*, an underground document, 1974.
[53] This statement should not be mistaken for the claim that individuals are drawn to the terrorist organization at random. Studies in the psychology of terrorism have shown certain peculiar commonalities among terrorists; see Jerrold M. Post, "Notes on a Psychodynamic Theory of Terrorist Behavior," *Terrorism: An International Journal* 7, no. 3

it involves a group of true believers who challenge authority long before they become terrorists, recruit followers, clash with the public agencies of law enforcement from a position of weakness, obtain a distinct collective world view, and, in time, radicalize within the organization to the point of becoming terroristic. The terrorist collectivity is almost always an elite group that is headed by well-educated middle-class or upper-middle-class young people, usually college students or dropouts.[54]

Although neither supernatural nor rationally inexplicable, the process that leads to ideological terrorism is nevertheless extraordinary, because for the people concerned it involves a remarkable personal and political transformation. An understanding of this group process and its painful developmental stages seems to be much more important than an understanding of the individual terrorists' personal psychology.[55] This understanding of the evolutionary group psychology of terrorists seems crucial for the explanation of the ease with which young, educated, middle-class, normal people with no previous experience with violence are able to desecrate all of the norms of organized society, commit the worst atrocities, and feel good about it all.

The experience of the Weatherman organization shows that the process of delegitimation, through which ideological terrorism is formed, can be divided into three stages: (1) crisis of confidence, (2) conflict of legitimacy, and (3) crisis of legitimacy. Each of these stages identifies a particular collective psychopolitical identity reached by an ideologically motivated group. This group identity, which changes rapidly as radicalization proceeds, contains a combination of political-behavioral components, ideological and symbolic tenets, and psychological traits. It appears that, as radicalization deepens, the collective group identity takes over much of the individual identity of the members; and, at the terrorist stage, the group identity reaches it peak.[56] The individual terrorists may not lose their former identity, but their actual behavior can best be explained by the psychology of the larger group.

(1984): 244–6. The argument is that these peculiarities *do not explain* the phenomenon of terrorism.

[54] For a comprehensive summary of the sociopsychology of radical students and young intellectuals, see Christopher A. Roots, "Student Radicalism: Politics of Moral Protest and Legitimation Problems of the Modern Capitalist State," *Theory and Society* 9 (1980).

[55] According to Jerrold M. Post, "The predominant determinant of terrorist action is the internal dynamic of the terrorist group"; see Post, "Group and Organizational Dynamics," p. 16. See also Crenshaw, "The Psychology of Political Terrorism," pp. 395–400; and Abraham Kaplan, "The Psychodynamics of Terrorism," *Terrorism: An International Journal* 1, no. 3/4 (1978): 248.

[56] See Knutson, "The Terrorists' Dilemmas," 212–15.

If this analysis is correct, then the study of ideological terrorism, including its psychological dimension, can proceed fruitfully without clinical interviews (which are, in any case, very hard to obtain). If much of the terrorist's activity is determined by group identity, an empirical examination of the following two variables may help a great deal:

1. The changing symbolic behavior of the activists involved—the ways in which they talk, categorize, theorize, and stigmatize the world, both their own and that of the enemy[57]
2. The changing political and legal behavior of the activists involved—the ways in which they interact with the prevailing political and legal system

An examination of the interplay of these two dimensions helps to identify the general features of the three stages of the process of delegitimation.

Crisis of confidence is the psychopolitical stage reached by a movement, or a challenge group, whose confidence in the existing political government is greatly eroded. Crisis of confidence implies a conflict with specific rulers or policies. It does not presume a structural delegitimation because, at this stage, the foundations of the established political system are not yet questioned or challenged. In many cases, crisis of confidence involves an angry critique of the established authorities or rulers from the very ideological assumptions on which the regime itself is founded. The existing "masters" are projected as wrong not because of some fundamental faults in the system itself but because of their own misleading behavior or misguided policies.

Although a crisis of confidence does not indicate a complete ideological break with the powers that be, it nevertheless represents a profound conflict with what is seen as "the establishment" and goes far beyond ordinary political opposition.

From an empirical perspective, the crisis of confidence is marked by the appearance of an enraged ideological challenge group (or movement, or counterculture) that refuses to play according to the established political rules of the game. The group will usually articulate its critique of the

[57] For a general theoretical elaboration on the meaning of symbolic behavior in politics see Murray Edelman, *Politics as Symbolic Action* (Chicago: Markham Publishing Co., 1971). For attempts to read the terrorists' minds through their own words and expressions, see Konrad Kellen, "Terrorists: What Are They Like? How Some Terrorists Describe Their World and Actions," in *Terrorism and Beyond: An International Conference on Terrorism and Low-Level Conflict,* edited by Brian Jenkins (Santa Monica: Rand Corporation, 1982); Bonnie Cordes, "Euroterrorists Talk About Themselves: A Look at the Literature," paper delivered at the International Conference on Terrorism Research, University of Aberdeen, Scotland, 15–17 April 1986; David C. Rapoport, "The World as Terrorist Leaders See It: A Look at the Memoirs," paper delivered at the American Political Science Association convention, 28–31 August 1986, Hilton Hotel, Washington, D.C.

establishment in ideological terms, will dissent from mainstream politics, and will engage in protests, demonstrations, symbolic resistance, and other forms of "direct action."[58] Although not illegal, its behavior, group mentality, and language are likely to be countersystemic. Early confrontations with the authorities and the police, including small-scale and unplanned violence, are very likely.

Conflict of legitimacy is the radicalized continuation of the crisis of confidence. It is the behavioral stage that evolves when a challenge group previously engaged in antigovernment criticism is ready to question the very legitimacy of the whole system. Conflict of legitimacy emerges when the challenge group discovers that the erroneous rulers are able to "mislead the people" not because they shrewdly manipulate the otherwise benign system but because the system itself is manipulative and repressive. The way to do away with the oppressive rulers is to transform the system altogether. Conflict of legitimacy implies the emergence of an alternative ideological and cultural system, one that delegitimates the prevailing regime and its code of social norms in the name of a better one.

The conflict of legitimacy is usually precipitated by a great disappointment on the part of the challenge group with its previous stage of radicalization. The formerly "moderate" radicals are frustrated either by the government's hostile (and sometimes excessively violent) response to their passionate critique or by their own failure to score successes. They develop a need to channel their frustration into a more extreme form of protest. What follows is the development of an ideology of delegitimation, which articulates a break with the prevailing political order.[59] The new frame of reference is, in most cases, an already-existing ideology. Very few radicals are capable, during their intense process of delegitimation, of developing a new system of critical thought that fits the new situation analytically and empirically. It is much easier to take over an existing ideology of delegitimation (such as Marxism, Maoism, or third-world Trotskyism) and to believe that it is relevant to the situation at hand. It is of some interest that the ideology adopted need not be foreign. If the national culture of the country involved contains historical images of successful revolutions (such as the French or the American), these images may be rediscovered and reused with great effectiveness.

The evolution of the conflict of legitimacy is marked not only by ideo-

---

[58] See April Carter, *Direct Action and Liberal Democracy* (New York: Harper and Row, 1973), 26–7; Donald Light, Jr., John Spiegel, et al., *The Dynamics of University Protest* (Chicago: Nelson-Hall Publishers, 1977), chapter 4.

[59] See Sprinzak, "Marxism as a Symbolic Action."

logical, symbolic, and psychological changes, but also by intense political action that ranges from angry protest (demonstrations, confrontations, and vandalism) to the application of small-scale violence against the regime.[60] The challenge group or the movement, which is the concrete collective carrier of the conflict of legitimacy, lives now in a stage of intense radicalization. It solidifies itself and closes ranks. The individuals involved are totally consumed by the great moments and emotionally change a great deal. Their language and rhetoric—which is the expression of their inner collective identity—is revolutionary, and their jargon is full of slanders and desecrations.

Crisis of legitimacy is the behavioral and symbolic culmination of the two preceding psychopolitical stages. Its essence lies in the extension of the previous delegitimation of the system to every person associated with it. Individuals who are identified with the rotten, and soon-to-be-destroyed, social and political order are depersonalized and dehumanized. They are derogated to the ranks of subhuman species. Dehumanization makes it possible for the radicals to be disengaged morally and to commit atrocities without a second thought. It bifurcates the world into the sons of light and the sons of darkness, and makes the "fantasy war" of the former versus the latter fully legitimate.[61] It makes the few radicals who have made it to the third stage of the process of delegitimation, usually a second generation of radicals, accomplished terrorists. Each person who belongs to the establishment, or who is perceived as belonging to it, becomes a potential target for assassination or indiscriminate murder.

The first external indication of the evolution of the crisis of legitimacy is linguistic and symbolic. Expressions of political delegitimation are no longer limited to political terms or social concepts but are extended to a language of objects, animals, or "human" animals. The regime and its accomplices are now portrayed as "things," "dogs," "pigs," "Nazis," or "terrorists." The portrayal is not accidental and occasional but repeated and systematic. It is part of a new lexicon. The "pigs," "Nazis," or "terrorist lackeys" can be killed or eliminated because they are, by definition, not human and do not belong to the legitimate community of "the people."

[60] See Carter, *Direct Action*, 74–7; and Rob Kroes, "Violence in America: Spontaneity and Strategy," in *Urban Guerilla*, edited by Joane Niezing (Rotterdam: Rotterdam University Press, 1974), 82–7.

[61] Franco Ferracuti, "A Sociopsychiatric Interpretation of Terrorism," *Annals of the American Academy of Sciences* 463 (September 1982): 136–7.

The crisis of legitimacy—which brings together all of the earlier clusters of the process of radicalization—presupposes an acute stage of psychological transformation. The group that undergoes this profound mental change often displays antinomian behavior.[62] Its members free themselves from the yoke of conventional morality and engage in sexual perversity, excessive drug orgies, and criminality of many forms. The boundaries between political and personal illegality are totally removed, and certain forms of deviant behavior are hailed as right and even sacred. A new revolutionary morality emerges, and an antinomian *Weltanschauung* is articulated.

The political manifestation of the crisis of legitimacy is strategic terrorism. It consists of the formation of a small terror underground that engages in unconventional attacks on the regime and its affiliates and that is capable of committing a wide range of atrocities. As a social unit, the terrorist underground is isolated from the outside world. It constructs a reality of its own and a whole new set of behavioral and moral standards that are strictly enforced. The members of the group are so involved with each other that every individual act has a collective meaning of utmost importance. The psychodynamics of the whole unit, including its acts of terrorism against the outside society, assume an internally consistent logic that may be unrelated to external factors.[63] Very few of the terrorists who reach the crisis of legitimacy, and are fully consumed by it, are capable of reversing their radicalization to the point of returning to normal life. Their immense personal transformation—which, in many cases, leads them to nihilism, despair, and extreme fear of the group's punishment—may drive them to suicide.

Although all three stages of the process of delegitimation can be seen in most modern ideological terrorist organizations, they need not be. First, groups may not develop beyond the first or second stage. And even if a group does move through all these stages, individual members of that group may not.

It is important to recognize that the conditions that promote the evolution of ideological terrorism are very different from the conditions that

---

[62] For the relationships between terrorism and antinomian ethos in messianic and millenarian movements, see David C. Rapoport, "Why Does Messianism Produce Terror?" paper presented at the American Political Science Association meeting, New Orleans, 27 August—1 September 1985, 12–13.

[63] See Jerrold M. Post, "Notes on a Psychodynamic Theory," 250–3; Knutson, "The Terrorists' Dilemmas," 211–5; Crenshaw, "The Psychology of Political Terrorism," 395–400; Fred and Phyllis Wright, "Violent Groups," *Group* 6, no. 2 (Summer 1982): 31–4.

promote the evolution of protest and extraparliamentary politics. Most
modern societies experience, at some time, some form of a crisis of confidence. The accepted repertoire of political action of modern democracy
includes extraparliamentary politics of different types. The growing literature on collective and political action is full of cases and useful examples of such politics.[64] Even groups that delegitimate each other often
coexist. Communists, third-world Marxists, extreme neofascists, and religious fanatics coexist in the margins of most modern societies. Many of
them are engaged in one or another form of antigovernment action or
are waiting for the opportunity to do so. For ideological terrorism to
develop, another set of conditions is required. It is one that entails a
perception of harsh governmental repression, and a profound disillusionment (as well as a sense of guilt) among idealistic and young middle-class
intelligentsia regarding society and their role in it.[65] External models of
revolt and terrorism also must be available.[66] The New Left terrorism
that emerged in the late 1960s doubtless could not have come to existence without two critical historical conditions: the disillusionment with
the war in Vietnam and the attractive models of terrorism and the urban
guerrilla that developed after 1950 in the third world.

Despite the image of a widespread New Left terrorism that prevailed
in the 1970s, it is important to remember that even at that time ideological terrorism was the exception rather than the rule. Most processes of
delegitimation never reach the full maturation necessary for the formation of terrorism.

It is also important to recognize that radicalization is a demanding
and dangerous process. The radicals are always outnumbered. The more
violent they become, the harsher the official reaction is likely to be. In
addition to the forceful response of the police and the military—which in
most cases outbrutalizes the brutality of the inexperienced activists—the
society around them is likely to remain unmoved and hostile. Very few
radicals, who usually come from the second generation that was social-

---

[64] See Carter, *Direction Action;* E. N. Muller, *Aggressive Political Participation* (Princeton,
N.J.: Princeton University Press, 1979); Neil Smelser, *Theory of Collective Behavior* (New
York: Free Press, 1962); Charles Tilly, *From Mobilization to Revolution* (Reading, Pa.:
Addison-Wesley, 1978).

[65] For an excellent discussion of the conditions for terrorism, see Martha Crenshaw, "The
Causes of Terrorism," *Comparative Politics* 13 (July 1981).

[66] Students of terrorism discuss this issue in relation to the "contagion" of terrorism; see
Manu I. Midlarsky, Martha Crenshaw, and Fumihico Yoshida, "Why Violence Spreads,"
International Studies Quarterly 24 (June 1980); Kent Layne Oots and Thomas C. Wei-
gele, "Terrorist and Victim: Psychiatric and Physiological Approaches From a Social Science Perspective," *Terrorism: An International Journal* 8, no. 1 (1985): 8–13.

ized directly to the "conflict of legitimacy," are capable of becoming terrorists and of adhering to terrorism over a long period of time.[67] Those who do display either reckless optimism or profound pessimism and helplessness. Terrorism is violent, cruel, antinomian, and, most of all, deadly. People get killed or mutilated. For the radicals involved, just as for their victims, this is by far the most dangerous form of political action or warfare.

Most of the radicals who do not achieve the stage of terrorism stay at the psychopolitical level of the crisis of confidence or at the level of the conflict of legitimacy. It is thus possible to distinguish between the avant garde of the process of delegitimation—the terrorists—and the rearguard, the great number of the other radicals who remain behind.[68] The terrorists are usually scornful and critical of the rearguard. They see themselves as the *crème de la crème* of the revolution and perceive the others as fakes or failures. But politically and operationally they need the rearguard a great deal. No terror underground is capable of sustaining itself without a nonterrorist support system—friends and accomplices who provide information, hideouts, escape routes, and supplies. To the degree that the New Left terrorists were able to survive, they did it with the support of the less-committed rearguardists.

Ideological terrorism does not emerge from a vacuum or from an inexplicable urge on the part of a few unstable radicals to go berserk. Rather, it is the psychopolitical product of a profound process of delegitimation that a large number of people undergo in relation to the established social and political order. Although most of the participants in this process are capable of preserving their sense of reality, a few are not. Totally consumed by their radicalism, they imagine a nonexistent "fantasy war" with the authorities and expend themselves in the struggle to win it. Ideological terrorism, in the final analysis, is the simulated revolution of the isolated few.

[67] See Crenshaw, "The Psychology of Political Terrorism," 398–9.
[68] For the development of the distinction between the avant garde of the process of delegitimation and its rearguard, see Sprinzak, *Democracy and Illegitimacy*, chapter 7.

6

Terrorism in democracies:
Its social and political bases

TED ROBERT GURR

The thesis of this chapter is that the campaigns of political terrorists in democratic societies almost invariably emerge out of larger conflicts, and that they reflect, in however distorted a form, the political beliefs and aspirations of a larger segment of society. Recognition of the changing nature of the relationship between violent activists and their community of support is essential to understanding the onset, persistence, and decline of terrorist movements. This thesis implies, among other things, that analysis of the ideologies and psychological traits of violent activists and of the sociodynamics of terrorist groups is incomplete unless we understand their reciprocal relations with larger publics.

Two problems are examined in the light of this thesis. The first consists of the circumstances under which the political culture of communal and political minorities comes to provide a supportive climate of belief within which terrorism emerges and persists. The second consists of the processes by which these supportive climates erode—which they usually do. The general arguments are derived from conflict theory and from the observation of the dynamics of groups that have used terrorism in Western societies. Evidence from some specific episodes is cited in support of the arguments, but it is suggestive, not decisive. The purpose here is to set up plausible theoretical arguments that can and should be examined in careful comparative studies.

The theoretical arguments are specific to democratic societies, that is, to societies in which (1) there is organized expression of contending po-

Walter Reich and Jeffrey Ian Ross offered useful comments on an earlier draft of this chapter.

litical views and (2) office holding and policy depend directly or indirectly on elections. Terrorist campaigns in authoritarian societies also require supportive climates of opinion, but police-state tactics ordinarily preclude any organized expression of oppositional opinion, especially its violent manifestations. The leaders of most authoritarian states have more latitude than elected officials in whether and how they respond to discontent and disorder. They are less concerned than democratic leaders with maintaining a politically acceptable balance between suppressing violence and accommodating or deterring those who support the purposes but not the tactics of terrorists.

The political context of terrorism's onset

The general proposition here is that violent activism in democracies requires a climate of acceptance of unconventional means of political action among a support group. The support group is any social segment— a communal group, faction, political tendency, or class—whose members seek a particular kind of political change. There are two main routes by which (some of the members of) such groups come to accept extreme means: radicalization and reaction.

Radicalization refers to a process in which the group has been mobilized in pursuit of a social or political objective but has failed to make enough progress toward the objective to satisfy all activists. Some become discouraged, while others intensify their efforts, lose patience with conventional means of political action, and look for tactics that will have greater impact. This is the kind of situation in which modeling or "imitative" behavior occurs. Impatience and frustration provide an expressive motivation (anger) and rationalistic grounds (dramatic episodes of violence elsewhere) that make it likely that some activists will decide to experiment with terror tactics. The choice is made, and justified, as a means to the original ends of radical reform, group autonomy, or whatever. And the dynamics of the process are such that the terrorists believe that they enjoy the support of some larger community in revolt.

Two North American terrorist groups of the 1960s and 1970s provide evidence of the process of radicalization and its bases of community support. The *Front de Liberation du Québec* (FLQ) had its origins in the separatist sentiment that become widespread among French-speaking Canadians in the late 1950s and early 1960s. Disaffection with the policies of governments then in power in Québec and Ottawa was particularly intense in the growing class of young, urban Québecois men in skilled and technical occupations and in the teaching and liberal professions. The first important separatist organizations were founded in 1960. The FLQ was established by dissatisfied members of these groups, twenty-four of whom met in November 1962 to develop more radical but nonviolent forms of action for the cause of independence. In February 1963 three members of this group in turn rejected nonviolence and formed the FLQ.

The violent actions of the FLQ occurred in two distinct waves, one of them beginning in 1963, the second in 1968. Initially, adherents of the FLQ bombed military targets; then they extended their campaign to government buildings, the economic infrastructure, and targets that symbolized the FLQ's support of striking workers. Before the conclusion of the FLQ campaign in 1972 (for reasons examined later), people acting in its name carried out 169 actions resulting in eight deaths. The strength of separatist sentiment, of which the FLQ's campaigns were an extreme manifestation, is evident from the electoral success of the separatist *Parti Québecois* (PQ), which won 23 percent of the provincial vote in the first election it contested, in December 1970.[1]

The Weather Underground, the second case examined here, was the lineal descendent of the Students for a Democratic Society (SDS), which was founded in 1959 as an alliance of students, blacks (who soon left), and peace groups intent on influencing the politics of the Democratic party. Radicalized by the Vietnam War and the failure of mass political action to alter U.S. policy, the SDS split in 1969 into various factions, one of which was the Weathermen, later named the Weather Underground, then the Weather People. Its leadership, the Weather Bureau, attempted mass revolutionary action in the streets of Chicago in October 1969. They judged the strategy a failure in the face of overwhelming police response and went underground. The membership was purged and the remainder, perhaps fifty in all, organized communes called "focals" to carry out urban guerrilla warfare. A four-year campaign followed, during which there were nineteen dramatic bombings aimed at corporate offices, New York City police headquarters, the Capitol, and the Pentagon.[2]

---

[1] This summary is drawn from Louis Fornier, *FLQ: The Anatomy of an Underground Movement* (Toronto: NC Press, 1984); and Jeffrey Ian Ross, "Domestic Political Terrorism in Canada 1960–1985: A Statistical and Critical Analysis," paper presented to the Annual Meetings of the Canadian Political Science Association, Hamilton, 6 June 1987.

[2] This sketch is drawn from more detailed summaries in T. R. Gurr, "Political Terrorism in

In Chapter 5 of this volume, Ehud Sprinzak analyzes the psychopolitical process through which the New Left passed during the 1960s, which he characterizes as a crisis of legitimacy. The essential point for the present analysis is that the New Left was a mass movement that led, and fed upon, growing public opposition to U.S. involvement in Vietnam. Between 1965 and 1970, more than 3 million people were estimated to have taken part in antiwar demonstrations in the United States.[3] By 1968–9 more than half of the respondents to public opinion polls expressed verbal opposition to that policy. Only a handful of the New Left were alienated enough to embrace revolutionary strategies, but many of them agreed with the objectives, if not the tactics, of the militant Weather People, and some provided active support for them. Testimony to the effectiveness of that support network is the fact that no Weather People were arrested during the early 1970s or after the voluntary cessation of their bombing campaign in 1975—except for those who chose, years later, to emerge from the underground.

Reaction is an analytically distinct process in which members of a regional, communal, or political group resort to terrorism in response to threatening social change or intervention by authorities. Whereas *radicalization* characterizes groups with future-oriented objectives, *reaction* occurs in defense of a group's threatened rights and status.[4] Right-wing terrorism often is reactive in this sense, for example, the terrorism practiced by the Ku Klux Klan. The first Klan was established by Confederate veterans in 1867 and, along with like-minded groups, carried out a four-year campaign of coercion, threats, and terroristic violence against the supporters and agents of the Reconstruction state governments, which the North had imposed on the defeated South. They acted on behalf of, and generally with the active support of, white southerners. Moreover, many of their goals were achieved when state governments were restored

the United States: Historical Antecedents and Contemporary Trends," in *The Politics of Terrorism*, Michael Stohl, ed., 3d rev. ed. (New York: Marcel Dekker, 1987), 549–78; and Nicholas Strinkowski, "The Organizational Behavior of Revolutionary Groups" (Ph.D. dissertation, Northwestern University, 1985).

[3] From data compiled and summarized in T. R. Gurr, "Political Protest and Rebellion in the 1960s: The United States in World Perspective," in *Violence in America: Historical and Comparative Perspectives*, edited by Hugh Davis Graham and T. R. Gurr (Beverly Hills, Calif.: Sage Publications, 1979, rev. ed.), 55.

[4] The distinction between radicalization and reaction parallels Charles Tilly's distinction between "modern" and "reactionary" collective violence as developed in "Collective Violence in European Perspective," in Graham and Gurr, *Violence in America*, 91–100. Like most categorical distinctions, this one is soft around the edges: the political processes that lead to terrorism may include elements of both. Some examples are cited later.

to white southern control in the early 1870s and blacks were effectively disenfranchised.

The resurgence of terrorism by white supremacists after 1957 was a traditional response to new pressures from civil rights workers and the federal government. Terror peaked in the early 1960s when civil rights marches and voter-registration campaigns were at their peak, but in this instance terrorism failed to reverse change. Although both these episodes of reactionary terrorism enjoyed support among many rural and small-town southerners, the violent white supremacists of the 1960s could not count on the backing of the southern political elite or the urban middle and professional classes.[5]

The question is whether there are analogues to reactionary, Klan-style terrorism in other democratic societies. One feature that distinguishes the process of reactionary terror is the fact that deadly violence is usually an early response to perceived threat rather than the culmination of a long process of radicalization. A related feature is the existence of a tradition of violent resistance in the affected community, which is more or less quickly activated by externally imposed change. An example of this is a small Canadian religious sect of Russian origin, the Sons of Freedom Doukhobors, who live in British Columbia. The Freedomites, as they are known, hold religiously conservative views, reject materialism, and oppose government regulation and public education. During episodes of purification and renunciation they have perpetrated waves of reactive terrorism against commercial and government buildings and against other Doukhobors; more than 120 such terrorist actions were carried out in the early 1960s.[6]

Terrorist actions on behalf of regional minorities—such as the German-speakers of the Alto Adige in northern Italy during the early 1960s, and Basques and Corsicans from the 1960s to the present—also have some reactive characteristics. The militants claim to act in defense of a larger community whose integrity and well-being is at risk. One does not have to accept such claims at face value to recognize that these com-

[5] Analyses of the political circumstances of Klan and other white-supremacist violence are provided by David M. Chalmers, *Hooded Americanism: The First Century of the Ku Klux Klan, 1865–1965* (Garden City, N.Y.: Doubleday, 1965); G. David Garson and Gail O'Brien, "Collective Violence in the Reconstruction South," in Graham and Gurr, *Violence in America*, 243–60; and C. Vann Woodward, *The Strange History of Jim Crow* (New York: Oxford University Press, 1966).
[6] A detailed account is George Woodcock and Ivan Avakumovic, *The Doukhobors* (Toronto: McClelland and Stewart, 1977). Data from the 1960s episodes are reported by Ross, "Domestic Political Terrorism."

munally based terrorists, by invoking traditions of group autonomy, often elicit some community support because of latent resentment of ancient injustices and modern inequalities.

The terrorism of some right-wing political groups in Continental democracies has reactive characteristics as well. Neo-Nazis in Germany and neo-Fascists in Italy are marginal groups with little or no prospects for political influence by conventional means. The processes of delegitimation and radicalization presumably evolve within small groups of believers, perhaps under the influence of old fighters who have never accepted the postwar political settlement. Their ideas are not tested in the democratic political arena because they reject its validity from the outset. When such groups do enter political combat, they tend to begin with violent means because they do not think other means are worth using.[7] Something similar has happened among some small, right-wing extremist groups in the United States, such as the Aryan Nations. But most of the terrorist activities of these kinds of right-wing groups in contemporary Europe and North America have been short-lived, because they had little public support for their purposes even at the outset. In this respect they are different from the communally based terrorists identified earlier, who generally can count on some sympathetic support.

The terrorist insurgency of Catholics in Northern Ireland provides a last example, one that combines elements of radicalization and reaction. The fundamental issues that divide Catholic from Protestant need not be repeated in detail here. What began in 1967–9 was a process of radicalization among Northern Irish Catholics who, taking their cues from events in the United States, initiated a civil rights campaign. Ultraloyalist Protestants responded with coercion and violence, which provided an opening for intervention by the Irish Republican Army (IRA) on behalf of threatened Catholics. Military intervention by the British government, and the 1972 killing of Derry civil rights marchers, confirmed for many Northern Irish Catholics the justice of resistance by all means against the loyalists and the British. Opinion polls throughout the years of violence have shown majorities among Northern Irish Catholics favoring union with the Republic of Ireland, while the militant Sinn Fein—closely associated with the Provisional IRA (PIRA)—still commanded 35 percent of

[7] Not all right-wing extremist groups in Western Europe avoid electoral competition. Those with a significant following, especially in France, have entered the electoral arena with passing successes. The xenophobic National Front in contemporary France is an example. The National Front's stake in electoral politics minimizes the attractions of violent means for its most extreme sympathizers.

the Catholic vote in 1983. Paul Power thinks that Catholics' ideological commitment to the Irish Republican cause is gradually eroding and being supplanted by a war-weary acceptance of reconciliation and reformism within the present political structure.[8]

The political psychology of terrorism's decline

Power's observation introduces the second topic, which is to specify the processes and conditions that undermine acceptance of violent political action by the terrorists' community of support. Most terrorist organizations have finite life spans, and their actions, plotted over time, represent one or a series of "waves" with distinctive phases of increase and decline. The life spans of groups using terrorist strategies are being assessed in a study-in-progress by Martha Crenshaw. She identifies thirty-one such groups that have been active in Europe and North American democracies since the 1950s. Twenty of those groups ceased to exist after an average of 6.5 years of activity. The most durable of the ongoing campaigns have been carried out on behalf of communal minorities like the Basques and the contending religious factions of Northern Ireland. ETA (see Chapter 2) has used terror on behalf of autonomy for Spanish Basques since 1959, and five terrorist organizations in Northern Ireland have been active for well over a decade.[9]

Most of the major terrorist campaigns that began in Western societies in the 1960s and 1970s have ended or are in the last stages of decline. The issues that animated them may again lead to terrorism by militants using new names; communal grievances and demands for autonomy are particularly likely to resurface in this way. Nonetheless domestic terrorism has been generally declining in most Western societies. Some quantitative documentation about particular movements illustrates this phenomenon:

Canada. Terrorist actions by Québec terrorists began in 1963 (twenty events), reached their highest level in 1968 (thirty-eight events), then de-

[8] Paul F. Power, "Political Violence, Systemic Issues and Human Rights in the Northern Ireland Conflict," paper presented to the Annual Meetings of the American Political Science Association, Chicago, 3–6 September 1987, 23.

[9] My calculations from information provided in Martha Crenshaw, "How Terrorism Ends," paper presented to the 1987 Annual Meetings of the American Political Science Association, Chicago, 3–6 September 1987.

clined to two in 1972 and, with the exception of a single bombing in 1980, have not recurred.[10]

United States. Terrorism by the revolutionary left in the United States began with the 1970–4 campaign of the Weather Underground. Five successor organizations, using a dozen different names, carried out bombings in the name of revolutionary causes into the mid-1980s, but with ever-fewer members and diminishing public attention. Federal Bureau of Investigation data show a decline in the number of incidents of political terrorism in the United States of all kinds from an average of 119 per year in 1975–7 to 12 per year in 1984–6.[11]

Puerto Rico. Puerto Rican nationalists on that island dependency have been responsible for the most deadly of contemporary terrorist campaigns in North America.[12] Since their first violent acts in 1950 they have been active sporadically on the island and the U.S. mainland. Major campaigns, which reached their peak in 1974–7, ended in 1980 on the mainland with a series of arrests but continued for several more years in Puerto Rico. After a lull of several years, terrorism resumed on the island in 1986, but at a low level.

Italy. Terrorist events of all kinds in Italy, most of them the work of the Red Brigades, numbered less than 400 per year in 1969–70, peaked at more than 2,000 actions annually in 1978–9, then declined to less than 100 per year in the mid-1980s, as Franco Ferracuti has pointed out earlier in this volume.

Northern Ireland. In this, the most enduring and deadly of all contemporary terrorist campaigns in Western democracies, 2,532 people—nationalists, loyalists, security forces, and passers-by—died between January 1969 and the end of 1986. Yet the trend is unmistakably downward. In 1971–3 the annual death toll averaged 300; in 1977–9 the average was 97; in 1984–6 it was 61.[13]

[10] From figure 2 in Jeffrey Ian Ross and T. R. Gurr, "Why Terrorism Subsides: A Comparative Study of Trends and Groups in Terrorism in Canada and the United States," *Comparative Politics*, 21 (July 1989): 412.
[11] Ibid., tables 2 and 3.
[12] Gurr, "Political Terrorism in the United States," table 3.
[13] Power, "Political Violence," tables 1 and 2.

The literature on terrorism tends to be preoccupied with its causes and says little about the general circumstances responsible for such declines. Insofar as the question is addressed at all, it is assumed that movements decline as a result of some combination of security countermeasures and failure to achieve publicity or larger political objectives. I doubt that these answers are sufficient. They certainly seem inadequate to explain, for example, why revolutionary terrorism repeatedly reemerges in West Germany despite its lack of achievements, many arrests, and intensive security measures; or why the Provisional IRA has continued a deadly campaign for seventeen years without appreciable gains; or, for that matter, why ETA has continued a campaign, now nearly thirty years in duration, despite the achievement by Spanish Basques of a substantial measure of regional autonomy.

I propose to examine the conditions and events likely to undermine the larger basis of group support which, I have argued, is essential to sustain terrorist activities. The erosion of political support is not an immediate cause of decline in terrorist campaigns but an underlying one, and conditions the effects of almost all public policies directed at terrorism. Three general kinds of processes contribute to the erosion of support: backlash, reform, and deterrence.[14]

Backlash is a widely observed phenomenon in the analysis of conflict processes. Acts of disruption and violence that are intended to attract favorable attention from a relevant public often have the opposite effect. Backlash has been evident in the German public's hardening attitudes toward "revolutionary" acts by the Baader-Meinhof group and its main successor, the Red Army Faction. But general public antagonism and its counterpart, support for strong countermeasures, have not proven fatal—evidently because a significant residue of sympathy for revolutionary action remains on the German left. A significant number of leftists with university backgrounds continue to be concentrated in some cities; their radical commitments and preferences for collective action provide a community of support for more violent militants. Konrad Kellen estimates, elsewhere in this volume, that 5 percent of the West German population think that the terrorists have some justification for their action.[15]

[14] The following discussion uses arguments and evidence from Ross and Gurr, "Why Terrorism Subsides."

[15] Survey research on political activists in West Germany provides more precise documentation; see Edward Muller and Karl-Dieter Opp, "Rational Choice and Rebellious Collective Action," *American Political Science Review* 80 (June 1986): 471–88. See also Ekkart Zimmermann, "Review Essay: Terrorist Violence in West Germany: Some Reflec-

Backlash within the group that initially supported the terrorists' cause is even more devastating to the militants than backlash among the larger public. If and when active support dries up, the group finds it increasingly difficult to attract new recruits, to get material resources, to find refuge among reliable sympathizers, or to avoid informants. Dramatic acts of violence directed against victims thought to be innocent are particularly likely to provide backlash. Sympathy and support also may be reduced through propaganda campaigns by public officials and the media that aim at discrediting terrorists' causes and their supposed allies. Support also can be undercut by counterterror strategies that raise the costs for ordinary citizens of tolerating the terrorists' presence.

The decline of support for the FLQ and the revolutionary left in the United States are illustrative. The decline of the FLQ in the early 1970s can be attributed directly to the successive kidnappings (by two separate FLQ cells) of James Cross, the British trade commissioner in Montreal, on 5 October 1970, and Pierre Laporte, the Québec minister of labor and immigration, five days later. The Ottawa government promptly proclaimed the War Measures Act, equivalent to a declaration of martial law, whereupon Laporte was killed and left in the trunk of an abandoned car. On 4 December, Cross's abductors traded his life for safe conduct to Cuba. Major labor unions in Québec formed a common front to denounce the FLQ, and the general public also seemed overwhelmingly in support of the emergency powers and the presence of the army in Québec.[16] Almost simultaneously, in December 1970, the separatist *Parti Québecois* (PQ) came in second in the provincial election. Its *Manifesto*, issued a year later, proclaimed the need for struggle for national independence but also condemned political violence as "humanly immoral and politically pointless."[17] In the Québec case it is evident that backlash did not discredit separatism as an objective; it discredited the FLQ and the use of terrorism as a means to greater autonomy.

The New Left in the United States, some members of which were revolutionaries and some reformers, never agreed on strategy. Many who advocated revolutionary objectives during the late 1960s thought revo-

tions on Recent Literature," *Journal of Political and Military Sociology* 14 (Fall 1986): 321–32, which provides a critical evaluation of the psychological and other evidence gathered by the West German Ministry of Internal Affairs and published in five volumes under the general title *Analysen zum Terrorismus*, 1981–4.

[16] James Stewart, *The FLQ: Seven Years of Terrorism* (Montreal: Simon and Schuster of Canada, for the Montreal Star, 1970).

[17] Fornier, *FLQ*, 281.

lution could be pursued nonviolently, whereas the handful who plotted strategies of violence sought conscientiously to avoid killing people. Nonetheless, a series of deadly episodes discredited revolutionary terrorism for virtually all the New Left. On 6 March 1970, before the Weather Underground planted its first bomb, three of its members died in accidental explosions that wrecked their bomb factory in a Greenwich Village townhouse. The next death also was accidental. Dr. Robert Fassnacht, a mathematics researcher at the University of Wisconsin, died on 24 August because he happened to be working late at the U.S. Army–supported Mathematics Research Center, where a bomb was set off by a free-lance radical, Karleton Lewis Armstrong. These deaths reportedly led to considerable soul-searching among militants and persuaded some activists to give up more violent kinds of activism.

The Weather Underground itself avoided risking lives after the townhouse explosion, but the Symbionese Liberation Army (SLA) had no such compunctions. In 1973–4 the SLA enjoyed a brief but spectacular career based on the exploits of its dozen members, white radicals of middle-class origin who had joined with black ex-convicts. The SLA echoed, almost parodied, the revolutionary rhetoric of the 1960s by advocating the "unity in love" of all oppressed people, redistribution of capital, dismantling of the prison system, and so forth. But the SLA's first revolutionary action was the 1973 murder of Oakland's black superintendent of schools, Marcus Foster, because he had cooperated with police in planning a school identity card system. This action was followed in early 1974 by the kidnapping and conversion of Patty Hearst, and in May of that year by the fiery shootout in Los Angeles in which six SLA members died.[18]

Shortly before the SLA's fatal denouement, *Ramparts* magazine, a journal of the New Left, wrote what seems in retrospect an epitaph for revolutionary action in the United States. It attributed the emergence of the SLA "to the collapse of the organized left at the end of the sixties, and its continuing failure to regroup itself and survive." The SLA itself was criticized as a "self-appointed vigilante group" and its murder of Marcus Foster condemned as an act of "desperate violence."[19] Although a few violent acts of would-be revolutionaries continued until 1985, there

---

[18] Summarized in J. Bowyer Bell and T. R. Gurr, "Terrorism and Revolution in America," in Graham and Gurr, *Violence in America*, 340–1.
[19] "The Symbionese Liberation Army: Terrorism and the Left," *Ramparts* 12 (May 1974): 21ff.

is little doubt that by 1974 events had helped discredit both revolutionary objectives and violent means for virtually the entire left.

Revulsion against deadly violence is not a sufficient explanation for the decline of militancy on the American left. Just as revolutionaries lost the support of the New Left, the larger political movement was itself eroding as a consequence of widespread changes in political attitudes. A larger cycle of political change was under way, one that Arthur Schlesinger, Jr., characterizes as a shift from "public purpose" to "private interest."[20] The 1960s were a time when public purposes prevailed, a time of rapid political change induced by pressures from below but also encouraged by the commitment of national leaders to social change. I suspect, without having solid evidence, that during such periods of rapid political change growing numbers of activists become convinced that all political ends are possible and that any means can be used in the pursuit of those ends.[21] The general public's reaction to the rhetoric, disorder, and violence of this era crystallized in the 1968 election of Richard Nixon as president. In the years that followed, Americans became increasingly preoccupied with the pursuit of private interests. The "me decade" of the 1970s was accompanied by widespread opposition to advocacy of radical social change and sharp resentment against groups making extreme demands or using disruptive or violent tactics.[22] In short, the immediate backlash against revolutionary rhetoric and action was part of a larger swing in public sentiment away from sympathy with any kind of radical purpose or campaign.

Reform also is likely to undermine support for terrorists in democratic societies. I use *reform* as a shorthand term for government policies and actions that meet some of the grievances of the groups on which terrorists rely for support, as well as for policies that open up alternative means to the attainment of group goals. Such reforms are unlikely to dissuade people who have already been recruited and socialized into isolated cells of militant true believers. There is ample evidence that exit from such cells of people committed to violent activism is psychologically very difficult as well as personally dangerous. Moreover, achievement of limited or tactical successes is more likely to increase the "utilities" they attribute

---

[20] Arthur Schlesinger, Jr., *The Cycles of American History* (Boston: Houghton Mifflin, 1986), chapter 2.

[21] Jeffrey Ian Ross suggests (personal communication) that the speeches of ideologists of the left and writings in the alternative media may have contributed to delusions of grandeur and feelings of omnipotence among some activists.

[22] See Christopher Lasch, *The Culture of Narcissism* (New York: Warner Books, 1979).

to terrorism (in rational-choice terminology) and to reinforce their dis-
position to choose violence in the future (in terms of learning theory).[23]

Political leaders rarely acknowledge the validity of terrorists' demands
or negotiate directly with them. The risks of doing so are too great: negotiation would add to the stature of terrorist groups and provide an
incentive for them to escalate violence as a bargaining tactic. The main
aim—and effect—of the process of reform is to undermine the political
basis of support for the terrorist group. Once it becomes evident to an
aggrieved minority that dominant groups are prepared to accommodate
some of their demands, most are likely to conclude that terrorism is a
less attractive strategy. For potential recruits, the relative utilities of terrorism may no longer compensate for its personal costs and risks. It becomes apparent to the nonmilitant majority that there are less costly ways
of achieving moderate but more certain gains for the group. For those
who share the cause advocated by terrorists but reject their tactics, the
continued operation of terrorists now becomes an active threat to the
process of accommodation. Thus, groups that once supported terrorists
may become politically mobilized against terrorists and actively assist
police in identifying them.

Richard E. Rubenstein has argued, on the basis of comparative studies, that reform is not enough to discourage young intellectuals from terrorism. They will resort to extreme means unless convinced that there are
opportunities for radical political change by nonviolent means. This may
be a correct assessment for the most ideologically committed people, but
it overlooks the fact that reformist strategies are likely to erode the basis
of political support that is essential for any sustained and significant terrorist action.[24] The tension between these two political processes may
account for the desperate and seemingly irrational escalation of terrorism
that sometimes accompanies or follows the introduction of reforms.

A prima facie case can be made that reforms contributed to the decline
of violent separatism in Canada. The province of Québec gained substantial autonomy from the federal government and increased control over
its own economy during the 1960s and 1970s.[25] Although these gains
were not nearly enough to satisfy the militants' demands for indepen-

---

[23] This is an application of a more general argument first developed in T. R. Gurr, *Why Men Rebel* (Princeton, N.J.: Princeton University Press, 1970), chapters 6 and 7.

[24] Richard E. Rubenstein, *Alchemists of Revolution: Terrorism in the Modern World* (New York: Basic Books, 1987).

[25] Kenneth McRoberts and Dale Postgate, *Québec: Social Change and Political Crisis* (Toronto: McClelland and Stewart, 1984, rev. ed.).

dence, the rise of the *Parti Québecois* offered a more promising alternative to FLQ terrorism, especially after the party won seven seats and second ranking in the December 1970 provincial elections. In 1971 and later, a number of activists left the FLQ and joined the PQ in decisions that seemed to be justified by the PQ's victory in the 1976 provincial elections. That victory demonstrated that "the struggle for independence did not necessitate acts of terrorism but could take place within the framework of democracy and the rule of the majority."[26] The irony of nonviolent separatism was that the *Québecois* majority in 1980 rejected the PQ's referendum on "sovereignty association," a watered-down form of autonomy. In other words, public support for the independence sought by the FLQ was not there—in fact, it had been eroded by the gains made toward political and economic autonomy for Québec and by fears about the economic consequences of complete independence.

Reforms also were relevant to the subsidence of revolutionary terrorism in the United States. Two immediate and personal reasons for militant opposition to the government disappeared with the end of the draft in 1972 and with the simultaneous signing of a peace treaty by the United States and the two Vietnamese regimes, which paved the way for American troop withdrawals. Many former antiwar activists joined the forces of reform within the Democratic party, which, operating under revised rules, succeeded in nominating a liberal peace candidate, George McGovern, for the presidency in 1972. Some activists kept their ideological commitment to the revolutionary transformation of America, but their support among college and university youth had largely vanished.

Puerto Rican nationalism was the other major issue responsible for terrorism in the United States during the 1970s, and, as noted above, it also declined—but not because of any major concessions to the *Independentistas* or, so far as I can judge, because of backlash in Puerto Rico. An appreciable minority of Puerto Ricans continue to support independence—6.5 percent voted for the Independence Party in 1976—and the subsidence in Puerto Rican terrorism is more likely explained by police and FBI actions than by the dissipation of political support.

Deterrence is the third factor that can alter the psychology of support for terrorism. Deterrence can rarely be observed directly, only its presumed causes and inferred consequences. Deterrence is assumed to increase when terrorists are imprisoned or killed, their targets hardened,

---

[26] Thomas H. Mitchell, "Politically-Motivated Terrorism in North America: The Threat and the Response" (Ph.D. dissertation, Carleton University, 1985), 143.

tough laws against terrorism enacted, and antiterrorist squads and tactics put in place. When terrorists defect and the incidence of violent acts tapers off in the aftermath of such events, security officials and many analysts assume that the antiterrorist policies were responsible. Franco Ferracuti, earlier in this volume, implies that legal changes in Italy—specifically the introduction in 1979 and 1983 of flexible judicial instruments that facilitated individual exits from terrorism—have been primarily responsible for the decline in Red Brigade terrorism.

The argument here is that deterrent policies are effective to the extent that they reinforce, and are reinforced by, other changes in the bases of support for terrorism among wider sectors of the population. This means that the effects of both backlash and reform must be considered. If the community that once tolerated or supported terrorism has already begun to reject it because of revulsion against violence and expectations of peaceful change, deterrence will enhance the process. But if support for the cause and tactics of terrorism is still substantial, the likely effect of apprehension and killings of terrorists, or tough new antiterrorist policies, will be the intensification of resentment among the support group. Whether and how they act on that resentment depends on how high the costs and risks seem to be: if resentment is high and widespread, the risks posed by security policies must appear very high in order for them to have a deterrent effect. Moreover, deterrent effects under such circumstances are likely to be transient. Potential terrorists have demonstrated that they will bide their time and start new campaigns when security relaxes. I suspect that these kinds of processes are responsible for the periodic resurgence of left-wing terrorism in West Germany and of nationalist terrorism among Puerto Ricans and other communal separatists. The communities of support, small though they are, have objectives that are beyond the reach of any generally acceptable reforms and tolerate the use of violence on behalf of those objectives. Hence security countermeasures have only temporary effects.

The Canadian and U.S. cases provide some suggestive evidence about the effects of deterrence. The arrest and conviction of twenty FLQ members in the aftermath of the Cross and Laporte kidnappings, and the detention of more than five hundred others, did not prevent a new wave of FLQ bombings and holdups, which began in March 1971 and lasted through the autumn. Hard-core activists were not deterred until a series of arrests in late 1971 and throughout 1972, aided by informants, put a decisive end to their actions. This fact leads to two inferences: one, that militants who escaped initial arrest were not deterred until actually apprehended; and second, that the declining political support enjoyed by the FLQ made it easier for police to gather intelligence about the cells and to penetrate them with informers.

Revolutionary terrorism by the two most active American groups of the 1970s, the Weather Underground and the New World Liberation Front, was never effectively countered by the authorities. Both groups voluntarily suspended campaigns of violence, in 1974 and 1978, respectively, without arrests of their members. The most that can be said about deterrence is that the Weather People were afflicted by paranoia about being penetrated or detected by the FBI and police. Their leaders' obsession with security had corrosive effects on morale and inhibited revolutionary actions. Smaller groups of revolutionary terrorists who operated during the 1970s and 1980s, including some activists from the organizations mentioned, were broken by the arrest (or, in the case of the SLA, the killings) of all of their key members.[27] As in the Canadian case, the supposition is that the New Left's rejection of revolutionary adventurism had much to do with the fact that these groups remained small, achieved little support, and were vulnerable to detection.

To summarize, counterterrorist policies in democracies, whether they emphasize traditional law-enforcement techniques or, as in Italy, incentives to defect, are most effective when they coincide with larger shifts in the climate of political opinion away from support for, or sympathy with, terrorist causes and tactics. Law-enforcement strategies may reinforce the erosion in support for radical action; they cannot create it.

Conclusions

The arguments of this chapter have substantial implications for the analysis of the onset and decline of terrorism. The understanding of the process that leads to episodes of terrorism in Western democracies requires an analysis of the political circumstances that create the political beliefs that encourage extremists. The explanation of the "exit from terrorism," a term used by Franco Ferracuti, requires a parallel analysis. Rational-choice explanations for why active terrorists give up armed struggle are not enough. We need to understand why ordinary people and activists stop giving credence and support to the ideological justifications and tactics of terrorism. And to understand this we have to examine the ways in which backlash, reform, and deterrence alter the psychological environment within which terrorists operate.

[27] Gurr, "Political Terrorism in the United States," table 4.

Backlash is crucial. Just as revolutionaries hope or expect that government repression will increase support for their cause, ill-conceived acts of terrorism can and do extend and solidify public antipathy for the terrorists and, by extension, their objectives. One can argue that in democracies, where most groups have ample opportunities for seeking redress of grievances, almost any widely publicized act of terror will have such a backlash effect. In the instance of the revolutionary left in the United States, the judgment is that deadly violence, especially the death of a mathematician in a bombing at the University of Wisconsin, was critical in undermining support for the movement among its radical sympathizers. In Europe, terrorist campaigns in West Germany, Italy, France, and Northern Ireland have been accompanied by increased general support for strong countermeasures by the state. Support for terrorists' objectives remains only among distinctive minorities: some Catholics in Northern Ireland and some of the radical left in West Germany.

Equally important is the public response to issues that provide activists with their rationale for opposing the regime. "Redress of grievances" is unlikely to change the views or actions of committed revolutionaries or terrorists, but it is likely to dry up the bases of their social and political support. Large-scale public efforts to reduce racial inequalities did contribute to the decline of racial violence in the United States.[28] Reform and the rise of a legitimate separatist party in Québec eliminated the rationale for continued violence by the FLQ.

A rational-choice perspective on public support for terrorism would emphasize the extent to which various publics think that their interests are served by terrorists. The line of analysis developed here is Weberian in its emphasis on group and community norms. Terrorist violence in democratic societies offends most of the members of those societies and undermines support not only for the groups using it but also their purposes. In these circumstances there will be no "third generation" of militants, terrorists will find fewer sympathizers among whom to take shelter, and security agencies will find it much easier to find informants and entice defectors. Therefore, most terrorist campaigns in democratic societies contain the seeds of their own demise. The exceptions are based on distinctive communal and political minorities with unsatisfied, and often unsatisfiable, goals of fundamental change.

[28] See James W. Button, *Black Violence: Political Impact of the 1960s Riots* (Princeton, N.J.: Princeton University Press, 1978).

7

Sacred terror:
A contemporary example from Islam

DAVID C. RAPOPORT

O believers, shall I direct you to a commerce that shall deliver you from a painful chastisement? You shall believe in God and His Messenger, and struggle in the way of God with your possessions and your selves. That is better for you, did you but know. He will forgive you your sins and admit you into gardens underneath which rivers flow, and to dwelling-places goodly in Gardens of Eden; that is the mighty triumph; and other things you love, help from God and nigh victory. Give thou good tidings to the believers!

Qur'an 61: 10, A. J. Arberry, trans.

The problem

A most arresting and unexpected development in recent years has been the revival of terrorist activities to support religious purposes or terror justified in theological terms, a phenomenon that might be called "holy" or "sacred" terror.[1] It is most striking in Islam among both Shia and Sunni. In India, Sikh terrorists have been attempting to create an independent state.[2] In Israel, Jewish messianists organized the "Temple Mount Plot," a conspiracy to blow up Muslim sacred shrines built on the re-

I am grateful to Gideon Aran, Ibrahim Karawan, Etan Kohlberg, Martin Kramer, Richard Martin, Walter Reich, and Khachig Tololyan for offering a variety of suggestions to improve the text. Not all of those suggestions were taken, and the shortcomings are still my own responsibility.

[1] For a discussion of the ancient forms of holy terror, see my "Fear and Trembling: Terror in Three Religious Traditions," *American Political Science Review* 78, no. 3 (September 1984): 658–77.

[2] See Mark Juergensmeyer, "The Logic of Religious Violence," *Journal of Strategic Studies* 10, no. 4 (December 1987): 172–93. I have edited this issue of the *Journal* as a separate volume. See my *Inside Terrorist Organizations* (New York: Columbia University Press, 1988).

mains of the Second Temple, Judaism's holiest site. The hope was that then, at last, the Third Temple could be built, an event that would precipitate the coming of the Messiah.[3] Other pious Jewish groups have mounted assaults on the secular character of the Israeli state.[4] Even in the United States, where the scale of terror in the last decade has been comparatively insignificant, elements of holy terror exist. Abortion clinic bombers regularly cite scripture, and several scripture-based messianic terrorist groups have emerged, the most prominent being "The Covenant, the Sword, and the Arm of the Lord" and "The Order."[5]

Although everyone has noticed the phenomenon, no one yet has distinguished the characteristics of holy terror from those of political or secular terror. My aim here is to discuss aspects of that problem by focusing on one group, popularly known as *Al-Jihad*. It called itself "The Islamic Group of Egypt," and its most spectacular feat was the assassination of President Anwar Sadat in 1981. I chose this group for several reasons. The most important one is that its leader, Abd Al-Salam Faraj, later executed, wrote a recently translated pamphlet, *The Neglected Duty (Al-Faridah al-Gha'ibah)*, which explains the group's justification and which the government considered the group's "constitution."[6]

The text, it seems, has had a remarkable effect on the religious establishment and on Egyptian society as a whole. At a time when only a few underground copies were available, the grand mufti of Egypt produced a point-by-point refutation of its contents, making it necessary for the mysterious work to be published, too, so that the military court and the public could understand the controversy.[7] Clearly, the text must have

[3] See Ehud Sprinzak, "From Messianic Pioneering to Vigilante Terrorism: The Case of the Gush Emunim," *Journal of Strategic Studies* 10, no. 4 (December 1987): 194–216, and in Rapoport, *Inside Terrorist Organizations*, 194–216.

[4] Haim Cohn, "Holy Terror," *Violence, Aggression, Terrorism* 1, no. 2 (March 1987): 1–12; and Menachem Friedman's seminal essay, "Religious Zealotry in Israeli Society" in *On Ethnic and Religious Diversity in Israel*, edited by Solomon Poll and Ernest Krausz (Ramat-Gan, Israel: Institute for the Study of Ethnic and Religious Groups, Bar Ilan University, 1975), 91–111.

[5] For an interesting discussion of the theological basis of these groups, see Leonard Zeskind, *The Christian Identity Movement* (Atlanta: Center for Democratic Renewal, 1986). See also Bruce Hoffman, "Right Wing Terror in the U.S.," *Violence, Aggression, Terrorism* 1, no. 1 (January 1987): 1–25.

[6] Johannes G. Jansen, *The Neglected Duty: The Creed of Sadat's Assassins and Islamic Resurgence in the Middle East* (New York: Macmillan, 1986). The government's initial description is cited in Hamied Ansarie, "The Islamic Militants in Egyptian Politics," *International Journal of Middle East Studies* 16 (March 1984): 141.

[7] Five hundred copies were printed with the intention of circulating them as a manifesto; however, all but fifty were destroyed when *Al-Jihad* decided too many copies available would jeopardize its security. Mohammed Heikal, *Autumn of Fury: The Assassination of*

seemed a serious challenge to the interpreters of the Islamic tradition, the *ulama* (religious sages) who were, indeed, chided by the government for having been lax in their responsibilities. The lawyers for the accused described the pamphlet as a "valid Islamic defense"—a self-serving claim, obviously, but the grand mufti's concern shows that it had some basis, and the text of the trial verdict devotes ample space to discussing and refuting Faraj's writing. Also, Johannes Jansen, who translated Faraj, finds his scholarship impressive even though the author was an electrician without a formal religious education—a pattern common throughout Sunni Islamicist movements, which, unlike their Shia counterparts, are profoundly hostile to the religious establishment:

When even a non-Muslim reader of *The Neglected Duty* has every now and then the impression that everything he has ever read from the *Qur'an*, the traditions, and the books of *fiqh* (learned religious commentators) suddenly falls into place, how much more will the text . . . evoke this feeling with Muslim readers? *The Neglected Duty* strongly suggests that it offers a comprehensive view of the history of Islam which is based on all relevant sources, and it does so impressively.[8]

Charles J. Adams, a prominent authority on Islam, describes its importance in another, less controversial way:

[It] presents the radical view in a forceful and vividly clear way, and it also lays out the ongoing conversation between the radical and other elements in the Egyptian Muslim community. Like radicalism itself, the alternative Muslim opinions against which the manifesto argues are found elsewhere in the Muslim countries. . . . The document is therefore a key to understanding Islamic radicalism wherever it may be found; in any event we have no other source of information of comparable authenticity and depth—hence, its great importance.[9]

There is a third reason for focusing on this group. We have much information about the members. The trials of Sadat's assassins received great publicity, and the transcripts became available in Beirut. Two scholars, a French political scientist[10] and an Israeli historian,[11] made the work and the group the focus of their insightful analyses of the Sunni Islamicist movement. We know something, too, about the radical milieu.

Sadat (London: Andre Deutch, 1983), 245. After the grand mufti produced his refutation, the defense lawyers gave the press a copy. Professor Richard Martin, who was in Cairo about that time, has informed me by private correspondence that copies were circulating "underground" and could be obtained. When he returned in 1986, he discovered that the grand mufti's refutation had been withdrawn from circulation.

[8] Jansen, *The Neglected Duty*, 152.

[9] Ibid., xv.

[10] Gilles Kepel, *Muslim Extremism in Egypt: The Prophet and the Pharaoh* (Berkeley: University of California Press, 1985).

[11] Emmanuel Sivan, *Radical Islam: Medieval Theology and Modern Politics* (New Haven: Yale, 1985).

Many members of a closely related group, the Society of Muslims (*Al-Jama'ah al-Muslimin*), popularly known as Excommunication and Emigration (*Al-Takfir wa'l-Hijra*), were imprisoned after an earlier assassination, and the government permitted a prominent Egyptian sociologist to interview them extensively.[12]

The main concern is the analysis of Faraj's text. I confess I spent many hours agonizing over whether anyone who is not a student of Islam could say anything useful about it. I decided to try because I have read many terrorist "texts," but never one like *The Neglected Duty*, and because the people who had analyzed it had considered it neither from the perspective of other terrorist documents nor in the context of other sacred and secular experiences—which are my special interests.

Before turning to Faraj, it will be useful to define the boundaries for discussion, the thesis, and the order of the argument. Until the last decade or so, many people were loath to believe that anybody nowadays kills for religious purposes, which may be one important reason why the concept of sacred terror is rarely discussed. In the case of *Al-Jihad*, although the assassins said that they killed Sadat because they wanted Egypt to be governed by Islam's sacred law (the *shar'ia*), Mohammed Heikal, Egypt's preeminent journalist and former minister of information, tells us that they could not really have meant it. "Decoded, [the] grievance can be summed up as the social and economic conditions in the country."[13] I take the language the participants use more seriously.

This chapter examines nonmillenarian sacred terror employed by Muslims against members of the community, usually other Muslims.[14] Because I understand the distinctive characteristic of the terrorist to be

---

[12] Saad Eddin Ibrahim, "Anatomy of Egypt's Militant Islamic Groups," *International Journal of Middle East Studies* 12 (1980): 423–53.

[13] Heikal, *Autumn of Fury*, 246. Heikal says that *all* the reasons given "can be summed up as the social and economic conditions in the country," but the other reasons, the peace treaty with Israel and the unjustified persecution of religious leaders, are self-explanatory. Why should we "decode"? Emmanuel Sivan tells us that the justification was taken seriously by the authorities. "The Egyptian government, jolted by the Sadat assassination, seemed to relinquish its delay tactics and gave the People's Assembly the green light to work out draft bills incorporating Islamic laws in certain criminal matters (adultery, robbery, wine drinking, etc.) [which fundamentalists] welcomed [as] the first step towards full-fledged application . . . of the *shari'a*, which should include review of all existing laws in order to amend or abolish those contradicting it." "The Two Faces of Islamic Fundamentalism," *Jerusalem Quarterly* 27 (Spring 1983): 137.

[14] Christian, Jewish, and Muslim millenarian experiences are discussed in my "Messianic Sanctions for Terror," *Comparative Politics* 20, no. 2 (January 1988): 195–213. I include the Assassins here because they are premillenarian; I do not include the Carmatians, who believed themselves directed by the Madhi (messiah).

the means employed, I make *means* the focus of attention. My thesis is that the principal difference in means between sacred and secular terror derives from the special justifications and precedents each uses. In effect, the two forms represent distinct traditions of discourse. Contemporary sacred terror has important affinities as well with earlier, premodern, or ancient expressions, affinities worth pondering because they help us understand each sacred expression better. This argument is developed here in four successive steps: a brief characterization of secular terror, a more detailed analysis of Faraj and *Al-Jihad*, a discussion of ancient sacred terror, and a recapitulation of themes in Islamic sacred terror. The descriptions of Faraj and ancient terror will be more extensive than a taxonomy of terror requires, for the purpose of the volume as a whole is to offer pictures of how terrorists look at the world.

Secular rebel terror (which began in the 1880s) has no binding precedents, which means that the terrorist group itself determines both the means and ends, or at least believes that it does and acts accordingly. Means (i.e., organizational structures, weapons, and tactics) are modified constantly, presumably to enhance effectiveness. To take one example, from 1881 to 1914, terrorists advanced their cause by assassinating prominent public figures. But the pattern changed partly in response to criticisms that there were advantages in allowing "despicable" individuals to survive as the symbols of a hated regime, that the cost of removing them was great, and that there were easier targets available. As the fates of Italy's Prime Minister Moro and Britain's Lord Mountbatten indicate, assassinations still occur nowadays; but no longer are they the major tactic, and terrorists are not bound by the fact that assassination was once a preeminent means.

A similar process is evident with regard to ends. Regardless of the purpose of early secular terrorists, terror now serves a variety of different ends. Anarchists with millenarian visions, anticolonialists with broad but realizable goals, and groups that simply want to call attention to particular situations they find offensive, all use terror. The recent history of the "Euro-terrorists" even shows that a group can move from issue to issue trying to *find* one that promises to gain them the most support![15]

Secular terrorists, thus, have produced a "culture" in which participants feel free to take their lessons from anyone, a "tradition" without

[15] Bonnie Cordes, "When Terrorists Do the Talking: A Look at Their Literature," *Journal of Strategic Studies* 10, no. 4 (December 1987): 150–71 and Rapoport, *Inside Terrorist Organizations.*

binding precedents that both reflects and caricatures a much observed tendency in the larger society—a tendency to subject all activities to standards of utility and efficiency.

Obviously, terrorists may not be intelligent about their ends and tools; but they *can* change them, and when they do, presumably it is because they believe there are benefits in doing so. This is why the need to make terror more and more efficient dominates the first modern terrorist text, Nechaev's *Revolutionary Catechism (1871)*: "The revolutionary [terrorist] knows only one science: the science of destruction. For this reason, and only for this reason, he will study mechanics, chemistry, . . . the leading science of peoples, their characteristics and circumstances and all the phenomena of the present social order."[16] Concerned *solely* with technique, Nechaev's text is a study of how "revolution can destroy the entire state to its roots, exterminate all imperial traditions, the whole social order, and all existing classes." Beyond the sentence, "The aims of our society are none other than the entire emancipation and happiness of the People," no statement of ultimate purpose is provided, and morality is redefined as "everything which contributes to the triumph of the revolution. Immoral and criminal is everything that stands in its way." *The Revolutionary Catechism* introduces a type of discourse that has been sustained throughout the nineteenth and twentieth centuries, for numerous successors have written in virtually an identical spirit, the latest and best known being Carlos Marighela's *Minimanual of Urban Guerrilla Warfare.*[17]

The Neglected Duty and Al-Jihad

The most reliable Speech is the Book of God and the best guidance is the guidance of Mohammed, may God's peace be upon him. The worst of all things are novelties (*bidah*) and every innovation is deviation and all deviation is in Hell.

(*The Neglected Duty*, para. 2)

Let us turn directly to *The Neglected Duty* and *Al-Jihad*. I want, first, to describe some general rhetorical features and standards of proof in the text and then to discuss specific textual arguments and their bearing on *Al-Jihad*'s activities.

[16] See my *Assassination and Terrorism* (Toronto: CBC, 1971), 79. The entire document is reproduced there. It should be added that although terrorists use the language of efficiency when they alter procedures and aims, that does not mean either that they are rational or that the activity can be made rational. These are separate questions discussed in the concluding portion of "Fear and Trembling."

[17] Marighela, *Handbook (Minimanual) of Urban Guerrilla Warfare*, in *For the Liberation of Brazil* (London: Penguin, 1971).

Readers unfamiliar with the way Islamic religious commentary is constructed will find *The Neglected Duty* very odd. The most recent event discussed is Napoleon's invasion of Egypt! In contrast, Marighela, who is virtually Faraj's contemporary, refers only to events within the five years before the *Minimanual*'s publishing date, 1971. Justification is Faraj's preoccupation; most, perhaps all, of his pages treat that issue. But his justifications are irrelevant to non-Muslims, because they are drawn from events in Islam's founding period and from the commentaries of religious sages (*ulama*). Marighela gives no justification whatsoever for the revolution he urges, and the rationale for particular kinds of violence is always that they produce desirable results. His text is "offered" to anyone who wants to overthrow "military dictatorships"; it would have been potentially useful even for *Al-Jihad*. Faraj establishes proof by finding the appropriate authority, the most persuasive being the *Qur'an* and the *hadith* (traditional sayings that present examples from Muhammed's life).[18] Marighela's book "contains the systematized results of the experiences of a group of men who have fought under arms in Brazil,"[19] and presumably its propositions would be modified with more experience. It must be conceded that the two works cannot be easily compared because the writers do not have identical purposes. But it is important to remember that no work propounding a strategy for secular terror treats justification seriously, and Faraj does treat tactics, the preoccupation of secular terrorists. In all probability the difficulty derives largely from the fact that the traditions typically produce different kinds of reflection and discourse.

The ultimate object of *Al-Jihad* is a world governed by the *shar'ia*. Early Islam under Muhammed and his first three successors in the caliphate during its first century (seventh century A.D.) is the model.[20] What structures does this aspiration entail? Egypt's chief justice, Said Al-Ashmawy, points out that no one today knows how that model worked. *Al-Jihad* certainly had no clear idea of how it should be organized.[21]

---

[18] There are four sources of authority, the *Qur'an,* the *Sunna* (traditions based on Muhammed's life and sayings), consensus of legal scholars, and analogies based on these works.

[19] Marighela, *(Minimanual),* 61–2.

[20] Faraj reminds readers, "The conquest of Constantinople came about 800 years after the Prophet's prediction. And also the conquest of Rome will be realized" (para. 11).

[21] "Islamic Government," *Middle East Review* 17, no. 3 (September 1986): 7–13. Beyond the establishment of a "Council of Men of Religion" and a "Consultative Council" which would govern, Nemat Guenena found no plan for the day after the assassination. "The Jihad: An Islamic Alternative in Egypt," *Cairo Papers in Social Science* (Summer 1986): 72. Emmanuel Sivan says that the unpublished materials of other Islamicist underground organizations in Egypt, Syria, Tunisia, and Morocco show the same problem. Published

Even if, for the sake of argument, we had, or they did formulate, a clear picture, we would still not know how the model could be adapted to modern circumstances.

The second article of the 1971 Egyptian constitution (which, ironically, Sadat introduced) pledges that in due course the *shar'ia* will be Egypt's law. Indeed, the major justification given by the assassins was Sadat's failure to make good on his promise. Because the constitutional provision presumably represents the desires of many, probably most, Egyptians, the assassins' deed might command popular support, or at least the assassins might believe so.

The title of the book *The Neglected Duty* does not refer to the lapse regarding the *shar'ia* but to a different one—namely the failure to participate in the *jihad*, or holy war, which lack, the author believes, is the cause of Islam's decline and despair. Returning to the *jihad*, he maintains, is *the* essential means for reviving Islam, making it the responsibility of all able-bodied men as it originally was and not that of the military as it has become. *Jihad* means "striving in the path of God," but generations of religious commentators, taking their cue from apathetic and timid governments, have interpreted *jihad* to mean primarily spiritual struggle against one's own evil nature. A glance at Muhammed's life and at the *Qur'an*, Faraj believes, establishes beyond doubt that striving is "fighting, which means confrontation and blood":[22] "Slay the polytheists wherever ye find them, seize them, beset them, lie in ambush for them everywhere" (*Qur'an* 9:5); "Fighting is prescribed for you" (*Qur'an* 2: 216); "Fight them and God will punish them at your hands, will humiliate them and aid you against them and bring healing to the breasts of people who are believers" (*Qur'an* 9:14, Jansen trans.).

As it is normally perceived, the *jihad* was waged against non-Muslim communities. The classical Sunni view is that the necessity for *jihad* would disappear only when Islam embraced the whole world,[23] but the more recent Sunni view, as Rudolph Peters demonstrates, is that *jihad* was

Islamicist texts are not much more helpful, and Sivan reminds us that Khomeini's *Islamic Government* written in 1970 has the same characteristic. "The Islamic Republic of Egypt," *Orbis* (Spring 1987): 45.

[22] Faraj, *Neglected Duty*, para. 84. When citing Faraj's text as distinguished from Jansen's commentary, I will refer to the paragraph number. Richard Martin argues that the *jihad* refers to a variety of contexts and that the use of the term for violent activity is a later usage. "Religious Violence in Islam: Towards an Understanding of the Discourse on *Jihad* in Modern Egypt," *Contemporary Research on Terrorism*, edited by Paul Wilkinson and A. M. Stewart (Aberdeen: University Press, 1987), 54–71.

[23] Majid Khadduri, *The Law of War and Peace in Islam* (London: Luzac, 1940), 30 ff.

designed to defend Islam from direct assault.[24] Faraj revives the classical notion but goes on to argue that Islam cannot make headway with its original mission until the *jihad* is used for internal purposes, too, a view that the Sunni tradition normally rejected but one that the Kharijites, the Shia (and through them the Assassins and other assassination sects), and various millenarian movements accepted.

According to the criteria established by Muslim jurists, we do not live in an Islamic state, in that our laws do not derive from Islam. Thus, it is "unsafe" to be a Muslim. The *Qur'an* is very clear on the status of such persons. "Whosoever does not rule by what God sent down, those are the Unbelievers" (5:440). In these respects our condition is analogous to that of the Muslims ruled by Genghis Khan, whose legislation came from pagan sources although the Mongols were nominally Muslim, and who, Ibn Taymiyah (a fourteenth-century jurist) said, "should be treated according to what is due them."

Apostates or unbelievers are the very epitome of evil. Muslims are obliged to wage a *jihad* against them, and although in a *jihad* the rights of noncombatants must be respected, enemies who are apostates are to be treated differently.

The Rulers of the Age are in apostasy from Islam. They were raised at the tables of Imperialism, be it Crusaderism or Communism or Zionism. They carry nothing from Islam . . . though they pray, fast, and claim to be Muslims. It is a well-established rule of Islamic law that the punishment for an apostate will be heavier than for [one] who is by origin an infidel. . . . An apostate *has* to be killed even if he is *unable* to go to war. An infidel who is unable to go to war should not be killed.[25]

Getting rid of the internal enemy is the fundamental task, because without apostates, external enemies are impotent. Hitherto, Islamicist movements had concentrated on the external enemy (Israel), which was the wrong enemy then and is the wrong one now:

To fight an enemy who is near is more important than to fight an enemy who is far.

To begin by putting an end to imperialism is not a laudatory and *not* a useful act. *It is only a waste of time.* . . . We have to establish the Rule of God's Religion in our own country first, and to make the word of God Supreme. . . . The first

[24] Rudolph Peters, *Islam and Colonialism: The Doctrine of Jihad in Modern History* (The Hague: Mouton, 1979).

[25] Faraj, *Neglected Duty*, para. 25. "Apostasy consists of abjuring Islam by intention or words or acts of rejection whether the words were said in jest, or contradiction, or belief. . . . An act making one an apostate is one based on an obvious mockery or denial." Muhyi Din al-Nawawi, quoted in John Alden Williams, ed., *Themes of Islamic Civilization* (Berkeley: University of California Press, 1971), 150.

battlefield for *jihad* is the extermination of these infidel leaders and to replace them by a complete Islamic Order.[26]

One by one, Faraj examines the mechanisms available for eliminating the apostates by using legal means, avenues that other Islamicist groups had used and were attempting to use still. Some had organized an Islamic political party only to have it co-opted by the state. Others created voluntary benevolent societies to educate the masses; but they had to register with the state and comply with its regulations, and they found themselves denied media access anyway. A third element thought that if enough good Muslims obtained important technical posts they would eventually capture the state, a view Faraj deems "absurd," largely because it is unsupported by the *Qur'an* or by example (of the Prophet).[27]

The obligation of a good Muslim in the circumstances Faraj describes would be emigration (a *hijra*). The importance of such an act to Muslims cannot be overestimated. The Muslim calendar begins with the date of the *Hijra* and not with the birth of Muhammed. The *jihad* doctrine itself was formulated in the *Hijra,* and rebel groups usually begin their career by means of a *hijra,* whereupon they try to create the model for the proper society.[28] Indeed, one contemporary group (Excommunication and *Hijra*) attempted to do this by withdrawing, settling first in caves and then in urban communes; Faraj seizes the opportunity provided by the destruction of this group to assail those who think that a *hijra* must be a precondition for revolution. A true *hijra* requires a preexisting independent population for support, such as Muhammed had in Medina. Because nothing like that is available now, people taking this route are thoughtlessly following a venerated model that, in effect, keeps them from pursuing their obligation to pursue the *jihad* now. No wonder the state was able to deal with them easily.

[26] Ibid., paras. 69 and 70.

[27] Ibid., para. 53. His final argument is that the government would never allow good Muslims to occupy significant positions. Kepel enumerates the relevant groups for each point Faraj addresses. *Muslim Extremism*, 199–201.

[28] Sivan provides a penetrating discussion of the *hijra* concept in contemporary Egyptian thought, *Radical Islam*, 85–90. For discussions of the *hijra* in other Islamic rebellions, see Hodgson, *The Order*, 77–80; Peter Von Sivers, "The Realm of Justice: Apocalyptic Revolts in Algeria (1849–1879)," *Humaniora Islamica* 1 (1973): 47–60; T. Hodgkin, "Mahdism, Messianism and Marxism in the African Setting" in *African Social Studies: A Radical Reader*, edited by P. Gutkind and P. Waterman (New York: Monthly Review Press, 1977); Michael Gilsenan, *Recognizing Islam* (London: Croom Helm, 1982); Marilyn Robinson Waldman, "The Popular Appeal of the Prophetic Paradigm in West Africa," *Contributions to Asian Studies* 18 (1983): 110–14; and my "Fear and Trembling" and "Messianic Sanctions."

Some say that they will emigrate to the desert and then come back and have a confrontation such as Moses did, and then God will make the ground swallow the Pharaoh up together with his army. . . . All these strange ideas only result from having forsaken the only true and religiously allowed road towards establishing an Islamic state. So what is the true road? God—Exalted He is—says: "Fighting is prescribed for you though it is distasteful to you. Possibly ye may dislike a thing, though it is good for you, and possibly ye may like a thing, though it is bad for you!"

(*Qur'an* 2:216, Jansen, trans.)

The last major subject is the tactics for this *jihad:*

With the advance of time and the development of mankind emerges a question we must ask ourselves. There is no doubt that the modern method of fighting differs to a certain extent from the methods . . . in the time of the Prophet. . . . What is the Muslim's method of fighting in this day and age? Can he use his own intellect and his own judgement?[29]

Faraj's argument here resembles that offered by Nechaev and Marighela. However, the authority for believing that the Muslim can use whatever method works is Muhammed's experience, not the terrorist's; and, whereas the secular writers describe and evaluate an array of different tactics that history and reason indicate will work, Faraj studies only the founding period for appropriate guidelines. He concludes that all a believer with few resources needs is intelligence and "deceit, which is victory with the fewest losses and by the easiest means possible."[30]

At least three of the four examples Faraj uses to show that Muhammed allowed Muslims to do whatever works involve conflicts with Jews.[31] (Jewish tribes were constituent elements of the original community at Medina and removing them was a precondition of establishing an "independent religion.")[32] Some Western students of Islam, "along with those in whose hearts is the sickness of doubt," consider traditions celebrating "perfidious and treacherous" deeds unworthy. "The refutation is that the infidel (the victim) had broken his pledge and devoted all his efforts to harm the Muslims."[33] What Faraj does not discuss, and what

[29] Ibid., *The Neglected Duty*, para. 62.
[30] Ibid., para. 106.   [31] Ibid.
[32] Frantz Buhl, "Muhammed," *Encyclopedia of Islam* (Leiden: E. J. Brill, 1936), vol. 3, p. 650.
[33] Faraj, *Neglected Duty*, para. 113. The chief example Faraj offers is the assassination of Ka 'b ibn al-Ashraf and he relies on the "*Sahih* of Al-Bukhari on the authority of Jabir Ibn Abdallah." In Faraj's account the assassin explicitly asks whether he can "say things contradictory to the belief in God so as to feign disbelief." In my version he asks the Prophet's permission "to say what I like" and tells the victim that the Prophet's demand for charity is troubling. See *Sahih of Al-Bukari*, edited by Muhammed Missi (Gujranwala, Pakistan: 1971) vol. 4, p. 167, and vol. 5, p. 248–50. In Ibn Hisham's version he asks

is much more pertinent, is that the authorized interpreters of the Islamic tradition never cite these precedents as acts to be emulated, for they were unique and, according to some traditions, ordered by an angel.[34]

Despite his claim that anything that works is permissible, Faraj does admit that there are moral limits. The *jihad,* in all of its forms, displays, after all, moral restrictions;[35] it would 'seem a defiance of tradition to urge a *jihad* without such restrictions. The limits discussed here concern warnings and innocent bystanders. Must the intended victim be warned? It is preferable to do so, but tradition tells us that warnings are not obligatory. Is the killing of the innocent justified? No, but there are two classes of innocents, those who have no relationship to the intended victim, who should *never* be attacked, and those who are dependents (entourage) and family, who should not be attacked if it is possible to avoid doing so. The victim with his entourage may be attacked at night, for example, in the full knowledge that it is impossible to distinguish targets clearly (as it would be later with the grenades thrown at Sadat on the reviewing stand).

Successful assassinations, Faraj's examples demonstrate, depend on infiltrating the apostate's retinue and pretending to join his forces, even if this means publicly denying one's own commitment as a believer. (The most effective surprise comes from those in whom the victim has mistakenly put his trust.) One should, if possible—and this is quite important— humiliate the victim as well as kill him. Should the assailant allow himself to be taken prisoner? Dying, Faraj's examples several times show, with its special reward of paradise, is very much preferable.

Surprisingly, Faraj offers no discussion of follow-up measures, carried out to make sure that the victim is not replaced by another apostate. Faraj indicates that a divine intervention will prevent the "inevitable." (The passage appears immediately before revolts are discussed.) The affirmation seems to contradict earlier scoffing at those who used the *hijra* precedent, expecting that "God will make the ground swallow Pharaoh

whether he can "lie" and is told "you are free in the matter." *The Life of Muhammed,* 367. The other instances of assassination Faraj describes are substantially the same as those of Ibn Hisham.

[34] Etan Kohlberg, personal correspondence, 11 May 1988.

[35] In Islamic law the fight against apostates has fewer restrictions than that against rebels and is basically the same as the *jihad* against polytheists. The goal is to kill, not persuade them. Apostates can be attacked from behind, their wounded and captured can be put to death, their families may be enslaved, and their property plundered. One can use polytheistic confederates or tolerated non-Muslims against them, one cannot make a truce with them, and one may destroy their territories. The dead bodies of apostates are not washed, and no prayers are to be said over them. Williams, *Themes,* 273.

up": The "Muslim has first of all the duty to execute the command to fight with his hands. [Once he has done so] God—Praised and Exalted He is—will then intervene and [change] the laws of nature."[36] The laws of nature referred to here govern social, not physical, phenomena:

This community differs from the other [religious] communities as far as fighting is concerned. [In the case of Judaism, God acted by means] of natural phenomena like the eclipses, floods ... storms. With regard to the community of Mohammed—God's Peace be upon Him—this differs, for God—Praised and Exalted He is—addressed them saying: "Fight them and God will punish them at your hands, will humiliate and aid you against them and will bring healing to the breasts of people who are believers."

(*Qur'an* 2: 216, Jansen, trans.)

No one should hesitate just because a plan to cope with the aftermath has not been made:

It is said that we fear to establish the state [because] after one or two days a reaction will occur that will put an end to everything we have accomplished.

The refutation is that the establishment of an Islamic state is the execution of a divine command. We are not responsible for its results. Someone who is so stupid as to hold this view—which has no use except to hinder Muslims from the prosecution of their religious duty by establishing the Rule of God—forgets that when the Rule of the infidel has fallen everything will be in the hands of the Muslims.

At the trial, the conspirators made it clear that they discussed the issue of what might happen afterwards. One wanted more time to plan a mass uprising in the wake of Sadat's death. But when Faraj accused him of "faint-heartedness"—no charge is more effective in discussions among terrorists[37]—he withdrew his objection, appreciating that Faraj as *Faqih* (one eminent for his religious erudition) had more authority than he, a lieutenant colonel in Egyptian military intelligence, did![38] When the court asked Faraj what he hoped to accomplish, he emphasized something not present in the text. That was the importance of the act as a "warning to all who came after him [Sadat], and our teaching them a lesson. My aim at this stage of the struggle is to deter all rulers."[39]

[36] Faraj, *Neglected Duty*, para. 65.
[37] See my "The International World as Some Terrorists Have Seen It: A Look at a Century of Memoirs," *Journal of Strategic Studies* 10, no. 4 (December 1987): 32–58, and in my *Inside Terrorist Organizations*, 32–58.
[38] Hiekal, *Autumn of Fury*, 252.
[39] Ibid., 265. The failure to apply the *shari'a* is the primary reason offered by all the assassins and is consistent with the text. Additional reasons offered by the chief assassin, Islambouli, were the treaty with Israel and the unjustified arrest of several *ulama*. Adel Hamouda, *Ightiyahl Ra'is [The Assassination of a President]*, 4th ed., translated by Ibrahim Karawan (Cairo: Sina [Sinai], 1986), 280–1.

A brief additional word on the assassination and the trial might help put *Al-Jihad* in better perspective. It appears that anyone who read *The Neglected Duty* carefully might have had a sense of subsequent events. The assassination occurred when Sadat was reviewing his troops, celebrating the anniversary of his greatest triumph (the crossing of the Suez Canal in the October 1973 war against Israel), and the ceremony was being televised in Egypt. The chief assassin was a military officer in the parade. Could there have been a more humiliating and psychologically devastating set of circumstances for the blow?

Yet there was considerable opposition to the conspiracy within *Al-Jihad,* and the outcome did not go according to plan. Dr. Omar Abdel-Rahmen, who provided legal opinions for actions (*fatwas*), refused to sanction the assassination, a refusal that led to his being pushed aside. (Interestingly, no rabbi would sanction the Jewish plot to blow up the Muslim mosque on the site of the Second Temple, and the plan was then abandoned.)[40] One element refused to participate in the assassination because it believed Sadat to be a tool of the Christians (Copts), who had become so aggressive that the *jihad* would have to be waged against them first. The objection to the plan, on the ground that an assassination by itself was not enough, was disregarded for two reasons. The first, as already indicated, was that the opposition forces felt they lacked a religious authority comparable to Faraj. The second reason was that they were convinced that the assassins would die in the attempt. The assassins agreed that if they were captured, they would deny *Al-Jihad*'s role.[41]

But the assassins were captured; under torture they did identify *Al-Jihad*'s role, and, surprisingly, began to fast or atone for the fact that they might have hurt innocent parties![42] (Seven were killed and twenty-eight were wounded, mostly by the grenades thrown at Sadat.) Throughout the trial the four assassins steadfastly claimed that they wanted to kill Sadat only, as Faraj's text suggests. One testified that he shouted to the minister of defense and to Vice President Mubarak (both were survivors), "Get out of my way. I only want the Pharaoh." Another claimed that he did not return fire from a nearby person because he wanted to kill Sadat only. When a third was asked why he did not realize that innocent parties would be killed, he responded: "In the *day* of Judgement God will deal with all according to their deeds and intentions—and if I

---

[40] Sprinzak, "Messianic Pioneering."
[41] Hamouda, *Ightiyahl Ra'is,* 125.
[42] Ibid., 129. None of my English sources mentions the fast.

have killed innocent people then God will deal with me accordingly."[43]
All the assassins said they stopped firing after being certain Sadat was
dead and before their ammunition was exhausted.

This desire to distinguish between the leader and others suggests a
view that the people are always more healthy than their leaders—a picture that does *not* clearly emerge in Faraj's text. However, when Saad
Ibrahim questioned members of a similar group—the Islamic Liberation
Society (popularly known as the Technical Military Academy Group)—
that attempted to seize Sadat in 1974, they pictured the people as the
"victim of unscrupulous and God-fearless leaders. Thus the victimized
society is seen as eager but unable to get rid of its victimizers. One sur-
viving leader said that the Egyptians were basically a 'religious people
who were the helpless victims of an ungodly regime which imposed non-
Islamic institutions on them!' "[44] One commentator describes *Al-Jihad*
members as likening society to a "fish which gets rotten in the head
first. If a society gets rid of its rotten head or ruler it would get better!"[45]

The assassins convinced onlookers that they believed that they had
earned the martyr's right to paradise. Hamouda, the author of an extremely well-received account of the incident, says their demeanor reflected "a sense of happiness, pride, displayed a jovial mood before the
zero hour," and a firm belief that the "gates of heaven opened for them
from the minute they decided to kill Anwar Sadat."[46] One wrote to his
wife asking her to pay all his debts "because paradise has been forbidden
for those who are indebted" and telling her not to weep at his grave
"because I consider myself a martyr and these things should not be done
for martyrs."[47] Another asked his parents' forgiveness for the trouble
caused them. "It was God who led us to this act and towards martyrdom
in the path of God."[48]

Ancient sacred terror

The Messenger of God said "A martyr has six privileges with God. He is forgiven
his sins on the shedding of the first drop of his blood; he is shown his place in
paradise; he is redeemed from the torments of the grave; he is made secure from
the fear of hell and a crown of glory is placed on his head of which one ruby is

[43] Ibid., 282.
[44] Ibrahim, "Anatomy of Egypt's Militant Islamic Groups," 442.
[45] Hamouda, *Ightiyahl Ra'is*, 84.   [46] Ibid., 209.
[47] Ibid., 216.   [48] Ibid., 214.

worth more than the world and all that is in it; he will marry seventy-two of the huris with black eyes; and his intercession will be accepted for seventy of his kinsmen."

(Al-Khatib Al-Tibrizi, *The Niches of Lamps,* John A. Williams, trans.)

In Faraj's writings there are striking similarities with the early instances of sacred terror, particularly those produced by Islam. The comparisons, it is true, are incomplete because we have no ancient terrorist texts. But we still have some sense of what the terrorists were about. In an earlier essay, "Fear and Trembling," I provided an account based on the three best known groups: the Zealots-Sicarii (from Judaism), the Thugs (from Hinduism), and the Assassins (from Islam), who seemed to embody systematically patterns displayed by other terrorists in their respective religions.[49] What follows is an elaboration of those conclusions.

The sacred terrorists believed that their ends and means were sanctioned by divine authority, which humans had no right to alter. Whereas their modern secular counterparts are concerned with the future, the sacred terrorists' eyes are on the past—on the particular precedents established in the religion's most holy era, the founding period when deity and community were on the most intimate terms and when the basic rules of the religion were established. Sometimes the terrorists' purpose and means seemed so fixed that scholars describe their acts as a form of religious ritual. Borrowing from terrorists in other religions is not evident; within a particular religious tradition, terrorist groups do resemble each other, more because they study the same sources than because they communicate with each other.

This last point can be put in another form: ways of acting in the founding period became sanctified, and subsequent generations interpret and reinterpret those roles. To borrow a phrase from Khachig Tololyan's remarkable essay, which shows how the religious martyrdom theme so crucial in forming the Armenian community in the fifth century has been embodied in terrorist activity during the nineteenth and twentieth centuries, we are speaking here of "projective narratives" that "tell a story of the past" and "map out future actions that can imbue the time with transcendent collective values."[50] No two interpretations are identical; even if all expressions of holy terror in a given culture were inspired by the same

[49] See note 1, above.

[50] Khachig Tololyan, "Cultural Narrative and the Motivation of the Terrorist," *Journal of Strategic Studies* 10, no. 4 (December 1987): 217–36, and in my *Inside Terrorist Organizations,* 217–36.

theme (and it is unlikely that they would be), there would still be variations, even very significant ones, in those expressions.

Sometimes, the relationship between terrorists and the founding period is established because the participants or authoritative parties in the tradition have identified it for us. In Judaism, the inspiration for Zealot and Sicarii practices, the rabbis say, derives from deed of Phineas, the high priest after Aaron, during the founding period in Sinai. On his own initiative Phineas killed a tribal leader and his foreign concubine who were desecrating a sacred place. The act gained him divine favor, averted a plague, and became the basis in Jewish law for killing without trial in three situations and later for limited violence practiced by a number of ultraorthodox Hasidic groups.[51] The Thugs themselves traced their activities back to instructions Kali gave when she created their order.[52] Christian terror, which is usually millenarian, is not related to actions in the past so much as it is to a vision of the Second Coming, particularly as it is spelled out in *The Book of Revelation*.

The issue of whether and how founding precedents shape sacred terror is more problematic in Islam, at least it is for me, because the secondary sources I necessarily depend on simply do not address the question. Still, evidence of a connection exists. The Islamic concept of the *Sunna* (i.e., traditions based on precedents established by Muhammed and his companions), the model for how Muslims should live, is very close to Tololyan's conception of "projective narrative." It is unlikely that this is an exception to the pattern manifest in other religious cultures, especially because no alternative explanation for the doctrinal source of ancient Islamic terror is available. To support their activities it is known that ancient terrorists cited both the *Qur'an*'s declaration that rulers who do not govern according to the *shar'ia* are unbelievers and the tradition built on it relating that the Prophet said, "Whoever amongst you sees something reprehensible, should set it aright with his hand; if he cannot do that let him do it with his tongue; if that is impossible let him do it with his heart."[53] This tradition, it should be noted, is very similar to the act

---

[51] See my "Fear and Trembling," 670. Haim Cohn gives a valuable account of Phineas and the Jewish legal tradition in "Holy Terror" and Menachem Friedman explains how ultraorthodox groups have used the Phineas precedent in "Religious Zealotry." The Gush Emunim and those who organized the Temple Mount Plot apparently did not use the Phineas precedent, Dr. Gideon Aran has informed me.

[52] See my "Fear and Trembling," 662.

[53] Ibid., 665.

of Phineas in its obvious invitation to direct action. Significantly, Faraj cites this verse, and Sunni Islamicists have found the tradition (*hadith*) very useful.[54]

Still, the ancient terrorists provide no *direct* citations from *acts* in the founding period. The attention *The Neglected Duty* gives acts of Muhammed is, therefore, important, though we must recognize that the "interpretations" of the precedents by sacred terrorists are quite idiosyncratic. The orthodox community either refuses to recognize the acts as precedents at all or believes that an altogether different one pertains.

Let us turn now directly to Islam and try to make these general characterizations more concrete. Islam's best-known holy terrorists were the Assassins (1090–1275) or *Nizari*—a branch of the *Ismaili*. (It is odd how often the public refuses to accept the name terrorists give themselves.)[55]

They "represent" also a "family" of Muslim, mostly Shia, terrorist groups with similar but not identical features, the most striking one being a proclivity to assassination. Assassination is common in other religious communities; but, as the examples of Judaism and Christianity show, these acts are usually undertaken by individuals and do not reflect the continuing policy of a movement. The exception seems to be the Jewish Sicarii in the great uprising against Rome, which culminated in the destruction of the Second Temple and the last stand at Masada. Their name means "daggermen" and indicates their special methods. But they were engaged in more gruesome forms of terror, too, and assassination was important only in the early phase of their existence.

Each religion seems to generate a characteristic form of terror. In Islam, ever since the *Kharijite* uprising shortly after Muhammed's death, virtually all rebels have employed assassination as an instrument; and, more important, "many sects and groups" were exclusively committed to it or, in effect, were assassination cults.[56]

Jewish and Christian terrorists (who are almost always millenarian) are antinomian, aiming at producing a catastrophic social struggle, acting as if they believed that Hell must precede Paradise. The Thugs, like the *Nizari*, circumscribed their means but they "represented" a religion (Hinduism) that does not visualize the possibility of social reconstruc-

---

[54] Sivan, *Radical Islam*, 117.

[55] Professor Richard Martin in private correspondence says that the same pattern may be observed among the world religions. Only Islam is known by the name it gave itself.

[56] Bernard Lewis, *The Assassins: A Radical Sect in Islam* (London: Weidenfeld and Nicholson, 1967), 128.

tion, and the Thugs acted secretly or did not seek public support, regarding their *victims* as sacrifices who merited Paradise as a reward.

The *Nizari* were the best-organized and most durable Islamic cult, clearly exhibiting features usually inchoate only in other groups. Arising in a time of internal disarray when the community seemed to have lost its capacity to expand, the Assassins aimed to purify Islam (whose political and religious institutions are inseparable), thus creating conditions for the arrival of the Madhi (Messiah, or Rightly Guided One), who would then authorize another form of terror. Initially, the Assassins acted in a "prescribed" way, "using their tongues." When this proved insufficient, they emigrated to *dar al-hijra*, "a deliberate imitation of that archetype from Mohammed's own career," fleeing to a more receptive Medina when he failed to convert his own people in Mecca. "Medina was the first *dar al-hijra* of Islam, the first place of refuge" from which the persecuted would "return in triumph to the unbelieving lands."[57] The *hijra*, a pattern of withdrawing when one is weak in order to begin again in more conducive circumstances, is a model that earlier Muslim sacred terrorists imitated—beginning with the first ones, who emerged soon after Muhammed's death—and, as we saw, one that figured in the debates and practices of contemporary sacred terrorists.[58]

The *Nizari* victims were prominent figures who were "responsible" for preventing the New Preaching from being heard and ignored warnings to change their behavior, the requirement for dealing with people regarded as apostates. To maximize their psychological impact and emphasize the victims' helplessness, the assassinations took place in front of numerous witnesses in venerated sites like mosques, where sanctity provided immunity, or in highly protected sites where loyal supporters surrounded the victim.

The weapon of the Assassins was "always a dagger." Poison or a missile sometimes might have been more effective, but a dagger increased possibilities that its wielder would be captured or killed. The Assassin "usually made no attempt to escape; there is even a suggestion that to survive a mission was shameful. The words of a 12th century Christian author are revealing, when, therefore, any of them have chosen to *die* in this way [the Chief] hands them knives which are 'consecrated.' "[59]

[57] M. G. S. Hodgson, *The Order of Assassins* (The Hague: Mouton, 1955), 79.
[58] The withdrawal pattern in order to gain vision and strength, of course, occurs in Judaism and Christianity, too, as the examples of Moses, John the Baptist, and Christ indicate. In Islam, a community withdraws; the resemblance to *Exodus* is striking.
[59] Lewis, *The Assassins*, 127.

Other Muslim assassination cults attached special significance to particular weapons, too. In the eighth century, members of one cult (the *Khunnag*) strangled their victims with scarves, and another (the *Kaysaniyya*) beat victims to death with wooden cudgels.[60] In each case, the weapon and site precluded the assailant's escape. The source of this practice seems to be a tradition that Muslims cannot use swords against Muslims until the Madhi arrives to cleanse the orthodox Islamic establishment.[61] Various groups apparently interpreted this to mean that other weapons could or perhaps *should* be used to expedite the arrival of the Madhi. The weapon chosen represents a theme common in most, perhaps all, of the groups: because the victims were considered apostates, they should be assaulted in special ways. Thus, Ibn Surayi "says that they should be beaten to death with a stick because that is slower than the sword and may lead them to repent."[62]

Martyrdom, the voluntary acceptance of death in order to "demonstrate the truth," is a central and perhaps critical element of the message-giving religions (especially Christianity, Islam, and, to a lesser extent, Judaism), for it dispels the doubts of believers and aids proselytizing efforts. In the Islamic and Christian traditions, those who fall in a "holy war" (*jihad*) are deemed martyrs, and the Assassins viewed their efforts as a *jihad*. The word designating the assailants—*fidayeen* (consecrated or dedicated ones)—indicates that they were considered religious sacrifices who freed themselves from the guilt of all sins and thereby "gained entry into paradise."[63] It is noteworthy that other Muslim rebels, beginning with the *Kharijites,* also perceived their undertaking as a *jihad,* their victims as hypocrites (*munafiqun*) or apostates, and the assassins as martyrs.[64]

Legends concerning the *Nizari* are revealing. The most remarkable

[60] I. Friedlaender, "The Heterdoxies of the Shi-ites in the Presentation of Ibn Hazm," *Journal of the American Oriental Society* 28 (1907): 1–80; 29 (1909): 1–183; and Montgomery W. Watt, *The Formative Period of Islamic Thought* (Edinburgh: University Press, 1973), 48.

[61] D. MacEion, "The Babi Concept of the Holy Way," *Religion* 12 (1982): 121. Al-Mawardi quotes the Prophet as saying "It is not permitted to shed the blood of a Muslim except for one of three (offenses): apostasy, adultery by a married man and murder unprovoked by murder." Williams, *Themes,* 274.

[62] Williams, *Themes.*

[63] Etan Kohlberg, "The Development of the Imami Shia Doctrine of Jihad," *Zeitschrift der deutschen morganlandischen Gesellschaft* 125 (1976): 72.

[64] Watt, *The Formative Period,* 9–38; Elie Adab Salem, *Political Theory and Institutions of the Khawarij* (Baltimore: Johns Hopkins Press, 1956); and G. Levi della Vida, "Kharidjites," *Encyclopedia of Islam* (Leiden: E. J. Brill, 1978) vol. 4, 1074–77.

involve the victim-*fidayeen* relationship. It was believed that the *Nizari* placed a youthful member in the service of a high official. Through devotion and skill over the years he would gain his master's trust and then, at the appropriate signal, the "faithful" servant would plunge his dagger into his master's back. So preternatural did this immunity from personal or ordinary feelings seem to orthodox Muslims that they described the group as "hashish eaters" (*hashashin*), the source of our term *assassin*. While no evidence exists that the *Nizari* used drugs, their isolated bases allowed them to develop a quasi-monastic form of life where they began training *fidayeen* as children, enhancing the possibility that unusual immunities could be developed.

The unvarying character of Assassin tactics is striking. Potential victims were always warned that they would be harmed *only* if they interfered with *Nizari* missionaries, encouraging one observer to liken the *fidayeen* to armed naval escorts that never engage the enemy unless the convoy itself is attacked first.[65]

One assassination might produce political advantages. But repeated assassinations must be counterproductive, because the population must identify with some leaders and because assassinations themselves always entail treachery. "There can be good faith," Hodgson argued, "even in war but not in unannounced murder. Though Muslims . . . commonly used assassination as an expedient, the adoption of a regular and admitted policy horrified them and has horrified men ever since."[66]

The orthodox responded by indiscriminately slaughtering sympathetic Shia and Ismaili elements. Occasionally, the *Nizari* were reported to have retaliated by firebombing orthodox quarters and committing other acts of urban terrorism; but these responses were very infrequent and, indeed, reports of them may have been fabricated by anxious governments. In any case, all the authorities agree that the normal reaction to massacres provoked by assassination was another assassination. The political consequences of this process were predictable; popular support for the Assassins, once significant, disappeared.

The unwavering commitment to assassination is puzzling, for the *Nizari* had military forces, which Christian Crusaders found formidable. (Other Muslim sacred terrorists did not feel themselves so bound.) Still, *Nizari* armies were not used against other Muslims except to defend bases

---

[65] Maurice Tugwell, *Revolutionary Propaganda and Possible Counter-Measures* (Ph.D. dissertation, Kings College, University of London, 1979), 62.
[66] Hodgson, *The Order*, 84.

and to make booty raids on caravans. Assassination and war seemed to be mutually exclusive alternatives; the dagger was reserved for those who betrayed the faith (hypocrites and apostates) and the sword for those who never accepted it (*kuffar*).

Scholars have not tried to explain the original doctrinal basis for this particular pattern or for the general significance of assassination in Islam. Hodgson's classic study begins the discussion of *Nizari* practices suggestively: "A number of Muslim sects had used assassination as a technique. It is recorded of Mohammed himself that on several occasions, he exclaimed that one or the other did not deserve to live; and was then gratified by one of his men finding ways of destroying the enemy."[67] But this argument (which understates Muhammed's involvement in assassination) is never developed, and Hodgson's later work moves in another direction altogether to emphasize the "prudential" and "practical" rationale for *Nizari* policy.[68] Bernard Lewis, who wrote the other major study of the movement, emphasizes the prevalence of assassination in early Islam but does not explain its origin or suggest that the pattern may be unusual.[69]

Hodgson's initial suggestion seems quite sound, especially in view of Muhammed's pattern in employing military forces and assassins during the *hijra*. Initially, the army was limited to defending the community against attack and raiding caravans for booty. Simultaneously, Muhammed authorized various assassinations of prominent persons within or on its fringes—"hypocrites" whose behavior provoked him. Their deaths released hitherto latent sympathies for Islam among their followers. The process of purifying or consolidating the original nucleus of believers seemed to be the precondition of its expansion later. Assassinations ceased when Muhammed decided the community was ready to incorporate new territories and the army was given its first offensive role.

The constituent elements of this assassination archetype were time, space, weapons, rewards, and culpability. The acts occurred during the *hijra*, when the community was weak and had to remove people who were not fully committed. To demonstrate commitment sufficiently profound to earn remission of all sins, the assassin violated what were con-

---

[67] Ibid., 82.

[68] See "The Ismà'ili State," in the *Cambridge History of Iran*, vol. V, edited by J. A. Boyle (Cambridge: University Press, 1968), 422–82. Lewis's discussion of origins simply regards the *Nizari* as part of a millenarian tradition that precedes Islam and continues in our own day. See his *Assassins*, 128.

[69] Lewis, *The Assassins*, 125–40.

sidered his most cherished bonds or personal feelings and struck victims in intimate encounters. Umayr ibn 'Adi, for example, the first assassin, killed his kinswoman (a poet who mocked Muhammed) "asleep with her children about her. The youngest, still at the breast, lay asleep in her arms."[70] Because the victim was struck in a context sacred to the old religion, a context that was also the source of power (family or tribe), she was humiliated.

Islamic terrorist groups seemed to interpret this archetype in various ways. The most obvious differences concern weapons, *hijra*, assassin-victim relations, and the links between assassination and other violent acts. For some obscure reason, the most ritualized behavior occurs among the *Nizari* and some other earlier assassination cults who act to prepare the way for a millenarian uprising.[71]

In the founding period of Islam, Muhammed's approval seemed sufficient reward; often the assassin was atoning for not showing sufficient ardor. Later, martyrdom was normally achieved by means of the assassin's death. Such an archetype would greatly encourage individuals to be assassins on their own initiative. (Assassinations occurred often in Islam's founding period because the founder instructed his followers or because he approved their initiative.) Could the archetype help explain the fact that 35 percent to 40 percent of the caliphs were assassinated? By way of comparison, James Westphall Thompson, the medieval historian, said that no monarch in Western Europe after the feudal system was established was assassinated by a vassal.[72]

[70] Maxime Rodinson, *Mohammed* (London: Penguin, 1971), 171. Ibn Hisham, the chronicler cited, does not actually describe the incident as the first but as a much later one. The scholarly consensus is that the other chroniclers discussing the incident were more accurate in believing it to be the first. See, however, Ibn Hisham's edition of Ibn Ishaq, *The Life of Muhammed*, introduced and edited by Alfred Guillaume (London: Oxford University Press, 1955), 364 ff. and 675–6. Various assassinations are discussed by Rodinson and by Montgomery W. Watt, *Mohammed at Medina* (Oxford: Clarendon, 1956). Rodinson groups them in a single chapter and provides more details; consequently, the patterns are easier to grasp. Most victims were Jews. Muhammed's Constitution of Medina shows that Jews were part of the original community, and his initial intention was to make Islam as close to Judaism as possible. When that failed, assassins (kinsmen of intended victims) were used to separate the two bodies and to gain converts out of the Jewish tribes, a process described by Ibn Hisham as the aftermath of 'Umayr's deed. "'Umayr had been among the first of them to become a Muslim. On the day the daughter of Marwan was killed, the men of Banu Khatma were converted because of what they saw of the power of Islam." Quoted in Rodinson, *Mohammed*, 171.

[71] Christian groups waiting for the millennium normally are pacifists, but when they believe the millennium to be imminent, they often adopt terrorist tactics. See my "Messianic Sanctions."

[72] Cited by Saul K. Padover, "Patterns of Assassination in Occupied Territory," *Public Opinion Quarterly* 7 (Winter 1943): 123. The calculation is very rough, based on the fifty-five

A review of the themes in Islamic sacred terror

Assassination like . . . war is the pursuit of political [religious?] ends by different means. Umayr's exploit (the assassination of his kinswoman, the poetess) is listed by the chroniclers among Mohammed's *expeditions*.

(Maxime Rodinson, *Mohammed*, 171; my emphasis)

Al-Jihad did not reintroduce assassination practices into Egypt. Elements of the Islamicist movement produced some striking incidents in the two preceding decades; and from 1938 the Muslim Brotherhood was prepared to use violence and was held responsible for a number of assassinations.[73]

Such facts tempt one to believe that, in Egypt, assassination is primarily associated with religious groups. But the phenomenon was rare in the nineteenth century, and when the modern wave did begin in 1910, the first assailant acted for secular (nationalist or anticolonial) reasons. He was educated in Europe, which was then in the midst of its "golden age of assassination" (1880–1914). Appropriately, Egyptian newspapers attributed assassinations to insidious European influences! "We have acquired the faults of Europeans instead of assimilating their good qualities; we imitate the examples of their anarchists and apaches."[74]

caliphs listed by Lane-Poole, which includes the first four, the "patriarchs," fourteen Umayyads, and thirty-seven Abbasids. The circumstances of death are not always clear in the secondary accounts (perhaps they are unclear in the primary sources, too) particularly when a caliph is killed in a civil disturbance. My calculations indicate that anywhere from eighteen (31 percent) to twenty-six (43 percent) were assassinated. The *lower* figure seems more reliable, and no doubt other factors contribute to these statistics. See Stanley Lane-Poole, *Mohammedan Dynasties* (Beirut: Khayat Book Publisher, 1966).

[73] In 1977, the Excommunication and Emigration group assassinated the former minister of religious endowment, Sheik Hussein Al Zahala. In 1965, members of the Muslim Brotherhood (the original home of the violent elements in the Islamicist movement) were executed for attempting to assassinate Nasser. Eleven years earlier (1954) leaders of the Brotherhood were convicted for the attempt by one member to assassinate Nasser. In 1948, Prime Minister Al-Nuqrashi Pasha was cut down by a Muslim Brother. In the same year, Muslim Brothers assassinated a prominent judge, Ahmed Khazender, and the Brotherhood was accused of being involved in at least two more incidents in which prominent figures—Salem Zaki, the chief of Cairo police, and the sultan of Yemen and his three sons—were murdered. In 1945, Prime Minister Ahmed Maher was shot dead in the Egyptian parliament, after reading the Declaration of War against the Axis, by an assassin from a group related to the Muslim Brotherhood.

The costs to each group have been enormous. The Excommunication and Emigration Group and *Al-Jihad* have been destroyed, and *Al-Jihad*'s successor group is likely to be. The Muslim Brotherhood was savagely repressed twice, its founder was assassinated, and many of its leaders executed or imprisoned.

[74] Quoted by Donald M. Reid, "Political Assassination in Egypt, 1910–54," *International Journal of African Historical Studies* 15, no. 4 (1982): 639. Because the murdered prime minister was a Copt, the assassin became a popular hero; songs and poems celebrated "The Mussulman hero who has killed the accursed Christian" (ibid., 628). The Muslim

In the first half of the twentieth century, Egyptian assassins acted mostly for secular purposes and accounted for at least as many victims as the religious assassins did later. Whatever its origin, assassination became a regular feature of secular politics; at least four premiers and two presidents (Nasser and Sadat) engaged in assassination plots *before* they gained high political office.[75]

It is common to describe assassinations associated with the Muslim Brotherhood as religiously inspired, but they should be distinguished from assassinations by Islamicists. Brotherhood victims were primarily non-Muslims; their assassinations were part of a terror campaign to establish national independence. (The Brotherhood did not generally acknowledge attacks on Muslims, most of which seemed to be acts of unauthorized individuals.) Interested in keeping a mass political party intact, the Brotherhood tried to operate within the existing framework, "playing the political game, establishing coalitions with semi-apostates and setting detailed programs from reforms." It was "never an authentic counter-society, either in concept or realization."[76]

Those Islamicists who left the Muslim Brotherhood did so because they believed that the parent organization failed to understand that their allies in the independence struggle—the apostates and hypocrites—who now controlled the state machinery were a much more dangerous threat to Islam than Britain ever was. To make credible the Islamicist claim that a government that ruled in the name of Islam was composed of apostates, it was necessary to challenge the established standards of orthodox Islam, and this could be done only by rediscovering the "true" meaning of religious sources. In its modern form, therefore, sacred terror is very recent. Some Islamicists see the assassination campaign of the Iranian *Fidaiyun Al-Islam* (1943–55) against prominent officials as its first expression.[77]

The most complete source document among the Sunni, nonetheless, is *The Neglected Duty*. A comparison of it with secular terrorist texts indicates that critical differences between contemporary sacred and secular

Brothers hailed the Pan Islamic activist Afghani as their forerunner. Expelled from Egypt in the 1870s, he apparently instigated the assassination of the shah of Persia in 1896.

[75] Ibid., 629 and 646.

[76] Sivan, *Radical Islam*, 113.

[77] Mehdi Mozaffari, *La violence shi'ite contemporaine: Evolution politique* (Aarhus, Denmark: Institute of Political Science, University of Aarhus, 1988); and N. R. Keddie and K. H. Zarunkud, "*Fidaiyyan I-Islam*," *Encyclopedia of Islam* (1960), vol. 2, 883. A more recent Iranian example is the *Moujahidin*, who have concentrated on members of the legislature.

terror exist—differences that stem from the diverse meanings attributed to justifications and precedents. Furthermore, even though we lack texts written by ancient terrorists, there is good reason to think that ancient and modern sacred terror are varieties of a single type. Only contemporary Muslims could understand or be persuaded by Faraj, and earlier Muslims were probably presented with interpretations similar to his. Certainly, all of Faraj's sources, except Ibn Tamiyah, were available earlier, and it is hard to imagine them being ignored, especially those decisive examples from Muhammed.[78] It is possible to believe that Faraj and the ancient terrorists were altogether wrong in identifying their victims as hypocrites and apostates, and still recognize that forms associated with the Islamic *jihad* against apostates simultaneously inspired and restricted their actions.

Anything that works, Faraj says, is appropriate for such a *jihad*, and in principle there is no reason why he needed to limit his tactics in the precise manner chosen. Still, the examples that give the original point its authority—chosen as they are from Muhammed's experiences—focus on assassinations followed by spontaneous favorable popular reactions. Wholly favorable reactions are not common in history, and *Al-Jihad* had good reason to doubt the value of the plot. Still, it does not appear surprising—perhaps, it seems "inevitable"—that the authority of its precedents would lead it to do exactly what it did do. Faraj's text indicates that one should expect a divine intervention after the assassination, a reversal of normal social expectations, and, hence, that rare event, a favorable popular reaction, would occur. At the trial Faraj claimed something else, that the blow was delivered to provide a lesson for other potential "pharaohs." But no serious plans were made for the aftermath of the assassination; nearly all the members of *Al-Jihad* were picked up immediately,[79] which leads one to conclude that the text is a better clue to original expectations.

[78] Ibn Tamiyah, interpreted as sanctioning rebellion against the Mongols because they were not really Muslims, is important to Faraj. This is because the fourteenth-century writer is recognized as authoritative for the Sunni and provides more credence to the Islamicist denial that they are *Kharijites* and thus wholly illegitimate, as the establishment routinely claims.

[79] As I have already indicated, some members thought that the group did not make adequate military plans to cope with the situation created by the assassinations. The political plans were vague (see note 20 above). This leads Jansen to say that Faraj's text confirms "the spectator's impression at that time that there was no plan for further action, once the assassination attempt had succeeded. . . . The assassins may have expected large and spontaneous popular action to follow. . . . In their own words: 'once they had punished

The proclivity for assassination—even assassination with no supporting measures or with grossly inadequate ones—characterizes the early sacred terrorists in Islam, too. There are other affinities: a desire to reorder priorities and to purify the community so that it could resume its original purpose, expressed in both cases through the cry to make the *shar'ia* the source of all rules. (The Assassins as premillenarians were an exception.) Withdrawal from existing society to form a model one is common. Then comes the effort to persuade a potentially sympathetic mass public that the methods the assassin is obliged to try first have been used and found wanting. As the circumstances of Sadat's death and the examples from the founding period suggest, the place and timing of the assassinations are important.[80]

The decision by *Al-Jihad* to use the trial in order to affirm responsibility seems consistent with the spirit of the early sacred terrorists. How one dies for one's faith is at least as important as how one kills for it. The Russians, who created modern secular terror, appreciated that axiom, too, but other considerations obscured it as secular terror developed;[81] perhaps the same pressures account for the fact that responsibility was going to be denied in *Al-Jihad*'s original plan.

The claim of Sadat's assassins that they took pains to avoid hurting others may or may not be true, but it is hard to find another contemporary terror group so "fastidious" or so concerned to make this particular point. Indeed, the picture of the assassins fasting to atone for striking innocent victims (mostly guards and high officials) seems quite outside the realm of secular terrorist experience.[82] The trial made the public more favorably disposed toward the assassins.[83] Can we attribute this response in part to the assassins' claim that they took extra risks to avoid hurting

Sadat for his alleged apostasy from Islam, God would do the rest!' " Faraj, *Neglected Duty*, para. 31.

Nemat Guenena, who makes no judgment about the adequacy of the plans, says that her examination of the "case file" indicates that Sadat's assassination and the assassinations of other designated prominent personalities (once the mass communication centers were seized) would provide the signal for an uprising. But the security forces aborted the plan. *The Jihad*, 70–4.

[80] Kepel says they "chose that symbolic date to act against the Egyptian state in the most spectacular way possible: by assassinating the president." *Muslim Extremism*, 191.

[81] The American Weather Underground members always claimed to be "framed" and most showed a willingness to plea-bargain.

[82] One is reminded of the early Russian terrorists who were concerned to strike only at officials as symbols and whom Camus calls "fastidious assassins" in *The Rebel*.

[83] Beirut *Monday Morning*, 22–29 March 1982, *Foreign Broadcasting Information Service* (FBIS) *Near East and Southeast Asia* V, p. D-22.

innocents? Did this make them appear to act in a more traditional Islamic mode?

We have become accustomed to terrorist campaigns, in which the object is to strike many defenseless individuals over a protracted time period. Could Faraj's argument against hurting innocent Muslims have prevented *Al-Jihad* (which had three to four hundred members) from considering this course? The originators of modern secular terror in Russia were also concerned to protect innocents, but their successors believed such restrictions to be counterproductive. Faraj indicates that Islamic sources could be interpreted to justify movement in a similar direction. This may occur, but in Egypt it has not happened yet. "Those Spared from Hell" *(Al-Najun Min al-Nar), Al-Jihad*'s immediate successor, described by the government as using *The Neglected Duty* as "its sacred constitution," continues in the same path; this group attempted to assassinate three prominent figures in the summer of 1987.[84] Their action emphasizes that although Faraj himself seemed obsessed with the pharaoh (Sadat), his text emphasizes the problem of "rulers."

In the eyes of two of the most prominent scholars of Egyptian Islamicism, "Faraj is the most articulate spokesman of the gospel for the youth of the 1980's"[85] and "may inaugurate a new era in Islamicist thought."[86] If this is true, we may expect many more attempts to interpret and act upon the meanings of his interpretations of ancient precedents. Just as ancient Islamic sacred terror had its variations, so must we anticipate that the modern sacred form will, too.

[84] Cairo *Mena*, 31 August 1987, *FBIS* V, p. C-4 and Cairo *Al Akhbar*, 1 September 1987; 3 September 1987, *FBIS* V, p. C-3.
[85] Sivan, *Radical Islam*, 127.
[86] Kepel, *Muslim Extremism*, 240.

8

The moral logic of Hizballah

MARTIN KRAMER

"And verily the party of God is sure to triumph." In 1982, a group of Lebanese Shi'ite Muslims first adopted this verse of the *Qur'an* as their slogan and declared themselves to be "the party of God." Supported by many followers in Lebanon's large centers of Shi'ite population, and backed by the Islamic Republic of Iran, "the party of God"—Hizballah—has since become a movement with which all other Lebanese factions must reckon. Its growing ideological and armed strength is evident in its original stronghold in the Biqa Valley and in the predominantly Shi'ite southern suburbs of Beirut. Its fighters do sporadic battle with the rival Lebanese Shi'ite movement, Amal; with the Israeli-backed and predominantly Christian South Lebanon Army; and with Syrian forces stationed in Lebanon. In such pursuits, Hizballah is akin to the various other armed Lebanese factions, all battling for some advantage in the seesaw struggle for an ungoverned land. Like them, Hizballah propagandizes through rallies and speeches, a newspaper, and a radio station. The movement maintains command centers, training bases, and an armed militia. And its leaders conduct diplomacy to secure weapons, money, and support from allied factions and states.[1]

[1] The secondary literature on Hizballah is limited but growing. For an account of Hizballah's genesis, see Shimon Shapira, "The Origins of Hizballah," *The Jerusalem Quarterly*, 46 (Spring 1988): 115–30. For a brief description of the movement in the context of Lebanon's other Islamic movements, see Marius Deeb, *Militant Islamic Movements in Lebanon: Origins, Social Basis, and Ideology,* Occasional Papers Series of the Center for Contemporary Arab Studies, Georgetown University (Washington, D.C., November 1986), 12–19. For the Lebanese Shi'ite background, see Fouad Ajami, *The Vanished Imam: Musa al Sadr and Shia of Lebanon* (Ithaca: Cornell University Press, 1986). For the evolution of Iranian policy toward Lebanon, see R. K. Ramazani, *Revolutionary Iran: Challenge and Response in the Middle East* (Baltimore: Johns Hopkins University Press, 1986), 179–95. Cf. journalistic accounts of Hizballah in books by Robin Wright, *Sacred Rage* (New York:

Yet Hizballah differs from other Lebanese militias in a fundamental respect. Its leaders, nearly all of whom are Shi'ite clerics, have fashioned in their own minds and in those of their followers a revolutionary vision of a new Lebanon. Hizballah's declared aim is the creation, sooner or later, of an Islamic state in Lebanon. Its mission is not to improve the relative position of one of Lebanon's constituent communities vis-à-vis all others but to make of Lebanon an ideal Islamic polity and society. In Hizballah's vision, Islam alone will redeem Lebanon from the ravages of civil war and foreign intervention, which are the consequences of Lebanon's attempt to assimilate the ways of the West.

It is certain that there is disagreement within Hizballah over how Lebanon's Islamic revolution should be hastened and whether this is an opportune moment to articulate a full plan. There are also differences on this score between certain leading figures in Hizballah and the movement's Iranian guides, who themselves are divided over how best to transform Lebanon. But for Hizballah's rank and file, these debates are of no great importance. The young men and women of Hizballah are fired by the pure image of a future Lebanon that will regain stability through Islamic law and justice and embark on a redeeming struggle against those who would banish Islam from this Earth.

The framework of Hizballah

It is a pervasive sense of divinely sanctioned mission that Hizballah's leaders invoke when they insist that their movement is something other than a mere political party or militia. Hizballah's official spokesman maintains that the movement is "not a regimented party, in the common sense," for the idea of an exclusive "party" is foreign to Islam. Hizballah is a "mission" and a "way of life."[2] Another Hizballah leader has insisted that Hizballah "is not an organization," for its members carry no cards and bear no specific responsibilities. It is a "nation" of all who believe in the struggle against injustice and all who are loyal to Iran's Imam Khomeini.[3] Still another Hizballah leader maintains that "we are not a party in the traditional sense of the term. Every Muslim is automatically a

Linden Press/Simon and Schuster, 1985) and Amir Taheri, *Holy Terror* (London: Century Hutchinson, 1987).
[2] Ibrahim al-Amin in *al-Harakat al-Islamiyya fi Lubnan* (Beirut, Dar al-Sanin, 1984), 145–6.
[3] Interview with Husayn al-Musawi, *al-Nahar al-arabi wal-duwali* (Beirut), 10 June 1985.

member of Hizballah, thus it is impossible to list our membership."[4] And in the mind of Iran's chargé d'affaires in Beirut, Hizballah is not "restricted to a specified organizational framework. . . . There are two parties, Hizballah or God's party, and the Devil's party."[5]

The idea of Hizballah as a pure calling did approximate truth in the first few months after the movement emerged in 1982. But since then, Iran has worked to make Hizballah an increasingly structured, centralized, and accountable organization. It is now governed by a select consultative council (the Lebanon Council) and three regional councils (for the Biqa Valley, Beirut, and the South). Seven committees now divide administrative work among them. The consultative council, composed primarily of Lebanese Shi'ite clerics, acts with the advice and agreement of representatives of Iran. Hizballah's 4,000-man militia is increasingly structured, and new recruits pass through probationary membership before they are admitted to full membership.[6]

Still, as a revolutionary party, Hizballah seeks to maintain as much secrecy as possible about the nature of authority within the movement. Because of the growing use of Hizballah's name by persons acting without the authorization of the consultative council, Hizballah appointed a spokesman and published an official manifesto in February 1985.[7] But Hizballah has made no other public acknowledgments concerning its structure. And although it is possible to compile a lengthy list of Lebanese Shi'ite clerics and others who are prominent in the movement's activities, it is impossible to assign to any of them a specific office within Hizballah.[8] The avowed repudiation of formal structure, identified by

---

[4] Interview with Abbas al-Musawi, *La Revue du Liban* (Beirut), 27 July 1985.

[5] Interview with Mahmud Nurani, *Monday Morning* (Beirut), 14 January 1985.

[6] Some details on the structure of Hizballah, provided by sources within the movement, appear in *al-Shira* (Beirut), 17 March 1986. This account may be regarded as substantially accurate.

[7] The manifesto appeared in the form of an "open letter" to the "disinherited of Lebanon and the world." The letter first appeared as a pamphlet entitled *Nass al-risala al-maftuha allati wajjahaha Hizballah ila al-mustad'afin fi Lubnan wal-alam* (n.p. [Beirut], 26 Jumada II 1405/16 February 1985). An English translation appears in Augustus Richard Norton, *Amal and the Shi'a: Struggle for the Soul of Lebanon* (Austin: University of Texas Press, 1987), 167–87. For a full discussion of Hizballah's principles of rule, see Martin Kramer, "Redeeming Jerusalem: The Pan-Islamic Premise of Hizballah," in David Menashri, ed., *The Iranian Revolution and the Muslim World* (Boulder, Colo.: Westview Press, forthcoming).

[8] This secrecy has recently come under the criticism of a member of Hizballah, who has compiled a new book on the movement's methods of mobilization. The argument here is that even the most secretive of Islamic movements, the Isma'ilis, made their leadership

Weber as a consistent feature of the charismatically oriented movement, sets Hizballah apart from the other large Lebanese factions, and particularly from the rival Shi'ite movement Amal, which is governed by an elaborate, formal hierarchy of elected and appointed officials.

But the refusal to acknowledge structure is deceptive. Hizballah is an overwhelmingly Shi'ite movement for the establishment of an Islamic state through the implementation of Islamic law. The authorities on that law are Shi'ite clerics—*ulama*—and they occupy roughly the same place of preeminence in Hizballah that the *ulama* occupy in Iran's ruling Islamic Republic Party. Among the *ulama* themselves there are informal yet complex patterns of deference. Hizballah began as a coalition of *ulama,* each of whom brought with him his circle of disciples; and although the movement's Iranian guides have sought to break down these intermediate allegiances in order to control the rank and file directly, the effort has met with only partial success. The individual adherent of Hizballah is likely to be a follower of the movement through a Lebanese Shi'ite cleric who serves as his guide. That cleric may himself be a follower of the movement through a cleric senior to him, and so on. These relationships, which extend at their highest levels to the Shi'ite world's foremost clerics in Iran and Iraq, provide Hizballah with enough informal structure to enforce a modicum of internal discipline, implement higher decisions, and raise needed funds.

There is also a parallel structure of authority in Hizballah, which is intrinsic to the large Shi'ite families of the Biqa Valley. The loyalty of these clans to Hizballah may owe more to intraclan alliances and rivalries than to Islamic commitment. Similarly, the pattern of identification with Hizballah in the Shi'ite villages of South Lebanon partly replicates established patterns of village loyalty. But in the southern suburbs of Beirut, where Shi'ites have shed their loyalties to clan and village, allegiance to Hizballah is generally expressed through submission to Shi'ite *ulama.* These thickly populated suburbs are now the most important bastion of Hizballah in Lebanon, and they constitute the movement's intellectual center.

The prominent *ulama* in Hizballah possess a collective élan rooted in a shared formative experience. Most are products of the once-great academies of learning in the Shi'ite shrine city of Najaf in Iraq. There, in a

known, at least to their own members. See Ali al-Kurani, *Tariqat Hizballah fil-amal al-islami* (Beirut: 1986).

setting of pious fastidiousness, they studied sacred law, theology, and philosophy, according to medieval pedagogical methods. From the late 1950s to the late 1970s, Najaf was also a place of great intellectual ferment, fueled by the fears of the *ulama* that their Islamic values and religious autonomy were threatened by Westernizing influences. Their response was to elaborate a theory of an Islamic state that could offer a satisfying alternative to the doctrines of nationalism and communism, which had made inroads even in Najaf. The *ulama* thought, lectured, and wrote on subjects such as Islamic government, Islamic economics, and the ideal Islamic state. The most notable of these theorists were Ayatollahs Muhsin al-Hakim and Muhammad Baqir al-Sadr, both of Iraq, who had many Lebanese students. Their teachings received an important endorsement in 1965, with the arrival in Najaf of Ayatollah Ruhollah Khomeini, who had been expelled from Iran for his agitation against the Shah's foreign and domestic policies. Khomeini spent the next thirteen years of his exile in Najaf. It was there, in 1970, that he delivered his landmark lectures on Islamic government and called on Muslim men of religion to lay exclusive claim to political rule.

All the Lebanese Shi'ite clerics who studied in Najaf during those years were indoctrinated to some extent with this ideal, at an impressionable moment and in austere conditions of intense Muslim piety. They came away from Najaf with a coherent criticism of the world as it is, an often revolutionary program for change, and friendships spanning the Shi'ite world of scholarship. The Iraqi security authorities have since cleared Najaf of its radical *ulama,* and some have been executed. But the personal and ideological ties forged there have never been stronger. It is the Najaf background of the leading Lebanese Shi'ite clerics in Hizballah that accounts for the movement's rapid and complete assimilation of the doctrines now championed by the Islamic Republic of Iran.[9]

This inculcated sense of sacred mission has led Hizballah to regard its struggle as transcending the narrow frontiers of Lebanon. For unlike the other armed factions, Hizballah cannot hope to attain its ultimate aim without defeating a constellation of external forces, all opposed more or less resolutely to the transformation of Lebanon into an Islamic republic. Foremost among them are the United States and Israel, which are abetted

---

[9] For the various Lebanese and Iraqi Shi'ite movements that trace their antecedents to Najaf, see Martin Kramer, "Muslim Statecraft and Subversion," *Middle East Contemporary Survey,* vol. 8: 1983–84 (Tel Aviv, 1986), 170–3.

by Arab regimes that are allegedly their dependencies. These are powerful adversaries, capable of intervening in Lebanon in countless ways, from centers of decision far beyond the limited reach of Hizballah.

The cause of warding off those who would thwart Hizballah's mission has been embraced by Islamic Jihad. Islamic Jihad claimed credit for the spectacular bombing attacks that helped to drive U.S. and Israeli forces out of Lebanon. Islamic Jihad has done much to purge Lebanon of foreign influence by waging a campaign of kidnapping against foreign nationals. It is difficult to say much that is authoritative about Islamic Jihad or to do more than speculate about the precise relationship between Hizballah and Islamic Jihad. Leading figures in Hizballah, as well as Hizballah's spokesman, disavow all knowledge of the persons behind Islamic Jihad. Western intelligence sources regard Islamic Jihad as a group of clandestine cells run by several of Hizballah's military commanders, in most instances in collaboration with Iran.[10] But conventional thinking on this matter has changed more than once. Those communications issued by Islamic Jihad that are deemed to be authentic are too brief to open a window on this closed universe of belief and action. The few details about three young men known to have carried out suicide attacks claimed by Islamic Jihad are too scanty for any precise reconstruction of the group's methods or affiliations.[11]

But Islamic Jihad need not interpret itself to the world, for this is done on its behalf and with great effectiveness by the leaders of Hizballah. Whatever the relationship of accountability between Islamic Jihad and Hizballah, their ideological compatibility finds daily expression in the public statements of Hizballah leaders. Husayn al-Musawi is the leader of Islamic Amal, a constituent part of Hizballah based in the Biqa Valley.

---

[10] The most renowned of these commanders is Imad Mughniyya, a Lebanese Shi'ite who is now in Iran. Mughniyya's name has appeared in connection both with the bombing attacks and kidnappings against Americans in Lebanon, and he was reportedly one of four persons indicted in the United States for his planning of the TWA jet hijacking of June 1985. For an American intelligence assessment of his role and character ("He is a violent extremist capable of impetuously killing the [American] hostages. Yet he does not operate without constraints."), see Charles Allen to Vice Admiral John Poindexter, 9 September 1986, quoted in *Report of the President's Special Review Board* (Washington, D.C.: U.S. Government Printing Office, 26 February 1987), B-153, n. 90. An unusual opportunity to break the circle of secrecy surrounding Islamic Jihad was reportedly lost in late 1985, when Mughniyya passed through France, and French authorities did not act on a request from the United States that he be detained and prosecuted; *New York Times*, 14 March 1986.

[11] But new material is still appearing on the "martyrs." For the interesting interview with the parents of the young man who carried out the attack on the Israeli military headquarters in Tyre in November 1983, see *al-Ahd* (Beirut), 14 November 1986.

At times he has also been singled out in the media as one of the minds behind Islamic Jihad, a charge he has consistently denied. But he and his followers do claim to have given Islamic Jihad "political and moral support so that it would not look as if their actions were of a criminal nature. In this sense if it had not been for our propaganda, their actions would have been condemned by the public as criminal acts. We have tried to make the public understand that their action was in the nature of a jihad, launched by the oppressed against the oppressors."[12]

Husayn al-Musawi and other Hizballah leaders invest otherwise anonymous acts with meaning, transforming apparent crimes into sacred deeds. Hizballah's leaders justify the extraordinary operations carried out in the name of Islamic Jihad by constructing moral "logics," which are valid not only for the wider public but for themselves and perhaps even for Islamic Jihad. Among these leaders are some of Lebanon's foremost Shi'ite clerics, men respected and renowned for their learning in Islam and its incumbent obligations. With their support, Islamic Jihad need give little or no account of itself, and it has generally preferred not to do so. And through the strength and resourcefulness of their moral logic, the leaders of Hizballah have created a climate that promotes the kinds of operations that have consistently turned back Hizballah's enemies and placed an Islamic state within grasp.

Two categories of action have posed unique challenges to these leaders, precisely because they employ methods that on their face seem to violate some principle of Islamic law—the very law that Hizballah has championed as a solution to all of Lebanon's ills. These are the suicidal bomb attacks and the kidnappings of foreigners. The arguments within Hizballah over both these extraordinary means provide much insight into how morality, law, and necessity may be distorted and remade under the relentless pressures of great collective distress.

Hizballah's spokesmen

Before passing to the substance of the arguments advanced within Hizballah regarding these two issues, it is necessary to introduce those who will speak. All of them share a vision of an Islamic Lebanon. Yet each reached Hizballah through his own personal odyssey, and each has a distinctive perspective on the mission of Hizballah. Some are more senior

[12] Interview with Husayn al-Musawi, *Kayhan* (Tehran), 29 July 1986.

in the struggle than others; some have wider followings than others; some are more independent of Iran and of other Hizballah leaders than others. And because all but one are Shi'ite clerics, they occupy different positions of rank in the informal hierarchy of Shi'ite learning.

In the Biqa Valley, where Hizballah operates in close collaboration with an Iranian Revolutionary Guards Corps contingent, Hizballah leaders speak with the most uniform voice. Husayn al-Musawi, already mentioned earlier, is the only one who is not a cleric. Born in the village of Nabishit in the Biqa Valley, Husayn al-Musawi, now in his forties, is a former literature teacher who later served as an official in the Amal movement. One of his tasks was liaison with Iran, which he visited frequently. In 1982 when Amal leader Nabih Berri decided to join the National Salvation Committee, Husayn al-Musawi broke with Amal, made for the Biqa Valley, and there established Islamic Amal. This is now subsumed organizationally in Hizballah, although it apparently remains under the personal authority of Husayn al-Musawi.

Hizballah in the Biqa Valley is under the spiritual guidance of two young Shi'ite clerics, both products of the Shi'ite academies of Najaf in Iraq. Shaykh Subhi al-Tufayli was born in 1948 in the village of Brital, also in the Biqa Valley. He spent nine years studying in Najaf and a brief time in Qom in Iran. Despite his youth, Tufayli enjoys considerable prestige as the Biqa Valley's most learned cleric. Sayyid Abbas al-Musawi, born in 1952 in Nabishit, spent eight years in the same Najaf academy before coming to Ba'labakk in 1978. Now he teaches in a local academy which he helped to found. The Biqa Valley clerics have no pretensions to independent leadership. As Tufayli says, "Our relationship with the Islamic revolution [in Iran] is one of a junior to a senior . . . of a soldier to his commander."[13]

In Beirut, the official spokesman of Hizballah is Sayyid Ibrahim al-Amin, born in 1953 in the village of Nabi Ayla near Zahla. He was educated first in Najaf but more thoroughly in Qom, and he once represented Amal in Tehran. Like Husayn al-Musawi, he, too, broke with Amal in 1982, coming first to the Biqa Valley and later making his way to Beirut. He has worked very closely with officials of the Iranian embassy in Beirut and is an effective preacher in his own right.

It is significant that the man most often named as the spiritual leader of Hizballah denies not only the title but all formal connection with Hiz-

---

[13] Interview with Tufayli, *Ettela'at* (Tehran), 20 August 1985.

ballah. Nonetheless, Ayatollah Sayyid Muhammad Husayn Fadlallah owes his political ascent in Lebanon to his undeniable influence over the movement. Fadlallah is the most senior Shi'ite cleric affiliated with Hizballah, and is unquestionably the most articulate and subtle advocate of Islamic Republicanism in Lebanon. Fadlallah was born in Najaf in 1935, but his father hailed from the village of Aynata in South Lebanon. In Najaf, Fadlallah studied under radical clerics, but he also felt the moderating influence of another teacher, Ayatollah Abu al-Qasim Kho'i, renowned for his apolitical devotion to scholarship. Fadlallah arrived in Beirut in 1966 and began a promising career in preaching, teaching, writing, and communal work. The Iranian revolution led Fadlallah to shed his political quietism. Following the Israeli invasion in 1982, he turned his pulpit into a platform for criticism of foreign involvement in Lebanon and appeals for the establishment of an Islamic republic.[14]

Fadlallah is a man of no small ambition who claims a following not only in Hizballah but in Amal and even among Shi'ites outside Lebanon. At the same time, his relationship with Hizballah's Iranian sponsors and guides has been a wary one, for his reading of the Lebanese situation has diverged significantly from theirs. It is Fadlallah's view that an Islamic Republic of Lebanon will be achieved later rather than sooner, given the certain opposition of several communities in Lebanon and their powerful foreign supporters.[15] That opposition cannot be reduced solely through intimidation and violence, but it can be eroded gradually through a campaign of persuasion. Fadlallah himself aspires to be Lebanon's great persuader, a man of religion who stands above the mire of Lebanese militia politics and to whom all will eventually turn for mediation.

Fadlallah thus has no interest in being singled out as the leader, spiritual or otherwise, of Hizballah. Because a substantial part of Hizballah is influenced directly by the Iranians, he sees no reason to take on himself the burden of responsibility for Hizballah actions decided by others. And he does not wish to disqualify himself from a future role that might establish his authority far beyond the confines of Hizballah.[16] So Fadlallah

---

[14] For a fuller biographical account, see Martin Kramer, "Muhammad Husayn Fadlallah," *Orient* (Opladen, West Germany) 26, no. 2 (June 1985): 147–9. Some of Fadlallah's theoretical writings, mostly from the 1970s, have been examined in two articles by Olivier Carré: "Quelques mots-clefs de Muhammad Husayn Fadlallâh," *Revue française de science politique* 37, no. 4 (August 1987): 478–501; and "La 'révolution islamique' selon Muhammad Husayn Fadlallâh," *Orient* 29, no. 1 (March 1988): 68–84.

[15] For a revealing discussion of Fadlallah's differences with Iran, even over Iran's decision to promote the establishment of Hizballah, see *al-Shira*, 4 August 1986.

[16] Fadlallah has taken the highly controversial position that there need not be only one final

has repeatedly declared that were he the leader of Hizballah, he would "have enough courage to own up to that fact. It is simply not so." This allows him to affirm that "I am not responsible for the behavior of any armed or unarmed group." And unlike those clerics who identify openly with Hizballah, Fadlallah does not regard the movement as different in kind from Lebanon's other militias: "Hizballah is a party, just like other parties in Lebanon which resort to the use of arms. It might be responsible for infractions and violations of the law, and they might have made mistakes, even though their mistakes are far less than those of others."[17] Fadlallah avers that he has a following within Hizballah, but he rejects even the label of "spiritual guide" of the movement.[18]

Yet for all that, Fadlallah stands atop the informal hierarchy of clerics associated with Hizballah. He is senior to them all in his learning and status. They turn to him for guidance, and he is a regular fixture at Hizballah rallies. Many who are devoted first and foremost to Fadlallah fill the ranks of Hizballah, and adherents of Hizballah fill his mosque in the Bi'r al-Abid quarter of Beirut. Hizballah uses his mosque for gatherings, and it may be Hizballah that guarantees Fadlallah's personal security against would-be assassins. There are close ties of mutual dependence among Hizballah's leaders, their Iranian guides, and Fadlallah; for all the jealousies they arouse in one another, a sense of shared purpose binds them. Hizballah's adherents pledge their ultimate allegiance to the Imam Khomeini, but he cannot address his Lebanese following directly, for his Persian oratory cannot transcend the linguistic frontier. And so Iran depends on Fadlallah's brilliant Arabic rhetoric to carry the message of Islamic republicanism to Hizballah. He is an imperfect medium, for Fadlallah has his own agenda; but no other Lebanese Shi'ite cleric comes close to rendering the service as effectively as he does.

There are many other noteworthy clerics affiliated with Hizballah. They include Shaykh Muhammad Isma'il Khaliq (Ayatollah Montazeri's representative in Lebanon and founder of an Islamic academy in Beirut), Shaykh Zuhayr Kanj (leader of a Hizballah-backed coalition of clerics), Shaykh Mahir Hammud (a Sunni from Sidon and a leader of that same

---

source of Shi'ite authority in matters of religious law; interview with Fadlallah, *al-Shira*, 26 May 1986. Fadlallah seems to be making a preliminary argument for a diffusion of authority that would allow him to stand as an equal to Khomeini's successor. Publication of this interview is said to have angered Iranian officials in Beirut.

[17] Interviews with Fadlallah, *Monday Morning*, 15 October 1984; *al-Nahar* (Beirut), 3 October 1984.

[18] Interview with Fadlallah, *al-Ittihad al-usbu'i* (Abu Dhabi), 30 January 1986.

coalition), Shaykh Muhammad Yazbak (founder of an Islamic academy in Ba'labakk), Sayyid Hasan Nasrallah (now very active in mobilizing Beirut Shi'ites for the struggle in the South), as well as a number of preachers in the towns and villages of South Lebanon. A complete analysis of Hizballah would take their opinions into account as well, but they tend to offer interpretations received from the movement's more visible representatives.

Suicide and martyrdom

Hizballah owes much of its reputation in the wider world to the unprecedented wave of suicidal bombings carried out by Lebanese Shi'ites from the spring of 1983 to the summer of 1985. These attacks were directed against U.S., French, and Israeli targets in Lebanon, and they met with astonishing success in bringing about policy reassessments by all these extraneous powers. In the best-planned of these operations, individual suicide bombers caused tens and even hundreds of casualties. Responsibility for most of the bombings was claimed by Islamic Jihad, and prominent figures affiliated with Hizballah were careful to disavow any involvement in the attacks. Nonetheless, it was Hizballah that most directly benefited from the suicide operations. The movement's own military capabilities were still very limited, and its militia had yet to take effective form. Yet the spectacular bombings suggested that religious fervor could compensate for small numbers and that Hizballah commanded a kind of devotion from its adherents that no other militia could claim. Hizballah could no longer be ignored. Its leading figures sought to assure this recognition even as they distanced themselves personally from the attacks, by justifying the operations as though they were Hizballah's own.

In one sense, it was an uncomplicated moral logic that justified the highly effective October 1983 suicide attacks against the U.S. and French contingents of the Multinational Force (MNF) in Beirut. Although he invariably denied any personal involvement in the attacks, Islamic Amal's Husayn al-Musawi saw the attacks as defensive acts against foreign occupation. "Even if we, the people of Islamic Amal, do not have relations with those who committed these attacks, we are nevertheless on the side of those who defend themselves, by whatever means they have chosen."[19] In his view, the MNF was a military force committed to armed struggle

---

[19] Interview with Husayn al-Musawi, *Le Monde*, 2 November 1983.

against Lebanon's Muslims, a view held widely in Beirut's southern suburbs and widely preached by Shi'ite clerics in mosque sermons throughout the country. "I accept these attacks," declared Musawi. "The French
and Americans came to Beirut to help the Phalangists and Israelis—our
enemies—against the Muslims. They evacuated the Palestinians to enable
the Israelis to enter Beirut."[20] Musawi denied knowing any members of
Islamic Jihad, which claimed credit for the attacks. But he would later
declare, "I supported their glorious attacks against the U.S. and French
forces in Lebanon. I have said repeatedly that I have no connection with
them, but we respect them and we support them fully and we bow our
heads to the greatness of their work."[21]

The Hizballah leader in the Biqa Valley, Sayyid Abbas al-Musawi, felt
justified in declaring that the attacks "represented the opinion of all Muslims. The MNF should not have acted the way it did. When you knock
on someone's door, you must wait for an answer before entering."[22] For
Sayyid Ibrahim al-Amin, spokesman of Hizballah in Beirut, this aggressive intrusion was part of a "war" with the United States, which had
"transformed Lebanon into a military test laboratory for their advanced
weapons." It was "our right to rise up against our enemies," and the
October 1983 attacks "deserve proper recognition, homage, and deference," for they were "unprecedented in the history of mankind."[23] Hizballah's leaders deemed the MNF a hostile force in time of war, not a
neutral force dispatched to preserve peace. Therefore, attacks against the
MNF were military operations against an enemy, not acts of terrorism
against political neutrals. And as spectacularly successful military operations, the attacks were widely applauded, not only by Hizballah but by
other Lebanese factions as well as by Iran and Syria. When attacks launched
against Israeli forces in Lebanon enjoyed comparable success, they met
with similar accolades.

The more complicated moral issue from Hizballah's point of view
concerned the method of the attacks, which depended on the premeditated sacrifice by Muslims of their own lives. The frequency with which
this issue was addressed by Shi'ite clerics following the attacks suggests
that resort to this method did not meet with universal approbation within
Hizballah, because of the strong Islamic prohibition against suicide.[24]

[20] Interview with Husayn al-Musawi, *Le Figaro*, 12 September 1986.
[21] Interview with Husayn al-Musawi, *Kayhan*, 29 July 1986.
[22] Interview with Abbas al-Musawi, *La Revue du Liban*, 27 July 1985.
[23] Interview with Ibrahim al-Amin, *Kayhan*, 19 October 1985.
[24] The accepted theological view is that suicide is a grave sin, and the person who commits

Some activists were also distressed that the method tended to obscure the message, because the many psychologists called upon to interpret the attacks suggested clinical rather than political interpretations for the motives of the perpetrators. These interpretations had some effect in the Shi'ite street, where it was rumored that the terrorists who had carried out the operations were possibly disturbed, making it necessary for Islamic Jihad to conceal their identities even after the attacks. If this had been the case, Islamic Jihad's operational planners had exploited the psychological distress of unbalanced youngsters, who had acted without the full possession of their faculties.

Sayyid Muhammad Husayn Fadlallah gave this issue the most systematic exposition in his interviews, speeches, and sermons. It was a subject he could not avoid, yet one that had to be addressed in cautious terms. Reports by the intelligence branches of the Lebanese army and the Lebanese Forces (Phalanges), which were leaked to the American press, had Fadlallah granting religious dispensation to the attackers on the eve of their mission.[25] He denied this accusation immediately and consistently, as the inevitable preface to his analysis of the moral implications of the attacks. This he made from the point of view of an interpreter of religious law, to whom persons both within and beyond Hizballah turned for judgment on the moral admissibility of the method employed in the operations.

Fadlallah's initial declaratory position was one of ambivalence toward the attacks. One of his professed doubts was strictly situational. In the immediate aftermath of the attacks, he expressed concern about possible retaliation against the southern suburbs and about the likelihood that the bombings might drive the United States to adopt a still more aggressive posture. The attacks were liable to create "a climate that makes it easier for imperialism to implement its plans. This is what happened with the two explosions. The United States benefited from them in invading Grenada and in exerting political pressure in Lebanon to further its interests."[26] But Fadlallah's concerns about the effect of the attacks on the resolve of the United States were soon dissipated; it rapidly became clear that the attacks had shattered that resolve and hastened the withdrawal of the MNF. Yet Fadlallah was still left with the complex moral and legal

suicide is doomed to continual repetition in Hell of the action by which he killed himself. Franz Rosenthal, "On Suicide in Islam," *Journal of the American Oriental Society* 66 (1946): 243, 245.

[25] The original story appeared in the *Washington Post,* 28, 30 October 1983.

[26] Interview with Fadlallah, *al-Khalij* (Sharjah), 14 November 1983.

issue of the method employed in the attacks, especially because he and other Shi'ite clerics who looked to him for guidance were besieged by believers' questions. Some of these wanted an explicit judgment based on religious law—a *fatwa*—sanctioning the method of suicidal attack.

Fadlallah knew the nuances of the law: He did not hesitate to declare that, "based on my individual interpretation of Islamic law, I have reservations about resorting to suicidal tactics in political action."[27] And so Fadlallah resisted all pressures to rule decisively on the matter. Although he publicly commented on the merit of individual operations, he generally avoided any blanket endorsement of the method, which remained highly problematic from the point of view of religious law. "In many cases, I stated that these martyrdom operations are not justified, except in very difficult cases. I can say that I have not issued any *fatwa* since the beginning of these operations and up to now. On the contrary, I am one of those who stood against all this commotion for *fatwas*. Despite the positive points which come out of this action, I believe that there are many negative points."[28] But this went without saying; it was his own philosophical assumption that "naturally, there is a positive aspect and a negative aspect to every event in the world,"[29] and "there is evil in everything good and something good in every evil."[30] No act of violence could be justified or condemned without knowledge of specific context. Having considered the specific circumstances of the operations, Fadlallah eventually gave them the fullest possible endorsement short of an explicit *fatwa*.

First, he said, no other means remained to the Muslims to confront the massive power commanded by the United States and Israel. In the absence of any other alternative, unconventional methods became admissible and perhaps even necessary. "If an oppressed people does not have the means to confront the United States and Israel with the weapons in which they are superior, then they possess unfamiliar weapons. . . . Oppression makes the oppressed discover new weapons and new strength every day."[31] The method itself redressed a gross imbalance in the capabilities of the competing forces. "When a conflict breaks out between oppressed nations and imperialism, or between two hostile governments, the parties to the conflict seek ways to complete the elements of their

---

[27] Interview with Fadlallah, *al-Khalij*, 14 November 1983.
[28] Interview with Fadlallah, *al-Mustaqbal* (Paris), 6 July 1985.
[29] Interview with Fadlallah, *al-Nahar al-arabi wal-duwali*, 21 July 1986.
[30] Fadlallah Friday sermon, *al-Ahd*, 6 December 1985.
[31] Interview with Fadlallah, *al-Ittihad* (Abu Dhabi), 7 June 1985.

power and to neutralize the weapons used by the other side. For example, the oppressed nations do not have the technology and destructive weapons America and Europe have. They must thus fight with special means of their own. [We] recognize the right of nations to use every unconventional method to fight these aggressor nations, and do not regard what oppressed Muslims of the world do with primitive and unconventional means to confront aggressor powers as terrorism. We view this as religiously lawful warfare against the world's imperialist and domineering powers."[32] The imbalance of power, coupled with the obligation of self-defense, therefore necessitated extraordinary and unconventional methods of waging war, because the oppressed stood at a distinct disadvantage in any face-to-face confrontation with the formidable forces of imperialism.

But although Fadlallah had established the need for unconventional methods, this did not constitute a clear endorsement of those unconventional methods that might also be in conflict with Islamic law, such as the self-destructive attack. One could not simply argue extenuating circumstances to a constituency devoted to the implementation of Islamic law. Here Fadlallah's argumentation became subtle. "These initiatives," he insisted, "must be placed in their context." If the aim of such a combatant "is to have a political impact on an enemy whom it is impossible to fight by conventional means, then his sacrifice can be part of a jihad, a religious war. Such an undertaking differs little from that of a soldier who fights and knows that in the end he will be killed. The two situations lead to death; except that one fits in with the conventional procedures of war, and the other does not."[33] Fadlallah, denying he had told anyone to "blow yourself up," did affirm that "the Muslims believe that you struggle by transforming yourself into a living bomb like you struggle with a gun in your hand. There is no difference between dying with a gun in your hand or exploding yourself."[34]

This point would ultimately constitute the crux of Fadlallah's argument: Deaths in suicide bombings are no different from more commonplace deaths of soldiers who enter battle knowing that some of them will

---

[32] Interview with Fadlallah, *Kayhan*, 14 November 1985; oppressed peoples "do not consider anything forbidden in the pursuit of these objectives. The legitimacy of every means stems from the legitimacy of the end sought"; interview with Fadlallah, *al-Majallah* (London), 1 October 1986.

[33] Interview with Fadlallah, *Politique internationale* (Paris) 29 (Autumn 1985): 268.

[34] Interview with Fadlallah, *Middle East Insight* (Washington, D.C.) 4, no. 2 (June–July 1985): 10–11.

not return but confident that their sacrifice will advance the common cause. "What is the difference between setting out for battle knowing you will die *after* killing ten [of the enemy], and setting out to the field to kill ten and knowing you will die *while* killing them?" Fadlallah argued that there was no difference. This the psychologists failed to understand. They had explained the operations as the necessary result of the "brain-washing" of the bombers, who had been "suspended in air in a magical paradise." But the psychologists knew nothing of oppression and how it moved men, for "he who has never known hunger in his life cannot understand the cries of hunger." There are Muslims who have set the aim of changing a certain political situation, and even if they die in doing so, their cause is advanced. The death of such persons is not a tragedy, nor does it indicate an "agitated mental state." Such a death is calculated; far from being a death of despair, it is a purposeful death in the service of a living cause. The suicide drivers who reportedly went "grinning" to their deaths were not contemplating paradise, as the media imagined, but were rejoicing in their hearts that they were able to advance their cause one step forward.[35]

Fadlallah thus retrospectively sanctioned operations that he believed had served the interests of Islam and had been carried out with full awareness of their purpose and consequences. But he himself would not issue a *fatwa;* nor would he acknowledge having sanctioned any operation in advance. He simply indicated that he had been approached by those willing to make such a sacrifice out of a full awareness and that these supplicants had been difficult to dissuade.[36]

Fadlallah's moral logic thus rested on two opposite but complementary assertions. The Muslims had just cause and need to resort to extraordinary means; yet the suicide bombings were not that extraordinary after all, and his closer analysis revealed that those Muslims who perished in such attacks died deaths that did not differ from battlefield deaths. These were the complex mechanisms of moral disengagement that permitted Islamic Jihad, in good conscience, to recruit and deploy young men in suicidal missions. Unlike simple mechanisms of disengagement, which

[35] Fadlallah lecture was delivered on 18 July 1984 and published in pamphlet form under the title *al-Muqawama al-Islamiyya fil-Junub wal-Biqa al-gharbi wa-Rashaya* (n.p., n.d.), 16–19; it was also reproduced in the collection of Fadlallah's sermons and lectures entitled *al-Muqawama al-Islamiyya: afaq wa-tatallu'at* (Beirut: 1986), 48–51.

[36] Interview with Fadlallah, *al-Majallah,* 1 October 1986. Here, too, Fadlallah criticized the American use of "psychologists and sociologists to come up with sensational phrases that will be popular with world public opinion."

culminate in dehumanization of "the other,"[37] these complex mechanisms allowed Hizballah's clerics to sanction the sacrifice of indisputably human—Muslim—lives. It was the specificity of those lives that posed the moral dilemma. Whereas a commander may know for certain that some of the soldiers in his charge may die in a conventional operation, he cannot know who among them will perish. It is God's will, or fate, or random luck that determines who will die, relieving the commander of direct and personal responsibility. But in the operations conceived by the commanders of Islamic Jihad, it was impossible to displace responsibility by the same simple process of dissociation. The clerics of Hizballah thus fashioned the necessarily complex logic that reached its highest refinement in the intellectualized reflections of Fadlallah.

Indeed, the moral logic of Fadlallah may have been too refined for Hizballah's rank and file, for his ideas were often simplified in the pronouncements of lesser clerics. A lesser cleric in Hizballah explained that suicide operations could neither be sanctioned nor banned absolutely, because their admissibility depended on circumstances and every Muslim was under a religious obligation to preserve his own life if possible. But those who carried out attacks for the good of Islam would go to paradise, and "we believe that those who carried out suicide operations against the enemy are indeed in paradise."[38] In contrast, Fadlallah never made explicit reference to the fate of the souls of those Muslims who died in the attacks. And others did not believe, as Fadlallah did, that his intellectual justifications were an adequate substitute for a formal legal ruling by a Muslim religious authority. According to one lesser cleric in Hizballah, acts of "self-martyrdom" (*istishhad,* as opposed to suicide, *intihar*) "were carried out by our youth under our inspiration. Some came to consult me about acts of self-martyrdom. I explained to them that this requires a *fatwa* from one of the highest authorities, that is, the Imams Kho'i or Khomeini, for a believer will do nothing without giving consideration to the principles of law." Three known men who carried out suicide operations against Israeli forces in South Lebanon were named as having "martyred themselves in accord with a *fatwa.*"[39] For these acts to be accepted as legitimate, many in Hizballah found intellectual justifications

---

[37] For the crucial role of moral disengagement in terrorism, see Albert Bandura's article in this volume (Chapter 9).

[38] Interview with Shaykh Ali Yasin, *al-Liwa* (Beirut), 9 July 1984. This person, originally from Majdal Silm, directs an Islamic institute in Tyre.

[39] Interview with Shaykh Yusuf Da'mush, *al-Safir* (Beirut), 14 August 1986. This person is the prayer leader of the village of al-Saksakiyya.

necessary but not sufficient; hence the popular clamor for formal *fatwas*, to which Fadlallah himself alluded. Still, the logic of such *fatwas* would not have differed in kind from the public statements by Fadlallah and Hizballah's other leaders justifying the suicide operations.

Following the withdrawal of the MNF and successive Israeli redeployments southward, the options for operations that would produce a high number of enemy casualties diminished. As time passed, similar operations were undertaken by groups that were not aligned ideologically with Hizballah. And because of various countermeasures, potential targets of such attacks became more difficult to reach and destroy, and some attempts took a significant toll in innocent Lebanese lives. At the same time, the fighters of Hizballah began to benefit from improved Iranian training in the Biqa Valley and were able to launch effective conventional operations against the South Lebanon Army.[40]

Under these altered circumstances, the method of the suicidal bombing attack was set aside. By late 1985, Fadlallah confirmed the change in approach: "We believe that suicide operations should only be carried out if they can bring about a political or military change in proportion to the passions that incite a person to make of his body an explosive bomb." Fadlallah deemed past operations against Israeli forces "successful in that they significantly harmed the Israelis. But the present circumstances do not favor such operations anymore, and attacks that only inflict limited casualties (on the enemy) and destroy one building should not be encouraged, if the price is the death of the person who carries them out."[41] Fadlallah, in essence, admitted that the legitimacy of this extraordinary method rested ultimately on its extraordinary success. When such success could no longer be assured, the many reservations that had been submerged beneath his moral logic reasserted themselves. Fadlallah and the Shi'ite clerics of Hizballah, men conscious of the dictates of Islamic law, could never allow that the mere success of these operations was their own justification. But once spectacular success began to prove elusive, all other arguments collapsed. Such attacks, done on what Fadlallah once described as "the Islamic pattern,"[42] were discontinued, and the issue ceased to figure in the running public commentary by the leaders of Hizballah.

---

[40] For Hizballah's own assessment of its military capabilities in the South (where it had about 500 men under arms), see *al-Ahd,* 12 December 1986.

[41] Interview with Fadlallah, *Monday Morning,* 16 December 1985. The Tyre and Metulla operations were those regarded as "successful."

[42] Interview with Fadlallah, *Kayhan,* 14 November 1985. Fadlallah specifically mentions the attacks on the MNF and the bombing of the "two Israeli spy centers."

Nevertheless, Sayyid Ibrahim al-Amin warned in 1986 that "suicidal operations may be used again" if opportunities presented themselves.[43] Hizballah's organization of a successful suicide bombing against Israeli forces in South Lebanon in October 1988 signalled that the method had been abandoned for tactical rather than moral reasons, and that it might be revived in changing circumstances.

Innocent hostages and Islamic morality

In July 1982, David Dodge, an American administrator at the American University of Beirut, was kidnapped by Lebanese Shi'ites with strong ties to Iran. Hostage taking had been part of the political repertoire of virtually all Lebanon's militias, but these had acted only against one another in order to intimidate opponents or to win the release of hostages held by Lebanese rivals. Foreigners felt secure from such assault, because they were not regarded by the local political factions as parties to the civil war for Lebanon. But the growth of Islamic republicanism among Lebanon's Shi'ites ended the idyll. Many of the foreigners in Lebanon were nationals of the United States and France, countries denounced by Iran as enemies of the cause of Islamic revolution in Iran, the Persian Gulf, and Lebanon. After the Dodge kidnapping, citizens of the United States and France were subjected to an intimidating campaign of hostage taking, done in part in the name of Islamic Jihad. As in the case of the suicide bombings, Hizballah's leaders consistently denied any knowledge of the persons or groups behind this campaign. But much evidence indicates that those who waged the campaign of hostage taking and hijacking were under the influence, and sometimes the control, of Iran and Hizballah.

Hostage taking and hijackings have served the cause of Islamic republicanism in Lebanon in many ways. First, the soldiers of the Islamic revolution do fall from time to time into hostile hands, and one way to secure their release is to seize and exchange hostages for Islam's prisoners of war—even when those prisoners are held elsewhere, as in the case of the Shi'ites under sentence in Kuwait for bombings committed in December 1983. The Lebanese Shi'ite who has directly controlled many of the American and some of the French hostages in Lebanon is reportedly a brother-in-law of one of the Kuwait prisoners, and his consistent demand has been their release. Second, hostages can conceivably be exchanged

---

[43] Interview with Amin, *Kayhan*, 9 February 1986.

for political or economic concessions from enemy governments; some have already been traded for U.S. arms and frozen Iranian assets. Third, the systematic taking of hostages may have the effect of driving out foreigners who come to fear for their safety. Their exodus undermines the security of local opponents who rely on foreign support and makes it more difficult for foreign spies to operate against the Islamic revolutionary party. Fourth, the holder of hostages may enjoy an immunity from attack or retaliation as long as hostages are under his roof. Fifth, the holding of hostages can make a great power appear helpless, boosting morale within the revolutionary movement. And last, the holding of hostages can bring wide attention to forms of injustice that go unnoticed unless they are dramatized.

But when hostages are innocent of all wrongdoing and are simply the means to an end, men who profess an absolute allegiance to law face a difficult dilemma. The seizure of innocents cannot be readily reconciled with Islamic law, even with the Islamic law of war. And because these acts are undertaken in the name of an Islamic cause, there is always the possibility that even fair-minded people will equate hostage taking and hijacking with Islam itself, thus doing damage to the image of Islam as a religion of tolerance and justice. Finally, as in the case of the suicide bombings, there is the ever-present danger that the method will obscure the message—that sympathy for the hostages will destroy all empathy for the Muslims whose victimization first prompted the hostage taking or hijacking.

Once again it fell to Hizballah to articulate a moral logic, this time for seizing and threatening the lives of foreigners. The simplest justification was to say that foreigners taken hostage were themselves guilty of some transgression against the Muslims, specifically that they were spies. According to Shaykh Subhi al-Tufayli, "Imperialism has agents and spies throughout the world. It is our right and the right of every person in the world to follow the moves of such agents and to arrest those who have been indicted." Such agents could hide behind a diplomatic or cultural guise, and arresting them was a matter of self-defense.[44] Husayn al-Musawi also approved of kidnappings "if the hostages are spies and agents and are there for mischief against Muslims."[45] But this justification was necessarily thin. For by its logic, all those taken hostage and then discovered not to be spies should have been released. And no one was so cred-

---

[44] Interview with Tufayli, *al-Ittihad al-usbu'i,* 4 December 1986.
[45] Interview with Husayn al-Musawi, *al-Ittihad,* 12 December 1986.

ulous as to believe that all the foreign hostages—including the hijacked passengers of TWA Flight 847 and persons snatched at random on West Beirut's streets—were indeed spies. The prolonged detention of foreigners who were personally innocent demanded a more complex justification.

Even the official spokesman of Hizballah had difficulty producing one. When Sayyid Ibrahim al-Amin was asked how Islamic law interpreted the kidnapping of foreign diplomats and journalists, he said that this was not his business and that the kidnappers themselves should be "asked about the question of Islamic law in this matter."[46] This kind of evasion did not befit a Shi'ite cleric, who is generally expected to have his own interpretation or to adopt an interpretation of a scholar whom he regards as more learned. Husayn al-Musawi also knew of no unequivocal justification in Islamic law for such an act. When asked about the Islamic view of holding innocents, he simply replied that "it is the same as with alcohol. Alcohol is forbidden under Islam, but when it is a medicine you are allowed to take as much as you need for your recovery."[47] It was a weak analogy, but Husayn al-Musawi had no schooling in Islamic law.

A cleric with Hizballah affiliations argued that the hostages were taken in order to assure the freedom of Muslim peoples from the "captivity" of colonialism. "Just as freedom is demanded for a handful of Europeans, it is also demanded for the millions of Muslims."[48] Yet it was well known that the most important demand of the hostage holders was the release of specific groups of Shi'ite Muslims held by Israel and Kuwait. Hizballah's own official statements regarding the TWA hijacking and the holding of French and American hostages simply argued that these acts were justifiable because of "extenuating circumstances." The TWA hijacking was sanctioned because it "awakened human consciences" to Israel's "abduction" of 700 Shi'ite detainees to "occupied Palestine." How could the United States approve of Israel's action, yet criticize the hijackers for holding only 40 hostages?[49] As for the kidnapping of Americans and Frenchmen, Hizballah determined that both countries had attempted to "drive the oppressed up against the wall," and their victims had "no other choice than to adopt this means."[50] Sayyid Abbas al-Musawi said

---

[46] Interview with Ibrahim al-Amin, *al-Majallah*, 19 March 1986.
[47] DPA (Beirut), 4 February 1987; quoted in *Daily Report: Middle East and Africa* (Washington, D.C.: Foreign Broadcast Information Service—FBIS), 5 February 1987.
[48] Interview with Sadiq al-Musawi, *al-Nahar al-arabi wal-duwali*, 28 July 1986.
[49] Hizballah statement, *al-Safir*, 29 June 1985.
[50] AFP (Beirut), 13 May 1986; quoted in FBIS, 14 May 1986.

the same, when asked whether the "oppressed" were responsible for the hostage taking: "Only the United States, France and Israel are responsible, since they provoke such actions by their hateful policy toward the Muslim people and their barbaric practices, the consequences of which they must accept."[51]

The thinness of this logic demonstrated a lack of intellectual resourcefulness and legal acumen—those very qualities that so clearly distinguished Fadlallah from Hizballah's other clerics and rendered him so indispensable to the movement. But Fadlallah himself would not provide a compelling moral logic for the hostage taking and kidnapping, because he had reached the conclusion that neither could be justified on Islamic moral and legal grounds. The sanction Fadlallah had bestowed upon the self-sacrificing bomber he withheld from the kidnapper and hijacker of innocents.

It was true that there were positive aspects to such acts; Fadlallah did not abandon his principle that "there is evil in everything good and something good in every evil." The Islamic movement indisputably benefited from using the hostages to exert pressure on the United States and France and force them to alter their policies.[52] Important issues were brought before world public opinion that otherwise would have been ignored.[53] These were pragmatic arguments in favor of the acts, but they could also be justified in limited moral terms. Those responsible for the hijacking of the TWA flight and the kidnapping of foreigners were in a "tight spot," anxious for the safe release of their own relatives; theirs was also a humanitarian cause. And who were the Americans and French to preach against hostage taking and hijacking—those who set up the kidnapping of Ben Barka and hijacked the plane of Ben Bella?[54]

The intractability of the hostage problem became the fault of the Americans, who created a deadlock by turning an apolitical bid for the release of relatives into a matter of principle in an American war against terrorism. Fadlallah saw the problem of kidnapped foreigners in the same light as the problem of kidnapped Lebanese: "We know that those who kidnap a Lebanese citizen in East or West Beirut do so in order to obtain the release of another kidnapped person." So it was when foreigners in

[51] Interview with Abbas al-Musawi, *La Revue du Liban*, 27 July 1985.
[52] Interview with Fadlallah, *La Vanguardia* (Barcelona), 9 November 1986; quoted in FBIS, 17 November 1986.
[53] Interview with Fadlallah, *al-Nahar al-arabi wal-duwali*, 21 July 1986.
[54] Interviews with Fadlallah, *al-Nahar al-arabi wal-duwali*, 1 July 1985; *al-Mustaqbal*, 6 July 1985; *al-Ittihad al-usbu'i*, 30 January 1986.

Lebanon were first kidnapped.[55] Had the Americans dealt with the matter in "a practical way," by accepting an exchange "according to the Lebanese practice," the hostage affair "would have ended and its file would have been closed without further suffering." Instead, the Americans hopelessly complicated the affair by placing it in the realm of international terrorism. The U.S. government could then use the hostage issue to generate a "political and security program" against the "Islamic movement" and then exploit it as a means to reopen a dialogue with Iran.[56]

Yet when all was said and done, Fadlallah's verdict went against the hijackers and hostage takers. His simplest objection was that these actions harmed the image of Islam and seriously undermined his own campaign to persuade all and sundry that an Islamic Lebanon would be a more just and equitable Lebanon, for Christian and Muslim alike. Opposition to Islamic republicanism fed on the perception of Islam as a faith of fanatic extremism. Fadlallah lamented that "in Western public opinion, it has become popular to think that terrorism is linked to the revival of Islam, and that extremism and related violence are natural Islamic traits, revealing the true face of the religion."[57] Fadlallah sought to dispel this image of Islam through a brilliant combination of candor and guile.

Since the deeds of hijackers and hostage takers seemed bold and courageous to many in Hizballah, Fadlallah first had to make the "nation" of Hizballah aware of their cost. Particular targets of hostage takers and even assassins were the faculty members of the American University of Beirut (AUB), an institution considered by many in Hizballah to be a bastion of corrupting influence. Fadlallah agreed that a conflict existed between the "Western system of education" and "Islamic ideology," but the haphazard kidnapping of professors would not bring about AUB's closure, and it cast Islam in an utterly negative light. The proper approach was to transform the university by transforming its students, through the confident preaching of Islam's message.[58]

Other common targets of hostage takers were the foreign correspondents stationed in Beirut; there was a widespread suspicion in Hizballah that hostile spies made extensive use of journalistic cover. But Fadlallah saw the role of journalists as an essential one in his campaign of persua-

---

[55] Interview with Fadlallah, *al-Hawadith* (London), 13 February 1987.
[56] Interviews with Fadlallah, *al-Ra'y al-Amm* (Kuwait), 3 April 1986; *al-Nahar al-arabi wal-duwali*, 9 February 1987.
[57] Fadlallah, "Islam and Violence in Political Reality," *Middle East Insight* 4, nos. 4–5 (1986): 7.
[58] Interview with Fadlallah, *al-Khalij*, 28 June 1986.

sion. Foreign journalists often sought him out, making him one of Lebanon's most interviewed personalities and providing Hizballah with access to readers and viewers throughout the world. In this light, the kidnapping of foreign journalists was positively harmful to the cause, even if there were some spies among them. In one instance, Terry Anderson, the bureau chief of the Associated Press in Beirut, was kidnapped "a day after he had interviewed me,"[59] a move that Fadlallah obviously regarded as a personal affront because it threatened his own easy access to the press. "We should help journalists in their task to inform, whatever the negative aspects may be."[60]

But Fadlallah invoked a more consequential logic for his stand, in his capacity as an authoritative interpreter of Islam's moral and legal precepts. The hijacking and kidnapping of innocent persons constituted wrongful punishment and contradicted the teachings of Islam. It was "forbidden to kidnap or kill an innocent person because one has a score to settle with a head of state."[61] The *Qur'an* taught that no one should take on himself the burden of another soul, that "if a father commits a sin you are not permitted to punish his son, because God has made everyone responsible for what he has done." Fadlallah explicitly defined hijacking and kidnapping as "inhumane and irreligious" and an "un-Islamic method." For all anyone knew, the victims "might be opposed to the regime against which the hijacking operation is directed" and "opposed to the policies of their own governments." These innocent persons bore no responsibility for the wrongs done to the Muslims. What was their crime? If they were indeed spies, as hostage takers sometimes claimed, they should immediately be tried for espionage. If they were not spies, they should be released, not bartered. Fadlallah adhered to this position not only in interviews with journalists but in his Friday sermons from the pulpit of his own mosque in Beirut's southern suburbs. He not only denied allegations of personal involvement in these acts but declared, "I would not have any self-respect if I had anything to do with them."[62]

Indeed, Fadlallah claimed to be actively working for the release of

[59] Interview with Fadlallah, *Kayhan International* (Tehran), 23 July 1985.

[60] Fadlallah on kidnapping of French television journalists, AFP (Beirut), 12 March 1986; quoted in FBIS, 12 March 1986.

[61] Fadlallah on fate of a French television journalist, AFP (Beirut), 15 March 1987; quoted in FBIS, 16 March 1987.

[62] Fadlallah, "Islam and Violence in Political Reality"; interviews with Fadlallah, *al-Nahar al-arabi wal-duwali*, 1 July 1985; *Kayhan International*, 23 July 1985; *Kayhan*, 14 November 1985; *al-Majallah*, 25 December 1985; Fadlallah Friday sermon, *al-Ahd*, 6 December 1985.

hostages, and he met with the many mediators who clamored to see him. His purpose, he declared, was to "create a psychological situation that would bring pressure to bear on the kidnappers themselves."[63] Fadlallah's denial of sanction for these acts left the justifications to Hizballah's lesser clerics, who were not up to the task and were reluctant to challenge directly Fadlallah's more authoritative reading of Islamic precepts. And so the hostage takers themselves were forced to plead their own case in any way they could, usually through letters to the Lebanese press and videotapes of the hostages reading messages from the captors. These became more lengthy and frequent, but they could not match the eloquent locutions of Fadlallah.

And so consensus eluded Hizballah regarding the extraordinary means of hostage taking. Fadlallah's preaching created a moral dilemma for Hizballah and necessitated a more careful reformulation of Hizballah's own position. Husayn al-Musawi continued to support the kidnapping of "spies or military personnel," actions that were "undoubtedly useful" to the cause. But hostage taking had gotten out of hand after "some excited Muslims in Beirut" began to take "anyone off the streets." No good had come of these ill-conceived operations, and Muslims were now widely regarded as kidnappers. Hostage taking had become "chaotic," overshadowing and tarnishing "the major acts of hostage taking which were done to serve the nation of Hizballah." Musawi's was a plea for discriminate rather than indiscriminate hostage taking, in accord with what he called "Islamic decision-making"—a euphemism in Hizballah's lexicon for Iran.[64] Musawi even reached the conclusion that if hostages were innocent, then "I am against hostage taking, even if the captives are American or French."[65] Subhi al-Tufayli also concluded that the hostage situation "harms the Islamic cause."[66]

The growing unease in Hizballah over the method of hostage taking had its origins in the moral logic of Fadlallah, who sought to serve as the movement's unacknowledged conscience. But if hostage deals should ever begin to provide substantial benefits to Hizballah, that may force a change in his moral logic by altering perceptions of cost and benefit in hostage taking. Fadlallah responded to the spectacular success of the suicide

[63] Interview with Fadlallah, *al-Hawadith*, 27 March 1987.
[64] Interview with Husayn al-Musawi, *Kayhan*, 29 July 1986.
[65] Interview with Husayn al-Musawi, *al-Ittihad*, 12 December 1986. Still, he favored the "abduction and trial" of Presidents Reagan and Mitterrand; interview with Husayn al-Musawi, *al-Nahar*, 1 November 1985.
[66] Tufayli on kidnapping, AFP (Beirut), 30 March 1987; quoted in FBIS, 31 March 1987.

bombings by overcoming his "reservations" and creating a moral logic that justified the attacks. If hostage taking were ever to be regarded in Hizballah as a great success in its own right, Fadlallah's moral objections might dissolve into simple reservations, permitting a reformulation of his moral logic in subtle but significant ways. For he is not locked into his current position. He has never issued a formal *fatwa* forbidding all hostage taking. He has even hesitated to issue a *fatwa* regarding proper conduct when a hostage falls seriously ill. Although Fadlallah has taken a position on hostage taking, he has not staked his professional reputation as a jurist on his stand. Those who actually hold the hostages have been able to resist the "psychological situation" that Fadlallah seeks to create, precisely because he has not issued a definitive ruling. Finally, Fadlallah is wary lest he be caught contradicting Khomeini, who never issued a ruling on hostage taking and whose silence has been understood by the hostage holders as an implicit endorsement. When they have given up hostages, it has been at the bidding of Iran, not Fadlallah.

Hizballah's continuing dialectic

Hizballah is divided over the question of hostage taking. That is perhaps inevitable, for Hizballah began as a coalition and it remains one. The movement is devoted to one purpose: the eventual establishment of an Islamic state in Lebanon. But its leaders continue to debate among themselves the morality and legality of the means to that elusive end. The extraordinary means employed by some within the coalition have prompted an extraordinary debate. It is unusual because in Shi'ite Islam, only the cleric can morally disengage the common believer from his acts. In that limited sense, bombers, hijackers, and hostage takers are morally dependent on Hizballah and Iran, and the verdicts of their learned scholars are hardly academic. Yet their interpretations of Islam's dictates often differ in important and even fundamental ways. The evidence for their debate in interviews and speeches only hints at what must be an intense internal disputation over the future course of the "nation" of Hizballah.

As a coalition, Hizballah is liable at any time to split. Yet Lebanon's tribulations seem only to strengthen it. Hizballah has seen its enemies retreat time and again, reinforcing its view that Lebanon's crisis will be resolved through Hizballah's ultimate triumph. But Syria proposes a very different resolution to that crisis, one in which Hizballah has no place. The movement cannot confront Syria in conventional ways and expect victory. Hizballah is also unlikely to succeed in its bid to rid South Lebanon of all Israeli political and military influence if it resorts only to conventional methods. The debate over extraordinary means will not soon end.

Part III

States of mind:
How do terrorists think? Which psychological
mechanisms enable them to do what they do?

9

Mechanisms of moral disengagement

ALBERT BANDURA

Self-sanction plays a central role in the regulation of inhumane conduct. In the course of socialization, people adopt moral standards that serve as guides and deterrents for conduct. Once internalized control has developed, people regulate their actions by the sanctions they apply to themselves. They do things that give them satisfaction and build their sense of self-worth. They refrain from behaving in ways that violate their moral standards, because such behavior would bring self-condemnation. Self-sanctions thus keep conduct in line with internal standards.

But moral standards do not function as fixed internal regulators of conduct. Self-regulatory mechanisms do not operate unless they are activated, and there are many psychological processes by which moral reactions can be disengaged from inhumane conduct.[1] Selective activation and disengagement of internal control permits different types of conduct by persons with the same moral standards. Figure 9.1 shows the points in the self-regulatory process at which internal moral control can be disengaged from destructive conduct. Self-sanctions can be disengaged by reconstruing conduct as serving moral purposes, by obscuring personal agency in detrimental activities, by disregarding or misrepresenting the injurious consequences of one's actions, or by blaming and dehumanizing the victims. The way in which these moral disengagement practices

Preparation of this chapter was facilitated by Public Health Research Grant MH-5162-25 from the National Institute of Mental Health. Some sections of this chapter include revised and expanded material from the book, *Social Foundations of Thought and Action: A Social Cognitive Theory* (Englewood Cliffs, N.J.: Prentice-Hall, 1986).
[1] A. Bandura, *Social Foundations of Thought and Action: A Social Cognitive Theory* (Englewood Cliffs, N.J.: Prentice-Hall, 1986).

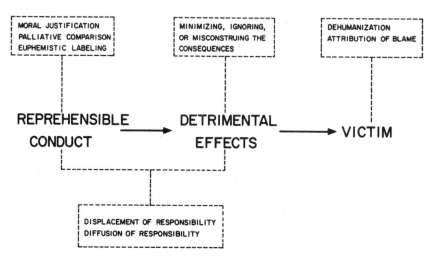

Figure 9.1. Psychosocial mechanisms through which internal control is selectively disengaged from detrimental conduct at three major points in the self-regulatory process. These include reconstruing conduct, obscuring causal agency, distorting consequences, and blaming and devaluating the targets.

operate in the execution of inhumanities is analyzed in considerable detail later in this chapter.

These psychosocial mechanisms of moral disengagement have been examined most extensively in relation to political and military violence. This limited focus tends to convey the impression that selective disengagement of moral self-sanctions occurs only under extraordinary circumstances. Quite the contrary: Such mechanisms operate in everyday situations in which decent people routinely perform activities that further their interests but have injurious human effects. Self-exonerations are needed to eliminate self-prohibitions and self-devaluation. This chapter analyzes how the mechanisms of moral disengagement function in terrorist operations.

Terrorism is usually defined as a strategy of violence designed to promote desired outcomes by instilling fear in the public at large.[2] Public intimidation is a key element that distinguishes terrorist violence from other forms of violence. In contrast to the customary violence in which victims are personally targeted, in terrorism the victims are incidental to the terrorists' intended objectives and are used simply as a way to pro-

[2] M. C. Bassiouni, "Terrorism, Law Enforcement, and the Mass Media: Perspectives, Problems, Proposals," *Journal of Criminal Law and Criminology* 72 (1981): 1–51.

voke social conditions designed to further their broader aims. Third-party violence is especially socially terrorizing when the victimization is generalized to the civilian population and is unpredictable, thereby instilling a widespread sense of personal vulnerability.

The term *terrorism* is often applied to violent acts that dissident groups direct surreptitiously at officials of regimes to force social or political changes. So defined, terrorism becomes indistinguishable from straightforward political violence. Particularized threats are certainly intimidating to the martial and political figures who are personally targeted for assassination and create some apprehension over destabilizing societal effects, but such threats do not necessarily terrify the general public so long as ordinary civilians are not targeted as the objects of victimization. (As is shown later, terrorist tactics relying on public intimidation can serve other purposes as well as a political weapon.)

From a psychological standpoint, third-party violence directed at innocent people is a much more horrific undertaking than political violence in which particular political figures are targeted. It is easier to get people who harbor strong grievances to kill hated political officials or to abduct advisers and consular staffs of foreign nations that support repressive regimes. However, to slaughter in cold blood innocent women and children in buses, in department stores, and in airports requires more powerful psychological machinations of moral disengagement. Intensive psychological training in moral disengagement is needed to create the capacity to kill innocent human beings as a way of toppling rulers or regimes or of accomplishing other political goals.

Moral justification

One set of disengagement practices operates on the construal of the behavior itself. People do not ordinarily engage in reprehensible conduct until they have justified to themselves the morality of their actions. What is culpable can be made honorable through cognitive reconstrual. In this process, destructive conduct is made personally and socially acceptable by portraying it in the service of moral purposes. People then act on a moral imperative. Radical shifts in destructive behavior through moral justification are most strikingly revealed in military conduct.

People who have been socialized to deplore killing as morally condemnable can be transformed rapidly into skilled combatants, who may feel little compunction and even a sense of pride in taking human life.

Moral reconstrual of killing is dramatically illustrated by the case of Sergeant York, one of the phenomenal fighters in the history of modern warfare.[3] Because of his deep religious convictions, Sergeant York registered as a conscientious objector, but his numerous appeals were denied. At camp, his battalion commander quoted chapter and verse from the Bible to persuade him that under appropriate conditions it was Christian to fight and kill. A marathon mountainside prayer finally convinced him that he could serve both God and country by becoming a dedicated fighter.

The conversion of socialized people into dedicated combatants is not achieved by altering their personality structures, aggressive drives, or moral standards. Rather, it is accomplished by cognitively restructuring the moral value of killing, so that the killing can be done free from self-censuring restraints.[4] Through moral sanction of violent means, people see themselves as fighting ruthless oppressors who have an unquenchable appetite for conquest, protecting their cherished values and way of life, preserving world peace, saving humanity from subjugation to an evil ideology, and honoring their country's international commitments. The task of making violence morally defensible is facilitated when nonviolent options are judged to have been ineffective and utilitarian justifications portray the suffering caused by violent counterattacks as greatly outweighed by the human suffering inflicted by the foe.

Over the years, much reprehensible and destructive conduct has been perpetrated by ordinary, decent people in the name of religious principles, righteous ideologies, and nationalistic imperatives. Throughout history, countless people have suffered at the hands of self-righteous crusaders bent on stamping out what they consider evil. Elsewhere, Rapoport and Alexander have documented the lengthy blood-stained history of holy terror wrought by religious justifications. Acting on moral or ideological imperatives reflects a conscious offense mechanism, not an unconscious defense mechanism.[5]

Although moral cognitive restructuring can easily be used to support self-serving and destructive purposes, it can also serve militant action aimed at changing inhumane social conditions. By appealing to morality, social reformers are able to use coercive, and even violent, tactics to force

[3] T. Skeyhill, ed., *Sergeant York: His Own Life Story and War Diary* (Garden City, N.Y.: Doubleday, Doran, 1928).
[4] H. C. Kelman, "Violence without Moral Restraint: Reflections on the Dehumanization of Victims and Victimizers," *Journal of Social Issues* 29 (1973): 25–61; and N. Sanford and C. Comstock, *Sanctions for Evil* (San Francisco: Jossey-Bass, 1971).
[5] D. C. Rapoport and Y. Alexander, eds., *The Morality of Terrorism: Religious and Secular Justification* (Elmsford, N.Y.: Pergamon Press, 1982).

social change. Vigorous disputes arise over the morality of aggressive action directed against institutional practices. Power holders often resist, by forcible means if necessary, making needed social changes that jeopardize their own self-interest. Such tactics provoke social activism. Challengers consider their militant actions to be morally justifiable because they serve to eradicate harmful social practices. Power holders condemn violent means as unjustified and unnecessary because nonviolent means exist to effect social change. They tend to view resorts to violence as efforts to coerce changes that lack popular support. Finally, they may argue that terrorist acts are condemnable because they violate civilized standards of conduct. Anarchy would flourish in a climate in which individuals considered violent tactics acceptable whenever they disliked particular social practices or policies.

Challengers refute such moral arguments by appealing to what they regard as a higher level of morality, derived from communal concerns. They see their constituencies as comprising all people, both at home and abroad, who are victimized either directly or indirectly by injurious social practices. Challengers argue that, when many people benefit from a system that is deleterious to disfavored segments of the society, the harmful social practices secure widespread public support. From the challengers' perspective, they are acting under a moral imperative to stop the maltreatment of people who have no way of modifying injurious social policies, either because they are outside the system that victimizes them, or because they lack the social power to effect changes from within by peaceable means. They regard militant action as the only recourse available to them.

Clearly, adversaries can easily marshal moral reasons for the use of aggressive actions for social control or for social change. Different people view violent acts in different ways. In conflicts of power, one person's violence is another person's selfless benevolence. It is often proclaimed that one group's criminal terroristic activity is another group's liberation movement fought by heroic freedom fighters. This is why moral appeals against violence usually fall on deaf ears. Adversaries sanctify their own militant actions but condemn those of their antagonists as barbarity masquerading behind a mask of outrageous moral reasoning.

Moral justification of counterterrorist measures

So far, the discussion has centered on how terrorists invoke moral principles to justify human atrocities. Moral justification is also brought into play in selecting counterterrorist measures. This poses more troublesome problems for democratic societies than for totalitarian ones. Totalitarian regimes have fewer constraints against using institutional power to control media coverage of terrorist events, to restrict individual rights, to sacrifice individuals for the benefit of the state rather than to make concessions to terrorists, and to combat threats with lethal means. Terrorists can wield greater power over nations that place high value on human life and are thereby constrained in the ways they can act.

Hostage taking has become a common terrorist strategy for wielding control over governments. If nations make the release of hostages a dominant national concern, they place themselves in a highly manipulable position. Tightly concealed captivity thwarts rescue action. Heightened national attention, along with an inability to free hostages independently, conveys a sense of weakness and invests terrorists with considerable importance and coercive power to extract concessions. Overreactions in which nations render themselves hostage to a small band of terrorists inspire and invite further terrorist acts. In contrast, hostage taking is stripped of functional value if it is treated as a criminal act that gains terrorists neither any coercive concessionary power nor much media attention.

Democratic societies face the dilemma of how to morally justify countermeasures that will stop terrorists' atrocities without violating the societies' own fundamental principles and standards of civilized conduct.[6] A set of critical conditions under which violent counterattacks are morally justified can be spelled out. It is generally considered legitimate to resort to violent defense in response to grave threats that inflict extensive human suffering or endanger the very survival of the society. But the criterion of "grave threat," while fine in principle, is slippery in specific application. Like most human judgments, gauging the gravity of threats involves some subjectivity. Moreover, violence is often used as a weapon against threats of lesser magnitude on the grounds that, if left unchecked, they will escalate in severity to the point at which they will eventually exact a high toll in loss of liberties and in suffering. Gauging potential gravity involves even greater subjectivity and fallibility of judgment than does assessment of present danger. Construal of gravity prescribes choice of options, but choice of violent options also often shapes construal of gravity. Thus, projected grave dangers to the society are commonly in-

[6]D. J. C. Carmichael, "Of Beasts, Gods, and Civilized Men: The Justification of Terrorism and of Counterterrorist Measures," *Terrorism* 6 (1982): 1–26.

voked to morally justify violent means that are used to squelch limited present threats.

It is hard to find any inherent moral rightness in violent acts that are designed to kill assailants or to deter them from future assaults but that inevitably risk the lives of some innocent people as well. Because of many uncertain factors, the toll that counterterrorist assaults take on innocent life is neither easily controllable nor accurately calculable in advance. To sacrifice innocent lives in the process of punishing terrorists raises fundamental moral problems. Democratic societies that happen to kill some innocent people in the process of counterterrorist actions find themselves in the vexing predicament of violating the values of their society in defense of those values. Therefore, the use of violent countermeasures is typically justified on utilitarian grounds—that is, in terms of the benefits to humanity and the social order that curbing terrorist attacks will bring. On the assumption that fighting terror with terror will achieve a deterrent effect, it is argued that retaliatory assaults will reduce the total amount of human suffering. As Carmichael notes, utilitarian justifications place few constraints on violent countermeasures because, in the utilitarian calculus, sacrificing the lives of some innocent persons can be greatly outweighed by the halt to repeated massacres and the perpetual terrorizing of entire populations.[7]

Public intimidation and judgments of retaliatory violence

Several features of terrorist acts give power to a few incidents to incite widespread public fear that vastly exceeds the objective threat. The first such feature is the unpredictability of terrorist acts. It is impossible to predict when or where a terrorist act will occur. When people are threatened by someone they know, their fears are circumscribed, because they can judge when they are safe and when they are at risk. In contrast, violent acts in which assailants pick victims and places of attack unpredictably instill the strongest phobic fear because everyone is continually vulnerable.[8]

The second feature is the gravity of the consequences. Terrorist acts maim and kill. People are unwilling to risk such threats even though the chance of being victimized by a terrorist attack is extremely low. Indeed,

[7] Ibid.
[8] L. Heath, "Impact of Newspaper Crime Reports on Fear of Crime: Multimethodological Investigation," *Journal of Personality and Social Psychology* 47 (1984): 263–76.

domestic crime takes an infinitely heavier toll on human life day in and day out than do the sporadic terrorist acts. But domestic crime arouses much less public fear because most homicides involve acquaintances. The incidence rates of terrorist acts, of course, increase substantially if the definition of terrorism is expanded to include state violence in which tyrannical regimes terrorize their own people.

A third feature of terrorist acts that renders them so terrorizing is the sense of uncontrollability that they instill. People believe that they can exercise no control over whether they might be victimized. Perceived self-inefficacy in coping with potential threats activates fear and self-protective courses of action.[9] The risk of being maimed or killed from driving an automobile is infinitely higher than from falling victim to a terrorist act. But people fear terrorists more than their cars, because they believe they can exercise personal control over the chance of injury by the care with which they drive. The combination of unpredictability, gravity, and perceived self-inefficacy is especially intimidating and socially constraining.

The fourth feature is the high centralization and interdependency of essential service systems in modern-day life. When people were widely dispersed in small communities, the consequences of a violent act affected mainly the persons toward whom the behavior was directed. In urbanized life the welfare of entire populations depends on functional communications, transportation and power systems, and safe water and food supplies. Because these service activities are controlled from centralized sources, they are highly vulnerable to disruption or destruction. A single destructive act that requires no elaborate apparatus to perform can instantly frighten or harm a vast number of people. Thus, for example, poisoning a few imported Israeli oranges aroused widespread alarm in the importing nations. Drugstore terrorism—the poisoning of a few packages of patent medicine—struck fear in an entire population and forced elaborate safeguards in packaging. People shun countries and airlines that have been the object of terrorist attacks. Airline hijacking and the development of sophisticated explosive devices have imposed escalating financial burdens on societies by requiring costly electronic surveillance and bomb detection systems. In short, the actual number of terrorist acts may be relatively few, but the fear of terrorism affects the lives of vast populations.

Efforts to reduce societal vulnerabilities with better counterterrorist

[9] Bandura, *Social Foundations of Thought and Action.*

technologies beget better terrorist tactics and devices. A security officer characterized such escalating adaptations well when he remarked, "For every 10-foot wall you erect, terrorists will build an 11-foot ladder." Technological advances are producing highly sophisticated terrorizing devices that increase societal vulnerability to attack. Supportive nations and former intelligence operatives who have become terrorism entrepreneurs—aided by international networks of former military officers, government officials, and weapons merchants—readily supply the world's terrorists with the most advanced lethal tools.

In coping with problems of terrorism, societies face a dual task: how to reduce terrorist acts and how to combat the fear of terrorism. Because the number of terrorist acts is small, the widespread public fear and the intrusive and costly security countermeasures pose the more serious problems. Utilitarian justifications can readily win the support of a frightened public for violent counterterrorist measures. A frightened and angered populace does not spend much time agonizing over the morality of lethal modes of self-defense. Should any concern arise over the taking of innocent lives, it can be assuaged by stripping the victims of their innocence by blaming them for not controlling the terrorists in their midst. The perturbing appearance of national impotence in the face of terrorist acts creates additional social pressures on targeted nations to strike back powerfully.

Extreme counterterrorist reactions may produce effects that are worse than the terrorist acts themselves. Widespread retaliatory death and destruction may advance the political cause of terrorists by arousing a backlash of sympathy for innocent victims and moral condemnation of the brutal nature of the counterreactions. To fight terror with terror often spawns new terrorists and provides new justifications for violence that are more likely to escalate terrorism than to diminish it. Indeed, some terrorist activities are designed precisely to provoke curtailment of personal liberties and other domestic repressive measures that might breed public disaffection with the system. Extreme countermeasures can, thus, play into the hands of terrorists.

Euphemistic labeling

Language shapes thought patterns on which people base many of their actions. Activities can take on a very different appearance depending on what they are called. Euphemistic language thus provides a convenient device for masking reprehensible activities or even conferring a respectable status on them. Through convoluted verbiage, destructive conduct is made benign and people who engage in it are relieved of a sense of personal agency. Laboratory studies reveal the disinhibitory power of euphemistic language.[10] Adults behave much more aggressively when given opportunities to assault a person when assaultive acts are given a sanitized athletic label than when they are called aggression. In an insightful analysis of the language of nonresponsibility, Gambino identifies the different varieties of euphemisms.[11] One form, palliative expressions, is widely used to make the reprehensible respectable. Through the power of hygienic words, even killing a human being loses much of its repugnancy. Soldiers "waste" people rather than kill them, intelligence operatives "terminate (them) with extreme prejudice."[12] When mercenaries speak of "fulfilling a contract," murder is transformed by admirable words into the honorable discharge of duty. Terrorists label themselves "freedom fighters." Bombing attacks become "clean, surgical strikes," invoking imagery of the restorative handicrafts of the operating room, and the civilians they kill are linguistically converted to "collateral damage."[13] Sanitizing euphemisms, of course, perform heavy duty in less loathsome but unpleasant activities that people are called on to do from time to time.

The agentless passive form serves as a linguistic device for creating the appearance that culpable acts are the work of nameless forces, rather than people.[14] It is as though people are moved mechanically but are not really the agents of their own acts. Gambino further documents how the jargon of a legitimate enterprise can be misused to lend an aura of respectability to an illegitimate one. Deadly activities are framed as "game plans," and the perpetrators become "team players" calling for the qualities and behavior befitting the best sportsmen. The disinhibitory power of language can be boosted further by colorful metaphors that change the nature of culpable activities.

[10] E. Diener, J. Dineen, K. Endresen, A. L. Beaman, and S. C. Fraser, "Effects of Altered Responsibility, Cognitive Set, and Modeling on Physical Aggression and Deindividuation," *Journal of Personality and Social Psychology* 31 (1975): 143–56.

[11] R. Gambino, "Watergate Lingo: A Language on Non-Responsibility," *Freedom at Issue* 22 (November–December 1973): 7–9, 15–17.

[12] W. Safire, "The Fine Art of Euphemism," *San Francisco Chronicle*, 13 May 1979, p. 13.

[13] S. Hilgartner, R. C. Bell, and R. O'Connor, *Nukespeak: Nuclear Language, Visions, and Mindset* (San Francisco: Sierra Club Books, 1982).

[14] D. Bolinger, *Language: The Loaded Weapon* (London: Longman, 1982).

Advantageous comparison

Whenever events occur or are presented contiguously, the first one colors how the second one is perceived and judged. By exploiting the contrast principle, moral judgments of conduct can be influenced by the expedient structuring of what it is compared against. Self-deplored acts can be made to appear righteous by contrasting them with flagrant inhumanities. The more outrageous the comparison practices, the more likely it is that one's own destructive conduct will appear trifling or even benevolent. Thus, terrorists minimize their slayings as the only defensive weapon they have to curb the widespread cruelties inflicted on their people. In the eyes of their supporters, risky attacks directed at the apparatus of oppression are acts of selflessness and martyrdom. People who are objects of terrorist attacks, in turn, characterize their retaliatory violence as trifling, or even laudable, by comparing them with carnage and terror perpetrated by terrorists. In social conflicts, injurious behavior usually escalates, with each side lauding its own behavior but condemning that of its adversaries as heinous.

Advantageous comparisons are also drawn from history to justify violence. Advocates of terrorist tactics are quick to note that the democracies of Britain, France, and the United States were born of violence against oppressive rule. A former director of the CIA effectively deflected, by advantageous comparison, embarrassing questions about the morality and legality of CIA-directed covert operations designed to overthrow an authoritarian regime. He explained that French covert operations and military supplies greatly aided the overthrow of oppressive British rule during the American Revolution, thereby creating the modern model of democracy for other subjugated people to emulate.[15]

Social comparison is similarly used to show that the social labeling of acts as terrorism depends more on the ideological allegiances of the labelers than on the acts themselves. Airline hijackings were applauded as heroic deeds when East Europeans and Cubans initiated this practice, but condemned as terrorist acts when the airlines of Western nations and friendly countries were commandeered. The degree of psychopathology ascribed to hijackers varied with the direction of the rerouted flights. Moral condemnations of politically motivated terrorism are easily blunted by social comparison because, in international contests for political power,

---

[15] Brief comment by Colby on television during the Irangate hearings.

it is hard to find nations that categorically condemn terrorism. Rather, they usually back some terrorists and oppose others.

Cognitive restructuring of behavior through moral justifications and palliative characterizations is the most effective psychological mechanism for promoting destructive conduct. This is because moral restructuring not only eliminates self-deterrents but engages self-approval in the service of destructive exploits. What was once morally condemnable becomes a source of self-valuation. After destructive means become invested with high moral purpose, functionaries work hard to become proficient at them and take pride in their destructive accomplishments.

Moral justifications and the media

The mass media, especially television, provide the best access to the public because of the media's strong drawing power. For this reason, television is increasingly used as the principal vehicle of social and moral justifications of goals and actions. Struggles to legitimize and gain support for one's causes, and to discredit the causes of one's foes, are now waged more and more through the electronic media.[16]

Terrorists try to exercise influence over targeted officials or nations through intimidation of the public and arousal of sympathy for the social and political causes they espouse. Without widespread publicity, terrorist acts can achieve neither of these effects. Terrorists, therefore, coerce access to the media in order to publicize their grievances to the international community. They use television as the main instrument for gaining sympathy and supportive action for their plight by presenting themselves as risking their lives for the welfare of a victimized constituency whose legitimate grievances are ignored. The media, in turn, come under heavy fire from targeted officials who regard granting terrorists a worldwide forum as aiding terrorist causes. Security forces do not like media personnel to track their conduct and broadcast tactical information that terrorists can put to good use, or to interpose themselves as intermediaries in risky negotiation situations. Social pressures mount to curtail media coverage of terrorist events, especially while they are in progress.[17]

[16] S. J. Ball-Rokeach, "The Legitimation of Violence," in *Collective Violence,* edited by J. F. Short, Jr., and M. E. Wolfgang (Chicago: Aldine-Atherton, 1972).
[17] M. C. Bassiouni, "Terrorism, Law Enforcement, and the Mass Media: Perspectives, Problems, Proposals," *Journal of Criminal Law and Criminology* 72 (1981): 1–51.

Displacement of responsibility

Another set of dissociative practices operates by obscuring or distorting the relationship between actions and the effects they cause. People behave in injurious ways they normally repudiate if a legitimate authority accepts responsibility for the consequences of their conduct.[18] Under conditions of displaced responsibility, people view their actions as springing from the dictates of authorities rather than from their own volition. Because they are not the actual agents of their actions, they are spared self-prohibiting reactions. In terrorism that is sponsored by states or governments in exile, functionaries view themselves as patriots fulfilling nationalistic duties rather than as free-lancing criminals. Displacement of responsibility not only weakens restraints over one's own detrimental actions but also diminishes social concern over the well-being of people mistreated by others.[19]

Exemption from self-devaluation for heinous deeds has been most gruesomely revealed in socially sanctioned mass executions. Nazi prison commandants and their staffs divested themselves of personal responsibility for their unprecedented inhumanities; they were simply carrying out orders.[20] Impersonal obedience to horrific orders was similarly evident in military atrocities, such as the My Lai massacre.[21] In an effort to deter institutionally sanctioned atrocities, the Nuremberg Accords declared that obedience to inhumane orders, even from the highest authorities, does not relieve subordinates of the responsibility for their actions. However, because victors are disinclined to try themselves as criminals, such decrees have limited deterrence without an international judiciary system empowered to impose penalties on victors and losers alike. In studies of the disengagement of self-sanctions through the displacement of responsibility, authorities explicitly authorize those who play the role of functionaries to carry out injurious actions and hold themselves fully accountable for the harm caused by those actions. However, in the sanctioning practices of everyday life, responsibility for detrimental conduct is rarely assumed so explicitly, because only obtuse authorities would leave themselves open to accusations of authorizing heinous acts. Actual

---

[18] Diener et al., "Altered Responsibility."

[19] H. A. Tilker, "Socially Responsible Behavior as a Function of Observer Responsibility and Victim Feedback," *Journal of Personality and Social Psychology* 14 (1970): 95–100.

[20] B. C. Andrus, *The Infamous of Nuremberg* (London: Fravin, 1969).

[21] Kelman, "Violence Without Moral Restraint."

authorities are concerned not only with adverse social consequences to themselves, should the courses of action they advocate miscarry, but with the loss of self-regard for sanctioning human atrocities in ways that leave blood on their hands. Therefore, authorities usually invite and support detrimental conduct in insidious ways that minimize personal responsibility for what is happening.

In the preceding chapter, Kramer described the great lengths to which Shi'ite clerics go to produce moral justifications for violent acts that seem to breach Islamic law, such as suicidal bombings and hostage taking. These efforts are designed not only to persuade the clerics themselves of the morality of the terrorists' actions but to preserve the integrity of the perpetrating group in the eyes of other nations. The religious code permits neither suicide nor the terrorizing of innocent people. On the one hand, the clerics justify such acts by invoking situational imperatives and utilitarian reasons, namely, that tyrannical circumstances drive oppressed people to resort to unconventional means in order to rout aggressors who wield massive destructive power. On the other hand, they reconstrue terrorist acts as conventional means in which dying in a suicidal bombing for a moral cause is no different from dying at the hands of an enemy soldier. Hostages simply get relabeled as spies. When the linguistic solution defies credibility, personal moral responsibility is disengaged by construing terroristic acts as dictated by the foe's tyranny. Because of the shaky moral logic and disputable reconstruals, clerics sanction terrorism by indirection, vindicate successful ventures retrospectively, and disclaim endorsing terroristic operations beforehand.

States sponsor terrorist operations through disguised, roundabout routes that make it difficult to pin the blame on them. Moreover, the intended purpose of sanctioned destructiveness is usually linguistically disguised so that neither issuers nor perpetrators regard the activity as censurable. When culpable practices gain public attention, they are officially dismissed as only isolated incidents arising through misunderstanding of what, in fact, had been authorized. Efforts are made to limit the blame to subordinates, who are portrayed as misguided or overzealous.

A number of social factors affect the ease with which responsibility for one's actions can be surrendered to others. High justification and social consensus about the morality of an enterprise aid in the relinquishment of personal control. The legitimacy of the authorizers is another important determinant. The higher the authorities, the more legitimacy, respect, and coercive power they command, and the more amenable are people to defer to them. Modeled disobedience, which challenges the legitimacy of the activities, if not the authorizers themselves, reduces the willingness of observers to carry out the actions called for by the orders of a superior.[22] It is difficult to continue to disown personal agency in the face of evident harm that results directly from one's actions. People are, therefore, less willing to obey authoritarian orders to carry out injurious behavior when they see firsthand how they are hurting others.[23]

Obedient functionaries do not cast off all responsibility for their behavior as though they were mindless extensions of others. If this were the case, they would do nothing unless told to. In fact, they tend to be conscientious and self-directed in the performance of their duties. It requires a strong sense of responsibility to be a good functionary. In situations involving obedience to authority, people carry out orders partly to honor the obligations they have undertaken.[24] It is therefore important to distinguish between two levels of responsibility, duty to one's superiors and accountability for the effects of one's actions. Self-sanctions operate most efficiently in the service of authority when followers assume personal responsibility for being dutiful executors while relinquishing personal responsibility for the harm caused by their behavior. Followers who disowned responsibility without being bound by a sense of duty would be quite unreliable.

Displacement of responsibility also operates in situations in which hostages are taken. Terrorists warn officials of targeted nations that if they take retaliatory action they will be held accountable for the lives of the hostages. At different steps in negotiations for their release, terrorists continue to claim that the responsibility for the safety of hostages rests with the national officials. If the captivity drags on, terrorists blame the suffering and injuries they inflict on their hostages on the officials for failing to make what they regard as warranted concessions to right social wrongs.

[22] W. H. J. Meeus and Q. A. W. Raaijmakers, "Administrative Obedience: Carrying Out Orders to Use Psychological-Administrative Violence," *European Journal of Social Psychology* 16 (1986): 311–24; S. Milgram, *Obedience to Authority: An Experimental View* (New York: Harper & Row, 1974); and P. C. Powers and R. G. Geen, "Effects of the Behavior and the Perceived Arousal of a Model on Instrumental Aggression," *Journal of Personality and Social Psychology* 23 (1972): 175–83.

[23] Milgram, *Obedience to Authority*, and Tilker, "Socially Responsible Behavior."

[24] D. M. Mantell and R. Panzarella, "Obedience and Responsibility," *British Journal of Social and Clinical Psychology* 15 (1976): 239–46.

Diffusion of responsibility

The deterrent power of self-sanctions is weakened when responsibility for culpable behavior is diffused, thereby obscuring the link between conduct and its consequences. Responsibility can be diffused in several ways, for example, by the division of labor. Most enterprises require the services of many people, each performing fragmentary jobs that seem harmless in themselves. The fractional contribution is easily isolated from the eventual function, especially when participants exercise little personal judgment in carrying out a subfunction that is related by remote, complex links to the end result. After activities become routinized into programmed subfunctions, attention shifts from the import of what one is doing to the details of one's fractional job.[25]

Group decision making is another common bureaucratic practice that enables otherwise considerate people to behave inhumanely, because no single person feels responsible for policies arrived at collectively. When everyone is responsible, no one is really responsible. Social organizations go to great lengths to devise sophisticated mechanisms for obscuring responsibility for decisions that will adversely affect others.

Collective action is still another diffusion expedient for weakening self-restraints. Any harm done by a group can always be ascribed, in large part, to the behavior of other members. People therefore act more harshly when responsibility is obfuscated by a collective instrumentality than when they hold themselves personally accountable for what they do.[26]

Disregard for, or distortion of, consequences

Additional ways of weakening self-deterring reactions operate through disregard for or misrepresentation of the consequences of action. When people choose to pursue activities that are harmful to others for reasons of personal gain or social inducements, they avoid facing or minimize the harm they cause. They readily recall prior information given to them about the potential benefits of the behavior, but are less able to remember

[25] Kelman, "Violence without Moral Restraint."
[26] A. Bandura, B. Underwood, and M. E. Fromson, "Disinhibition of Aggression Through Diffusion of Responsibility and Dehumanization of Victims," *Journal of Research in Personality* 9 (1975): 253–69; E. Diener, "Deindividuation: Causes and Consequences," *Social Behavior and Personality* 5 (1977): 143–56; and P. G. Zimbardo, "The Human Choice: Individuation, Reason, and Order Versus Deindividuation, Impulse, and Chaos," in *Nebraska Symposium on Motivation,* edited by W. J. Arnold and D. Levine (Lincoln: University of Nebraska Press, 1969), 237–309.

its harmful effects.[27] People are especially prone to minimize injurious effects when they act alone and thus cannot easily escape responsibility.[28] In addition to selective inattention and cognitive distortion of effects, the misrepresentation may involve active efforts to discredit evidence of the harm they cause. As long as the detrimental results of one's conduct are ignored, minimized, distorted, or disbelieved, there is little reason for self-censure to be activated.

It is relatively easy to hurt others when their suffering is not visible and when causal actions are physically and temporally remote from their effects. Our technologies for killing people have become highly lethal and depersonalized. Mechanized weapons systems and explosive devices, which can cause mass death by destructive forces unleashed remotely, illustrate such depersonalized action. Even a high sense of personal responsibility is a weak restrainer when aggressors do not know the harm they inflict on their victims.[29] In contrast, when people can see and hear the suffering they cause, vicariously aroused distress and self-censure serve as self-restraining influences. For example, in his studies of commanded aggression, Milgram obtained diminishing obedience as the victims' pain became more evident and personalized.[30]

Most organizations involve hierarchical chains of command in which superiors formulate plans and intermediaries transmit them to executors, who then carry them out. The further removed individuals are from the end results, the weaker is the restraining power of the foreseeable destructive effects. Kilham and Mann set forth the view that the disengagement of personal control is easiest for the intermediaries in a hierarchical system—they neither bear responsibility for major decisions nor are a party to their execution.[31] In performing the transmitter role, they model dutiful behavior and add legitimacy to their superiors' social policies and practices. Consistent with these speculations, intermediaries are much

[27] T. C. Brock and A. H. Buss, "Dissonance, Aggression, and Evaluation of Pain," *Journal of Abnormal and Social Psychology* 65 (1962): 197–202; and T. C. Brock and A. H. Buss, "Effects of Justification for Aggression and Communication with the Victim on Postaggression Dissonance," *Journal of Abnormal and Social Psychology* 68 (1964): 403–12.

[28] C. Mynatt and S. J. Herman, "Responsibility Attribution in Groups and Individuals: A Direct Test of the Diffusion of Responsibility Hypothesis," *Journal of Personality and Social Psychology* 32 (1975): 1111–18.

[29] Tilker, "Socially Responsible Behavior."

[30] Milgram, *Obedience to Authority.*

[31] W. Kilham and L. Mann, "Level of Destructive Obedience as a Function of Transmitter and Executant Roles in the Milgram Obedience Paradigm," *Journal of Personality and Social Psychology* 29 (1974): 696–702.

more obedient to destructive commands than are people who have to carry them out and face the results.[32]

Diverse functions and consequences of terrorism

The term *terrorism* is most commonly applied to surreptitious acts of violence in which dissidents attack a state by victimizing citizens. However, like other forms of coercive and aggressive conduct, terroristic violence involves varied targets and serves diverse functions. Variation in purpose alters the readiness with which causal responsibility is acknowledged and the way in which the consequences of terrorist acts are represented. Terrorism directed by states at their own people is designed to eliminate internal opposition and squelch peaceful dissent and social activism against the ruling cliques who use force to keep themselves in power. The punitive consequences for challenging the regime are publicized in order to deter potential opponents, but the mechanisms and brutality of tyranny are concealed. State-sponsored international terrorism seeks political gains through surreptitious underwriting of terrorist operations performed by surrogate groups. The sponsors go to great lengths to distance themselves publicly from the pernicious operations and the havoc they wreak. However, the public appearance of noninvolvement in international terrorism is difficult to pull off for states that provide the training sites and sanctuaries for known terrorist groups.

Politically motivated terrorism carried out against a state in the name of liberation movements is designed to gain widespread media dissemination of grievances. Terrorists therefore actively seek publicity for their cause in the effort to enlist popular support for the social or political changes they desire. They often attempt to minimize, or deflect attention from, the harm inflicted through their terrorist acts by centering attention on the inhumanities perpetrated on their compatriots by the state.

Some terrorist violence is carried out by self-appointed crusaders who act on behalf of oppressed people with whom they identify. They are motivated, in large part, by ideological imperatives and mutual reward of their efforts by fellow members. Their tactics are often calculated to expose the weaknesses of power holders and to provoke them to foolish actions and repressive security measures. Such counterreactions will presumably create widespread public disaffection and outrage, discredit the

[32] Ibid.

power holders' own leadership, and thus help bring about their own downfall and the regime over which they preside. Such groups readily take responsibility for their terrorist acts. Their eye is on the radicalization of the "consciousness of the masses" rather than on the carnage inflicted on those victimized by their actions.

Shared fervent belief sustains terrorist activities. The power of belief to sustain a program of political activism offering little hope of quick successes operates in virtually all groups seeking to effect social change and is not peculiar to terroristic groups that have little prospect of inciting the intended popular uprising.[33] Were social reformers to be entirely realistic about the prospects of transforming social systems during their operative period they would either forgo the endeavor or fall easy victim to despair.

A fair amount of terrorism is performed for financial gain that is justified on political grounds. Executives of foreign corporations and advisers of powerful and wealthy nations are favorite targets of terrorist acts. The particular victims are depersonalized as mere symbols of imperialism. People are more subject to self-reprimands for inflicting human suffering than for extracting money from prosperous, faceless corporations. Moral self-sanctions are therefore more easily disengaged from destructive conduct directed at a despised system than at a person. Lucrative ransom and extortion payments make this form of terrorism profitable.

Another tactic of terror that quickly spreads when it pays off involves the abduction of foreign advisers and diplomats in order to force release of jailed "political prisoners."[34] Abduction is a highly efficacious weapon for dissident groups as long as governments are willing to negotiate. Abductors view their action as a political bargaining tool rather than as an act of terrorism, especially if they gain release of their jailed compatriots without having inflicted physical injury on their captives.

Some people are motivated by bizarre and malevolent beliefs to commit acts that terrorize the public. Such idiosyncratically motivated acts are illustrated in recent incidents of drugstore terrorism, in which isolated individuals indiscriminately took the lives of several people by lacing bottles of patent medicine with poison. Once the idea of such an act is planted in the public consciousness, it is not uncommon for new variants of death threats involving food substances to appear. Through the

---

[33] Bandura, *Social Foundations of Thought and Action.*
[34] A. Bandura, *Aggression: A Social Learning Analysis* (Englewood Cliffs, N.J.: Prentice-Hall, 1973).

influence of modeling, terrorist acts that were originally politically motivated may be adopted by individuals for their own idiosyncratic purposes.[35] The rapid spread of airline hijacking internationally is illustrative of this modeling process.

As previously noted, the task of psychologically circumscribing and
sanitizing destructive effects presents special problems for democratic societies when they resort to violent counterterrorist actions that take the
lives of some innocent people. Counterattackers try to minimize the brutal aspects of such assaults by depicting them as "surgical strikes" that
wipe out only terrorists and their sanctuaries. The targets of violent retaliation try to arouse worldwide condemnation of such attacks through
graphic media portrayals of the carnage inflicted on women and children.
Some nations pursue the policy that terrorist acts will be promptly answered with massive deathly retaliation, whatever the cost might be, on
the ground that this is the price that must be paid to check terrorism.
Opponents of such policies argue that overkill countermeasures only fuel
greater terrorism by creating more terrorists and increasing public sympathy for the causes that drive them to terroristic violence. Vigorous verbal battles are fought over immediate results and long-range effects of
such violent countermeasures.

Dehumanization

The final set of disengagement practices operates on the targets of violent
acts. The strength of self-censuring reactions to injurious conduct depends partly on how the perpetrator views the people toward whom the
harmful behavior is directed. To perceive another person as human enhances empathetic or vicarious reactions through perceived similarity.[36]
The joys and suffering of similar persons are more vicariously arousing
than are the joys and suffering of strangers or of persons who have been
divested of human qualities. Personalizing the injurious effects experienced by others also makes their suffering much more salient. As a
result, it is difficult to mistreat humanized persons without risking self-
condemnation.

Self-sanctions against cruel conduct can be disengaged or blunted by

---

[35] Bandura, *Aggression: A Social Learning Analysis.*
[36] A. Bandura, "Social Cognitive Theory and Social Referencing," in *Social Referencing and Social Construction of Reality,* edited by S. Feiman (New York: Plenum, 1989).

divesting people of human qualities. Once dehumanized, the potential victims are no longer viewed as persons with feelings, hopes, and concerns but as subhuman objects. They are portrayed as mindless "savages," "gooks," "satanic fiends," and the like. Subhumans are regarded as insensitive to maltreatment and capable of being influenced only by harsh methods. If dispossessing antagonists of humanness does not blunt self-reproof, the self-reproof can be eliminated by attributing bestial qualities to the antagonists. It is easier to brutalize victims, for example, when they are referred to as "worms."[37] Studies of interpersonal aggression give vivid testimony to the self-disinhibitory power of dehumanization.[38] Dehumanized persons are treated much more punitively than persons who have not been divested of their human qualities. When punitiveness fails to achieve the desired result, the terrorists view this outcome as further evidence of the unworthiness of dehumanized persons, thus justifying their even greater maltreatment. Dehumanization fosters different self-exonerative patterns of thought. People seldom condemn punitive conduct—in fact, they create justifications for it—when they are directing their aggression at persons who have been divested of their humanness. By contrast, people strongly disapprove of punitive actions and rarely excuse them when they are directed at persons depicted in humanized terms.

Under certain conditions, the exercise of institutional power changes the users in ways that are conducive to dehumanization. This happens most often when persons in positions of authority have coercive power over other persons and when adequate safeguards for constraining the behavior of power holders are lacking. Power holders come to devalue those over whom they wield control.[39] In a simulated prison experiment, even college students, who had been randomly chosen to serve as either inmates or guards given unilateral power, began to treat their charges in degrading, tyrannical ways as guards.[40] Thus, role assignment that authorizes use of coercive power overrode personal characteristics in promoting punitive conduct. Systematic tests of relative influences similarly

[37] J. T. Gibson and M. Haritos-Fatouros, "The Education of a Torturer," *Psychology Today* (November 1986): 50–8.
[38] Bandura et al., "Disinhibition of Aggression."
[39] D. Kipnis, "The Powerholders," in *Perspectives on Social Power*, edited by J. T. Tedeschi (Chicago: Aldine, 1974), 82–122.
[40] C. Haney, C. Banks, and P. Zimbardo, "Interpersonal Dynamics in a Simulated Prison," *International Journal of Criminology and Penology* 1 (1973): 69–97.

show that social influences conducive to punitiveness exert considerably greater sway over aggressive conduct than do people's personal characteristics.[41]

The overall findings from research on the different mechanisms of moral disengagement corroborate the historical chronicle of human atrocities: It requires conducive social conditions rather than monstrous people to produce heinous deeds. Given appropriate social conditions, decent, ordinary people can be led to do extraordinarily cruel things.

Power of humanization

Psychological research tends to focus extensively on how easy it is to bring out the worst in people through dehumanization and other self-exonerative means. The sensational negative findings receive the greatest attention. Thus, for example, the aspect of Milgram's research on obedient aggression that is most widely cited is the evidence that good people can be talked into performing cruel deeds. However, to get people to carry out punitive acts, the overseer had to be physically present, repeatedly ordering people to act cruelly as they voiced their concerns and objections. Orders to escalate punitiveness to more intense levels are largely ignored or subverted when remotely issued by verbal command. As Helm and Morelli note, this is hardly an example of blind obedience triggered by an authoritative mandate.[42] Moreover, what is rarely noted is the equally striking evidence that most people steadfastly refuse to behave punitively, even in response to strong authoritarian commands, if the situation is personalized by having them see the victim or requiring them to inflict pain directly rather than remotely.

The emphasis on obedient aggression is understandable, considering the prevalence and harmfulness of people's inhumanities to one another. However, of considerable theoretical and social significance is the power of humanization to counteract cruel conduct. Studies examining this process reveal that, even under conditions that weaken self-deterrents, it is difficult for people to behave cruelly toward others when the potential victims are humanized or even personalized a bit.[43]

[41] K. S. Larsen, D. Coleman, J. Forges, and R. Johnson, "Is the Subject's Personality or the Experimental Situation a Better Predictor of a Subject's Willingness to Administer Shock to a Victim?" *Journal of Personality and Social Psychology* 22 (1971): 287–95.

[42] C. Helm and M. Morelli, "Stanley Milgram and the Obedience Experiment: Authority, Legitimacy, and Human Action," *Political Theory* 7 (1979): 321–46.

[43] Bandura et al., "Disinhibition of Aggression."

The moderating influence of humanization is strikingly revealed in situations involving great threat of violence. Most abductors find it difficult to harm their hostages after they have come to know them personally. Calm, patient negotiations with captors, therefore, increase the likelihood that captives will survive the ordeal. With growing acquaintance, it becomes increasingly difficult to take a human life cold-bloodedly.

Humanization, of course, is a two-way process. Captives may also develop some sympathy for their captors as they get to know them. Unfortunately, this phenomenon is sometimes called into question in analyses of terrorism by identifying it with the Stockholm syndrome. In the incident that spawned this "syndrome," people who were held hostage for six days by bank robbers began to sympathize with their criminal captors and sided with them against the police.[44] This hostage incident included several features that are conducive to the development of an affinity with the captors. The hostages were under extended siege by a horde of police seeking opportunities to shoot the robbers, depriving the group of food and other necessities to force their surrender, and poking holes in walls to gas the robbers into submission. The captors often acted as the hostages' protectors against the frightening maneuvers by the police. The refusal by the police to make concessions angered the hostages, who began to blame the police for their terrifying plight. ("It is the police who are keeping me from my children.")

As previously noted, construal of events is strongly colored by contrast effects. The chief captor in the bank-robbery case aroused strong feelings of gratitude in his captives by coupling brutalizing threats with seeming acts of considerateness. For example, he informed one of the hostages that he would forgo his plan to kill him to force police concessions, but instead would shoot him in the leg and have him pretend that he had been killed. This hostage expressed a strong sense of gratitude even long after the ordeal was over. ("How kind that he would shoot only my leg.") Another hostage was similarly overcome with gratitude over her captor's considerateness of her claustrophobic dread of sleeping in the bank vault. The "benevolent" gesture that won him good will consisted of placing a rope around her neck and letting her out of the vault on a thirty-foot leash. ("He was very kind to allow me to leave the vault.") The captors often consoled their captives when they were distraught, comforted them when they were physically miserable, and personalized

[44] D. A. Lang, "A Reporter at Large: The Bank Drama (Swedish Hostages)," *New Yorker* 50 (40) 1974: 56–126.

themselves by empathetic self-disclosures of their own human longings and feelings. The contrasting treatment led the hostages to perceive the police as the inhumane ones. ("I remember thinking, why can't the police be considerate like that?") Whether captivity produces sympathy for captors is determined by several factors—the extent to which captors personalize themselves and their plight, show some compassion toward their captives, portray the hostages' country as disregarding their welfare or jeopardizing their lives by reckless countermeasures, and act as their protectors.

Ideological terrorists are more likely to harass, browbeat, and degrade their hostages than to console them. Therefore, people who are subjected to terrifying political captivity rarely ally themselves with their abductors. But this does not mean that hostages never develop any sympathy for their captors' cause or plight, or that personalization never moderates captors' cruelty toward the people they hold hostage. When an important psychological phenomenon is linked to an example of questionable similarity, such as the Stockholm set of reactions, the aggression-restraining power of humanization may be inappropriately dismissed through improper comparison.

Attribution of blame

Imputing blame to one's antagonists is still another expedient that can serve self-exonerative purposes; one's own violent conduct can then be viewed as compelled by forcible provocation. For example, when power holders willfully disregard legitimate grievances concerning maltreatment, terrorists can easily persuade themselves that their actions are motivated by self-protection or desperation. Oppressive and inhumane social conditions and thwarted political efforts breed terrorists who often see foreign governments' complicity in their plight through support of the regime that they believe victimizes them. People who become radicalized carry out terrorist acts against the regime as well as the implicated foreign nations. When the social conditions breeding discontent and violent protest are firmly entrenched in political systems that obstruct legitimate efforts at change, governments readily resort to violent countermeasures in efforts to control terrorist activities. It is much easier to attack violent protesters than to change the sociopolitical conditions that fuel the protests. In such skirmishes, one person's victim is another person's victimizer.

Destructive interactions usually involve a series of reciprocally esca-lative actions, in which the antagonists are rarely faultless. A person can always select from the chain of events an instance of the adversary's de-fensive behavior and view it as the original instigation. Injurious conduct thus becomes a justifiable defensive reaction to belligerent provocations. People who are victimized are not entirely blameless, because, by their behavior, they contribute partly to their own plight. Victims can there-fore be blamed for bringing suffering on themselves. Terrorists can achieve self-exoneration by viewing their destructive conduct as forced by cir-cumstances rather than resulting from a personal decision. By blaming others or circumstances, not only can they excuse their own actions, but also they can even feel self-righteous in the process.

Terrorist acts that take a heavy toll on civilian lives create special per-sonal pressures to lay blame elsewhere. In 1987, Irish Republican Army (IRA) guerrillas planted a large bomb that killed and maimed many fam-ily members attending a war memorial ceremony in a town square.[45] The guerrillas promptly ascribed the blame for the civilian massacre to the British army for having detonated the bomb prematurely with an elec-tronic scanning device. The government denounced the "pathetic attempt to transfer blame" because no scanning equipment was in use at the time.

Observers of victimization can be disinhibited in much the same way as perpetrators are by the tendency to infer culpability from misfortune. Observers who see victims suffer maltreatment for which the victims themselves are held partially responsible leads observers to derogate the victims.[46] The devaluation and indignation aroused by ascribed culpabil-ity, in turn, provides moral justification for even greater maltreatment. The fact that attribution of blame can give rise to devaluation and moral justification illustrates how the various disengagement mechanisms are often interrelated and work together in weakening internal control.

Gradualistic moral disengagement

The aforementioned disengagement devices will not instantly transform a considerate person into a ruthless one who purposely goes out to kill other human beings. Terrorist behavior evolves through extensive train-

---

[45] "IRA 'Regrets' Bombing, Blames British for Civilian Toll," *San Francisco Chronicle*, 10 November 1987, p. 19.
[46] M. J. Lerner and D. T. Miller, "Just World Research and the Attribution Process: Look-ing Back and Ahead," *Psychological Bulletin* 85 (1978): 1030–51.

ing in moral disengagement and terrorist prowess, rather than emerging full blown. The path to terrorism can be shaped by fortuitous factors as well as by the conjoint influence of personal predilections and social inducements.[47] Development of the capability to kill usually evolves through a process in which recruits may not fully recognize the transformation they are undergoing.[48]

The disinhibitory training is usually conducted within a communal milieu of intense interpersonal influences insulated from mainstream social life. The recruits become deeply immersed in the ideology and role performances of the group. Initially, they are prompted to perform unpleasant acts that they can tolerate without much self-censure. Gradually, through repeated performance and repeated exposure to aggressive modeling by more experienced associates, their discomfort and self-reproof are weakened to ever higher levels of ruthlessness. The various disengagement practices form an integral part of the training. Eventually, acts originally regarded as abhorrent can be performed callously. Escalative self-disinhibition is accelerated if violent courses of action are presented as serving a moral imperative and the targeted people are divested of human qualities.[49] The training not only instills the moral rightness and importance of the cause for militant action, but also creates a sense of eliteness and provides the social rewards of solidarity and group esteem for excelling in terrorist exploits.

Sprinzak, in Chapter 5 of this volume, traces the gradual evolution of the Weatherman terrorist group. The process of radicalization began with opposition to particular officials and social policies; grew to increasing estrangement from, and eventual rejection of, the whole system, a process fueled by disillusionment, embittering failures, and hostile confrontations with authorities and police; and culminated in terroristic efforts to destroy the system and its dehumanized rulers. To inculcate the revolutionary morality and eliminate any residual self-censure and revulsion over ruthless behavior, the Weatherman group created small, isolated collectives where they eradicated their "bourgeois morality" with a vengeance.[50]

---

[47] A. Bandura, "The Psychology of Chance Encounters and Life Paths," *American Psychologist* 37 (1982): 747–55.

[48] Bandura, *Social Foundations of Thought and Action;* L. Franks and T. Powers, "Profile of a Terrorist," *Palo Alto Times,* 17 September 1970, pp. 26–28; and J. T. Gibson and M. Haritos-Fatouros, "The Education of a Torturer."

[49] Bandura et al., "Disinhibition of Aggression."

[50] Franks and Powers, "Profile of a Terrorist."

The preceding analyses have been concerned mainly with how disengagement mechanisms operate in removing moral impediments to terrorist violence and in combatting terrorism by violent means. These same mechanisms are also heavily enlisted by terrorist entrepreneurs, who supply militant states with the lethal tools to terrorize their own people or to equip the terrorist groups they sponsor. Frank Terpil, who became a terrorist entrepreneur after he fell from grace at the CIA, provides vivid testimony to these psychological mechanisms.[51]

Terpil shrouded his clandestine death operations in the euphemisms of a legitimate business fulfilling "consumer needs" under the appellation Intercontinental Technology. To spare himself any self-censure for contributing to human atrocities, he actively avoided knowledge of the purposes to which his weaponry would be put. ("I don't ever want to know that.") When asked whether he was ever haunted by any thoughts about the human suffering his deathly wares might cause, he explained that banishing thoughts of injurious consequences frees one's actions from restraints of conscience. ("If I really thought about the consequences all the time, I certainly wouldn't have been in this business . . . you have to blank it off.")

Efforts to probe for any signs of self-reproach brought self-exonerative comparisons. When queried concerning any qualms he might have felt about supplying torture equipment and tactical advice to Idi Amin in Uganda, Terpil countered with the view that the employees at Dow Chemical were not beset with guilt over the havoc wreaked on the Vietnamese population by the napalm they produced. ("I'm sure that the people from Dow Chemical didn't think of the consequences of selling napalm. If they did, they wouldn't be working at the factory. I doubt very much if they'd feel any more responsible for the ultimate use than I did for my equipment.") When pressed about the atrocities committed at Amin's "State Research Bureau" torture chambers, Terpil reiterated his depersonalized stance. ("I do not get wrapped up emotionally with the country. I regard myself basically as neutral and commercial.") To give legitimacy to his "private practice," he claimed that he aided British and American operations abroad as well.

The merchandising of terrorism is not accomplished by a few individuals. It requires a worldwide network of reputable, high-level operators who, by fractionation of function, perspective, and responsibility, amass

[51] D. Schorr, *Frank Terpil: Confessions of a Dangerous Man* [Film] (Boston: WGBH Educational Foundation, 1982).

arsenals of destruction, find places to store them, procure export and import licenses from different countries, obtain spurious end-user certificates that conceal the true destination of the shipments, and ship the arsenals around via circuitous itineraries. The cogs in this multifaceted network include weapons manufacturers, former government officials who have the useful political ties, ex-military and intelligence officers who provide valuable skills and contacts, weapons merchants, and shippers. By fractionating the enterprise, most of the participants see themselves as decent, legitimate practitioners of their own particular trade rather than as parties to a death operation.

Moral disengagement and self-deception

Does the disengagement of self-censure involve self-deception? Because of the incompatibility of being simultaneously a deceiver and the person deceived, literal self-deception cannot exist.[52] It is logically impossible to deceive oneself into believing something while knowing it to be false. Efforts to resolve the paradox of how anyone can be the agent and the object of deception at the same time have met with little success.[53] These attempts usually involve creating split selves and rendering one of them unconscious. The split-self conceptions neglect to specify how a conscious self can lie to an unconscious self without some awareness of what the other self believes. The deceiving self has to be aware of what the deceived self believes in order to know what kind of deceptions to concoct.

Different levels of awareness are sometimes proposed as another possible solution to the paradox. It is said that "deep down" people really know what they believe. Reacquainting the split selves only reinstates the paradox of how a person can be a deceiver and the person deceived at the same time. People, of course, often misconstrue events, lead themselves astray by their biases and misbeliefs, and act without first becoming informed. However, to be misdirected by one's beliefs or ignorance does not mean that one is lying to oneself.

Self-deception is often invoked when people choose to ignore possibly

[52] S. Bok, "The Self Deceived," *Social Science Information* 19 (1980): 923–36; T. S. Champlin, "Self-Deception: A Reflexive Dilemma," *Philosophy* 52 (1977): 281–99; and M. R. Haight, *A Study of Self Deception* (Atlantic Highlands, N.J.: Humanities Press, 1980).
[53] Bandura, *Social Foundations of Thought and Action*.

countervailing evidence. It could be argued that they must believe in its validity in order to avoid it, because otherwise they would not know what to shun. This is not necessarily so. Staunch believers often choose not to waste their time scrutinizing opposing arguments or evidence because they are already convinced of their fallacy. When confronted with evidence that disputes their beliefs, they question its credibility, dismiss its relevance, or twist it to fit their views. However, if the evidence is compelling, they alter their original beliefs to accommodate the discrepant evidence.

People may harbor some doubts concerning their beliefs but avoid seeking certain evidence because they have an inkling that the evidence might disconfirm what they wish to believe. Indeed, they may engage in all kinds of maneuvers, both in thought and in action, to avoid finding out the actual state of affairs. Suspecting something is not the same as knowing it to be true. Inklings can always be discounted as possibly being ill-founded. So long as a person does not find out the truth, what the person believes is not personally known to be false. Both Haight and Fingarette give considerable attention to processes by which people avoid painful or incriminating truth by not taking actions that would reveal the truth or not spelling out fully what they are doing or undergoing that would make it known.[54] They act in ways that keep themselves intentionally uninformed. They do not go looking for evidence of their culpability or the harmful effects of their actions. Obvious questions that would reveal unwelcome information remain unasked, so they do not find out what they do not want to know. Implicit agreements and social arrangements are created that leave the foreseeable unforeseen and the knowable unknown.

In addition to contending with their own self-censure, people are concerned about how they appear in the eyes of others when they engage in conduct that is morally suspect. This concern adds a social evaluative factor to the process. Haight argues that, in much of what is called self-deception, persons are aware of the reality they are trying to deny, but they create the public appearance that they are deceiving themselves.[55] Others are thus left uncertain about how to judge and treat persons who seem to be sincerely deluding themselves in efforts to avoid an unpleasant

[54] H. Fingarette, *Self-Deception* (New York: Humanities Press, 1969); and M. R. Haight, *A Study of Self Deception.*
[55] Haight, *A Study of Self Deception.*

truth. The public pretense is designed to head off social reproof. When people are caught up in the same painful predicament, the result may be a great deal of collective public pretense.

The mechanisms of moral disengagement involve cognitive and social machinations but not literal self-deception. In moral justification, for example, people may be misled by those they trust into believing that violent means are morally right because the means will check the human suffering of tyranny. The persuasive depictions of the perils and benefits may be accurate or exaggerated, or they may be just pious rhetoric masking less honorable purposes.

The same persuasion process applies to weakening of self-censure by dehumanizing and blaming adversaries. In the rhetoric of conflict, opinion shapers ascribe to their foes irrationalities, barbarities, and culpabilities that color public beliefs.[56] In these instances, people who have been persuaded are not lying to themselves. The misleaders and the misled are different persons. When the misleaders are themselves operating under erroneous beliefs, the views they voice are not intentional deceptions. They seek to persuade others into believing what they themselves believe. In social deception, public declarations by others may belie their private beliefs, which are concealed from those being deceived.

In reducing self-censure by ignoring, minimizing, or misconstruing the injurious effects of their actions, people lack the evidence to disbelieve what they already believe. The issue of self-dishonesty does not arise so long as people remain uninformed or misinformed about the outcomes of their actions. When moral disengagement is promoted by diffused and displaced responsibility, functionaries carry out the orders of superiors and often perform only a small subfunction of the enterprise. Such arrangements enable people to think of themselves merely as subordinate instruments, rather than as agents, of the entire enterprise. If they regard themselves as minor cogs in the intricate social machinery, they have little reason to believe otherwise concerning their initiatory power. This is not to say that disengagement of self-censure operates flawlessly. If serious disbeliefs arise, especially at the point of moral justification, people cannot get themselves to behave inhumanely. If they do, they pay the price of self-contempt.

[56] R. L. Ivie, "Images of Savagery in American Justifications for War," *Communication Monographs* 47 (1980): 270–94.

Conclusion

The massive threats to human welfare stem mainly from deliberate acts of principle rather than from unrestrained acts of impulse. The principled resort to destructiveness is of greatest social concern, but, ironically, it is the most ignored in psychological analyses of human violence. Given the existence of so many psychological devices for disengagement of moral control, societies cannot rely entirely on individuals, however righteous their standards, to provide safeguards against destructive ventures. Civilized conduct requires, in addition to humane personal codes, social systems that uphold compassionate behavior and renounce cruelty.

Monolithic political systems that exercise concentrated control over the major vehicles of social influence can wield greater justificatory power than pluralistic systems that represent diverse perspectives, interests, and concerns. Political diversity and toleration of public expression of skepticism create conditions that allow the emergence of challenges to suspect moral appeals. If societies are to function more humanely, they must establish effective social safeguards against the misuse of institutional justificatory power for exploitive and destructive purposes.

10

The readiness to kill and die:
Suicidal terrorism in the Middle East

ARIEL MERARI

Suicidal terrorism—the readiness to die in the process of committing a terrorist act—has attracted considerable public attention in recent years. In addition to evoking a widespread sense of horror, such terrorism has had significant strategic outcomes. For example, some high-casualty suicidal terrorist attacks on American and French targets in Lebanon contributed to the decisions of those countries to withdraw their forces from Lebanon, decisions that may have influenced the future of Lebanon for a significant period of time.

Nor have fear and concern been limited to the Middle East, where the most publicized suicidal attacks have occurred. Government buildings in Washington, D.C., as well as U.S. embassies around the world, have been fortified so as to prevent cars bearing bombs from being driven into them by drivers intent on suicidal attacks. Indeed, threats to carry out such attacks have been issued by various sponsors of terrorism. The media have reinforced these threats by reporting on the training of many terrorists in Middle Eastern countries for suicidal missions. On several occasions hundreds of zealots vowing to sacrifice themselves for the sacred cause have been shown on television.

In recent years, suicidal terrorism of the Middle Eastern variety has been attributed, by and large, to religious fanaticism, sometimes with significant political and strategic conclusions flowing from this attribution. The notion of an overwhelming wave of self-immolating Shi'ite fanatics permeated a recent article by an Israeli military commentator who analyzed the chances for success of various American responses to the persistent kidnapping of American citizens in Lebanon. He wrote:

One of the sources of the strength and attractiveness of Shi'ite fanaticism is the absolute disregard with which its followers view death and earthly vanities. This is proven by Shi'ite suicidal terrorism which was directed against the IDF [Israel Defense Forces] and against the Americans while they were in Lebanon. This fact sheds doubt on the utility of another mode of operation against Shi'ite terrorism now under consideration [referring to an American military operation].[1]

Others have regarded suicidal attacks as characteristic of contemporary terrorism in general, arguing that they necessitate a complete revision of antiterrorist measures. In a newspaper article, for example, Lord Chalfont, one authority, was quoted as saying:

The whole time that I have been involved in terrorist operations, which now goes back to 30 years, my enemy has always been a man who is very worried about his own skin. You can no longer count on that, because the terrorist [today] is not just *prepared* to get killed, he *wants* to get killed. Therefore, the whole planning, tactical doctrine, [and] thinking [behind antiterrorism measures] is fundamentally undermined.[2]

Clearly, understanding of the sources, nature, and scope of suicidal terrorism is important for reasons that exceed pure academic interest, because interpretations of this phenomenon may influence decisions with far-reaching political and strategic consequences.

The first part of this chapter offers a conceptual framework of suicidal terrorism; the second surveys and discusses its Middle Eastern manifestations.

Problems of definition

Many authors have noted the immense methodological difficulties inherent in defining suicidal behavior. Lester and Lester, for example, list difficulties stemming from differences in the manifestation of the suicidal behavior (e.g., attempted versus completed suicide), uncertainty about the true intention behind the act, and the degree of consciousness preceding the act.[3]

In the context of the specific subject of this chapter, there are three sources of confusion: (1) the problem of differentiating between being ready to die and seeking to die; (2) the difficulty of differentiating between people who wanted to die and those whose death was interpreted as suicide but who were actually fooled into suicide by those who sent

[1] R. Ben-Yishai, "Beirut Is Not Entebbe," *Yediot Aharonot Saturday Supplement,* 6 February 1987 [Hebrew].
[2] R. Kidder, "The Terrorist Mentality," *Christian Science Monitor,* 15 May 1986.
[3] G. Lester and D. Lester, *Suicide* (Englewood Cliffs, N.J.: Prentice-Hall, 1971).

them; and (3) the variability of the situational context of the suicidal act, particularly the need to differentiate between terrorists who merely killed themselves and those whose suicide was part of an act of killing others.

BEING READY TO DIE VERSUS SEEKING TO DIE. The difficulty of assessing whether the suicide really wanted to die has been pointed out by many suicidologists.[4] In the context of terrorism this difficulty is deepened, because the perpetrator is usually sent by an organization. Whereas in a case of a "private" suicide it can usually be assumed that both the decision-making process and the actions involved in carrying out the suicide involved only the individual, this assumption is untenable in most cases of terrorist suicide.

Furthermore, the term *suicidal attack* has been used in describing cases in which the terrorists actually killed themselves (e.g., activated a car bomb while driving it), but also in cases in which terrorists carried out high-risk attacks in which some of them were killed by security forces. Palestinian terrorists, for example, have often referred to barricade-hostage incidents which they carried out in Israel as "suicide operations." Indeed, the great majority of the Palestinian hostage takers in Israel were killed in rescue assaults by Israeli security forces. Yet in almost all these incidents the terrorists demanded safe conduct to an Arab country as a condition for the release of the hostages. At least consciously, they wanted to live, even though they were willing to take a high risk of dying. Obviously, proneness to suicide is a continuum rather than an absolute trait, and one might argue that people who volunteer for extremely high-risk missions have more than a streak of suicidal tendency. Nevertheless, for the sake of clarity this chapter deals only with events in which the terrorists actually killed themselves rather than with those in which they fought to the death.

GENUINE SUICIDES VERSUS REMOTE-CONTROL MARTYRS. In several cases, the apparent suicides were actually fooled by their senders, who led them to believe they would survive the operation even as they made sure that they would actually die and that the attack would appear to be a suicide.

For example, on 17 October 1985 a team of four members of the Lebanese Communist party tried to bomb the Voice of Hope radio station in Lebanon, near the border of Israel. Each of the team's members

[4]Ibid., 10.

carried about thirty kilograms of explosives and hand grenades. The station's guards noticed the attackers and opened fire. The explosive charges carried by two of the attackers went off and three of the team's members were killed in the explosion. The fourth terrorist, a twenty-two-year-old man by the name of Nasser Harfan, was captured. According to his story, the team's senders promised them that the explosive charges had been equipped with fuses with a ten-minute delay so that the team could escape after placing them.[5] Actually, however, the fuses were designed to detonate the explosives with no delay at all.

Before they went on their mission, the team's members recorded a last message on video tape. They were told that the recording was made just in case something went wrong. As it turned out, something indeed went wrong, albeit in a way different from what the planners had imagined. Because the attackers were discovered by the guards and were under fire, instead of placing the explosive charges at the same time as had been planned, the team's members decided that two of them would place the explosives first while the other pair returned fire. Only this on-site change of plans enabled one of the team to survive the mission to tell the story. Had the original plan been fulfilled to the letter, this event would undoubtedly have been counted as a clear case of terrorist suicide attack, authenticated by the dead men's video-taped message.

In several cases of attempted car-bomb attacks in Lebanon it was discovered that the explosive charge hidden in the car was intended to be detonated by a remote control operated from the following vehicle. In some of these cases this seemed to be a "safety" measure, put in place in case the intended suicides were to change their mind at the last moment. In other cases, however, the car-bomb drivers were told that their role was merely to smuggle the car bomb through security check points; thus the drivers did not know that they had been chosen to become martyrs by remote control.

It is noteworthy that in the case of the truck bombing of the American embassy in Kuwait on 12 December 1983, the truck's driver jumped out of the truck seconds before the explosion and ran a few steps away from the truck—not far enough, however, to escape death. This incident was registered as a case of suicidal car bombing, but we shall probably never know what actually happened. Was the driver fooled and the truck detonated by remote control? Did the driver himself detonate the explosives,

---

[5] *Ma'ariv*, 27 October 1985 [Hebrew].

having been fooled to believe that there would be sufficient time for him to escape? Or was he originally willing to die, changing his mind only belatedly?

On the plausible assumption that not all cases of fooled martyrs have been exposed, the number of genuine suicidal attacks is probably smaller than it appears to be.

Suicide with or without homicide

Terrorists have committed suicide under various circumstances. In some cases terrorists have taken their own lives without attempting to harm others. Such were the cases of Holger Meins, a member of the West German Red Army Faction who died in jail in 1974 as a result of a hunger strike; of Ulrike Meinhof, the ideological founder of the group, who hanged herself in prison in 1976; and of another four members of the same group, including Andreas Baader and Gudrun Ensslin, who committed suicide in jail in 1977 following the failure of an attempt to extort their release through the kidnapping of Dr. Schleyer and the hijacking of a Lufthansa airliner. The best-remembered case of this kind is probably the chain suicide of eleven Irish Republican Army (IRA) members who starved themselves to death in a Belfast prison in 1981.

Suicides of this type do not belong to the narrow definition of this chapter's topic, which deals with terrorists' suicides carried out in the context of violence against others. Nevertheless, of the two necessary elements of a suicidal terrorist attack—the willingness to kill others and the willingness to die—the latter is certainly of greater interest. The willingness of terrorists to kill others is much more common and much less surprising than their willingness to kill themselves. It is the self-sacrificial rather than the homicidal aspect of suicidal terrorist attacks that evokes scientific curiosity and public concern. For this reason, cases of terrorist suicide that have not been committed in a homicidal context are referred to in this chapter, although they are not counted for statistical purposes.

Constituents of suicidal terrorism

Factors influencing suicidal terrorism can be divided into four general categories: cultural factors, indoctrination, situational factors, and personality factors. These categories are discussed in this section.

CULTURAL FACTORS. Several studies have mentioned cultural factors as a major source of influence on suicidal behavior.[6] With regard to suicidal terrorism, as in other contexts of sacrificial self-destruction, culture (including religion) may affect behavior in two main ways: by setting norms regarding the circumstances under which a person may commit suicide and sometimes delineating the manner of doing it (e.g., actively or passively); and by influencing people's concepts (and expectations) concerning the question of what happens after death.

Norms concerning suicide exist in all major religions. Judaism, like other monotheistic religions, condemns suicide to the extent that suicides must be buried not in the community's cemetery but outside its wall. Jewish philosophy dictates that preservation of life (*piku'akh nefesh*) supersedes all religious and social dicta with the exception of those forbidding murder, incest, and the worship of false gods. It should be emphasized that even with regard to these three circumstances, Judaism does not permit active suicide but speaks of being killed rather than being forced to commit the sin. The Shi'ite survival code, the *taqiyya* (carefulness), is even more demanding concerning the preservation of life: a Shi'ite is even allowed to pose as a Sunni in order to survive persecution.[7] The only sin specifically forbidden, even at the cost of one's own life, is to kill another Shi'ite.

All monotheistic religions promise life after death. Hypothetically, they may thus encourage suicidal behavior, especially if the suicidal act is carried out for a righteous cause. Yet Catholicism, like Judaism, saw fit to prevent a voluntary departure to better pastures by professing that those who commit suicide are doomed to Hell. The concept of *shahid* (martyr) in Islam does not contradict Christian and Jewish belief. Whereas being killed by the enemy in *jihad* (holy war) guarantees paradise, suicide is strictly forbidden. *Shahid* is the warrior who was killed by the enemy in battle, not the one who killed himself.

Observers who emphasize the importance of cultural factors in suicidal terrorism have often used the behavior of Iranian soldiers in the war with Iraq as an example and proof. The apparently suicidal attacks

[6] See, for example, T. G. Masaryk, *Suicide and the Meaning of Civilization* (Chicago: University of Chicago Press, 1970); L. Dublin and B. Bunzel, *To Be or Not to Be* (New York: Harrison Smith and Robert Haas, 1933); M. L. Farber, *Theory of Suicide* (New York: Funk and Wagnalls, 1968); and J. M. A. Weiss, "Suicide," in *American Handbook of Psychiatry*, 2d ed., edited by S. Arieti (New York: Basic Books, 1974), 3: 743–65.

[7] E. Kohlberg, "Ha'Shia: si'ato shel Ali," in *Mekha'a u'mahapekha ba'islam ha'shi'i [Protest and Revolution in Shi'i Islam]*, edited by M. Kramer (Tel Aviv: Ha'Kibutz Ha-'Meukhad, 1985) [Hebrew].

of thousands of Revolutionary Guards, which continued despite heavy casualties, made a great impression on some Western observers, who viewed those attacks as a large-scale case of suicidal terrorism.

Two points should be emphasized in this regard. First, the soldiers of the Iranian Islamic Revolution have no monopoly on human-wave attacks against heavy fire. The most stunning examples of this form of large-scale daredevil attacks have apparently been carried out by modern Western armies, whose motivation had nothing to do with religious frenzy. For example, the rate of casualties sustained by Iran during its long war with Iraq does not approach the losses sustained by France in the four years of World War I. By the end of the fifth year of the Iran-Iraq war, Iran, with a population of about 40 million, suffered an estimated 250,000 casualties,[8] whereas France, with a population of about 55 million, sustained more than 1.35 million deaths.[9] Of course, similar disregard for casualties was displayed by other Western armies as well. In one day of the Somme offensive, for instance, the British army suffered 57,000 casualties—"the biggest loss ever suffered by any army in a single day."[10]

Second, heroic behavior by soldiers in battle is fundamentally different from a suicidal terrorist attack and cannot serve as a proper model for such attacks. In the military context, at the moment of truth, the dominant motivating forces are probably discipline and group cohesiveness, which influence soldiers' behavior in a direct and immediate way. Soldiers *must* obey orders and they are part of a formation. It probably takes more courage to stay behind when one's platoon rises for assault than to charge with the others. These crucial factors do not exist in the individual terrorist attack situation. This difference explains the practice of remote-control activation of the car bombs whose "suicidal" drivers proved insufficiently suicidal. Presumably, the senders of the suicide perpetrators believed in the power of religious conviction with some (apparently justified) reservations.

The widespread notion of the powerful influence of religious beliefs on the willingness of Iranian youth to die for the cause has undoubtedly been cultivated by Iranian authorities as a means of psychological war-

---

[8] A. Levran, "The Military Balance in the Fifth Year of the Iran-Iraq War," in *The Middle East Military Balance 1985*, edited by M. A. Heller (Boulder, Colo.: Westview Press, 1986).

[9] A. Golenpaul, ed., *Information Please Almanac* (New York: Information Please Almanac, 1977).

[10] N. F. Dixon, *On the Psychology of Military Incompetence* (New York: Basic Books, 1976), 82.

fare. This notion has not only been repeatedly conveyed by sensation-seeking mass media, it has also permeated some of the better writing on Iran and the Islamic Revolution. Robin Wright, for example, quotes a story about a fifteen-year-old Iranian prisoner of war captured by the Iraqis who wept because he had not been killed in battle. She also describes scores of boys who volunteered to walk through Iraqi mine fields in the role of live mine detectors, to clear the way for the advancing Iranian troops.[11] Again, phenomena of this kind have been seen in many wars throughout the ages, with no relation whatsoever to religious motivation. The more impressive aspect of these stories is, perhaps, the relentless use of young boys for what is usually accepted as a man's duty. Moreover, foreign observers have not been able to move freely in Iran, and it is probable that at least some of the heroic stories have been exaggerated, if not completely fabricated, by the Iranian authorities for their propaganda value.

INDOCTRINATION. Indoctrination may play a role in terrorist suicide in two ways. The first is essentially an educational process in which a person is convinced of the importance of the cause and of the means necessary for its implementation. Agents of influence in this phase, which is usually a long one, may be hard to identify, and may include parents, friends, teachers, writers, and other agents of socialization.

The second type of indoctrination is the mission-oriented persuasion of the person intended for suicide, usually by a charismatic political, military, or religious leader. This type of indoctrination is relatively brief and takes place shortly before the time of the suicide mission. Practically all Palestinian groups have used this kind of indoctrination for terrorist teams sent on high-risk *fedayeen* ("self-sacrifice") missions. Thus, Abu Jihad (Khalil al-Wazir), who, until he was assassinated in April 1988, was the revered military commander of *Al-Fatah*, the largest of the groups within the Palestine Liberation Organization, delivered a farewell speech to almost all such teams as they were ready to depart for hostage-taking incursions into Israel. Fundamentalist Shi'ite terrorists who have gone on suicidal car-bombing missions are said to have received last blessings from an Imam or an admired sheikh.

This kind of indoctrination has nothing in common with the "brain-washing" phenomenon as described by Shein and Lifton.[12] The Chinese

[11] Robin Wright, *Sacred Rage* (New York: Linden Press/Simon & Schuster, 1985), 36–7.
[12] See E. H. Shein, "The Chinese Indoctrination Program for Prisoners of War: A Study of

method of inducing a coercive change of a whole set of attitudes, opinions, and beliefs, which was the subject of these works, was a long and elaborate process involving both physical and mental measures intended to effect a permanent replacement of old concepts, loyalties, and behavior patterns with new ones (with very meager long-term success). Indoctrination of terrorists for suicidal missions, in contrast, is almost by definition meant to be short term (the indoctrinated persons are not expected to survive the mission) and is essentially a process of preaching to the converted, in the sense that it is addressed to preselected "volunteers."

It is difficult to assess the relative importance of indoctrination among the factors that push a terrorist to suicidal behavior. In the broad sense of education and assimilation of behavior patterns, as well as with regard to the development of cultural values, the concept of indoctrination is very close to the idea of cultural influence discussed earlier. In the more specific sense of the direct, immediate, and short-term persuasion by a charismatic agent of influence, indoctrination may serve as an ancillary factor by strengthening already-existing convictions and behavior tendencies and by adding an element of personal commitment to the persuader to carry out the mission. Nevertheless, it is conceivable that indoctrination of this kind cannot *create* suicidal behavior in the absence of other, more important elements.

SITUATIONAL FACTORS. This group of factors includes the conditions and circumstances under which the suicidal act is committed. An essential question in many—perhaps most—cases of terrorist suicide concerns the alternative to death. In an extreme situation, when this alternative is torture or a long period of imprisonment, suicide seems to be a reasonable choice for many persons who would not consider it an option under normal circumstances. Two examples of such a situation are the cases of Feinstein and Barazani, one of them a member of the *Irgun Zva'i Leumi* (National Military Organization) and the other of *Lohamei Herut Israel* (Fighters for Israel's Freedom), who, having been sentenced to death by a British mandatory court in 1947 for their activities as members of those underground Jewish military organizations, committed joint suicide. Other situational factors include group suicide, chain suicide, and the effect of audience.

Attempted 'Brainwashing,' " *Psychiatry* 19 (1956): 149–72 and R. J. Lifton, *Thought Reform and the Psychology of Totalism* (New York: W. W. Norton, 1961).

Group suicide. There are a few examples of mass suicide in history. Not one of these cases has been a terrorist suicide, but they seem relevant to the present discussion because they indicate the power of group pressure in generating extreme behavior. The most dramatic, albeit not the most bizarre, example of this kind is the communal suicide at Masada.

In A.D. 73, during the Jewish revolt against the occupying Roman forces, the tenth Roman legion, commanded by Flavius Sylva, was about to break into Masada, the last fortress of the rebels, after a three-year siege. Within the walls of Masada there were hundreds of *Kana'im* (Zealots) and their families—altogether nearly 1,000 men, women, and children. When it became clear that nothing could prevent the fall of the fortress the next morning, the leader of the Zealots (El'azar Ben Ya'ir) convened his followers and persuaded them to commit suicide rather than be captured by the Romans and suffer torture and slavery. Following his speech, the men slaughtered their families, killed each other, and the last took his own life. Only two women and five children hid and survived the carnage.

Among the 960 suicides in Masada there were certainly many—perhaps a majority—who did not wish to die. Why, then, did they agree to commit suicide? Undoubtedly, the influence of a charismatic leader played an important and probably crucial role in this case. Even more important, however, was the group pressure once the communal decision had been reached. This pressure was not necessarily coercive. There is no indication that persons were murdered because they refused to participate in the communal suicide. The critical factor probably was the individuals' feeling of commitment to the group as a social system and a strong sense of common fate.

It should be noted that, on the individual level, the act of suicide in Masada, probably like other cases of mass suicide, was passive. Except for the last warrior who actually killed himself, all others were killed by relatives and friends. In this regard, cases of communal self-destruction cannot be considered "pure" suicides. Not only is the element of individual freedom of choice questionable in these cases, the final auto-implementation of the decision is absent. This may well be the difference between the readiness to die and a true willingness to die. From another aspect, the difference between the passive nature of communal suicide and the usually active nature of individual suicide may reflect the disparity between the ideational willingness to die espoused by the many and the actual execution of the death wish implemented by the few.

Chain suicide. A special case of group influence on self-destruction is reflected in the phenomenon of chain suicide. The most dramatic example of this sort was the chain suicide of the eleven IRA members mentioned above. Unlike communal suicide, in this case suicide was actively committed by each of the eleven persons involved. Moreover, it is hard to imagine the will power necessary for committing this terrible form of suicide, which involves a protracted and painful process of consecutive deaths, all in the face of the implorings of relatives and priests. As in a situation of concurrent mass suicide, commitment to a group has an important role in chain suicide. In the latter situation, however, this commitment is made even more binding by the death of the first in the chain. The partners' agreement that each one will kill himself in turn becomes irreversible upon the death of the first in the series. The first cannot release his partners from their part of the agreement post mortem.

The effect of audience. Suicide conducted for the purpose of furthering a political cause is a demonstrative act by definition. As such, it requires the presence of an audience. In the era of electronic media this requirement is fulfilled more efficiently by television reporting than by the physical presence of spectators. Presumably, however, for the person committing the suicide the actual presence of a crowd may have a stronger ancillary influence than the assumption that the act would be reported by the media.

PERSONALITY FACTORS. The simple fact that most terrorists—Shi'ite, Japanese, Irish, or German, regardless of the conditions under which they have lived and fought—have neither committed suicide nor tried to do so attests to the importance of personality characteristics in the phenomenon of suicidal terrorism.

Most psychological theories of suicide view personality characteristics and intrapsychic processes as the most important factors in self-destructive behavior. Weiss, for instance, considers personality disintegration to be the single most important factor in suicide.[13] However, different writers emphasize different characteristics and processes in trying to identify the making of a suicidal personality. A survey of the various approaches is beyond the scope of this chapter.

The study of the personalities of suicidal terrorists is almost impossi-

[13] Weiss, "Suicide."

ble. In addition to the obvious fact that people who have actually committed suicide are unavailable for interviews and tests, in the case of terrorists, more than in ordinary suicides, the histories of the individuals
involved are usually unavailable. The rarity of suicidal terrorist attacks
further precludes any hope of reaching firm conclusions on the basis of
accepted scientific methods. Some inferences can be made using the scanty
information available, but they must be regarded as partial and tentative
at best. The most consistent element in the few cases in which the personal history is known seems to be a broken family background.

Terrorist suicide in the Middle East: A factual examination

Although there were cases of violent Palestinian terrorist suicide in the
1970s, widespread interest in this phenomenon was aroused in the wake
of the spectacular, high-casualty car-bombing attacks carried out by fundamentalist Shi'ites in 1983. These attacks included the suicidal car
bombings of the U.S. embassy in Beirut on 18 April 1983 (80 dead and
142 wounded); the attack on the U.S. Marines' headquarters in Beirut
on 23 October 1983 (273 dead and 81 wounded) and the concurrent
attack on the French paratroopers' headquarters there (58 dead and 15
wounded); an attack on the Israeli government building in Tyre on 4
November 1983 (88 dead and 69 wounded); and an attack on the American embassy in Kuwait on 12 December 1983 (4 dead and 15 wounded).

Bearing in mind the problems of definition already discussed, I have
included in this survey of suicidal Middle Eastern terrorist attacks only
those cases in which the perpetrators undertook a mission that would
result in certain death. High-risk missions—such as the attacks in the
Rome and Vienna airports on 27 December 1985, in which the deaths of
the perpetrators was a high probability but not a certain consequence—
were not counted. Therefore, suicidal car bombing is the only mode of
operation included in this sample.

Thirty-one cases of suicidal terrorist attacks were registered between
1983 and 1986. This count includes only those incidents in which the
perpetrators were actually killed. In two additional cases, the perpetrators were caught or escaped before carrying out the suicidal mission. In
two of the thirty-one attacks the perpetrators were evidently fooled by
their senders, who led them to believe that they would survive the mission. Because in most cases it is impossible to differentiate between genuine suicide events and those that were carried out by fooled couriers of

explosives detonated by remote control, it was decided to include in the list also the incidents that were exposed as false suicides ex post facto but would have otherwise been counted as true self-destruction.

CHANGES OVER TIME. Suicidal car-bomb attacks started in Lebanon in April 1983. By the end of the year, four additional attacks of this kind had been committed, all perpetrated by fundamentalist Shi'ites. These attacks caused heavy casualties, a total of 503 in 1983. However, despite the immense publicity and the deep concern generated, only two suicidal attacks were carried out in 1984—one of them by Amal, a mainstream Shi'ite organization, and the other by a fundamentalist Shi'ite group. The number of casualties in that year dropped to a total of twenty-three. A new flurry of suicidal car bombings occurred in 1985—twenty-two attacks in all. Twenty were perpetrated by pro-Syrian groups and reflected a central Syrian effort to use this spectacular form of terrorism to promote Syrian interests in Lebanon. One of the remaining incidents was carried out by Amal and the other by a fundamentalist Shi'ite group. Suicidal attacks in 1985 resulted in seventy-two fatalities. The number of suicidal car bombings declined again in 1986: Only two attacks were committed, both by pro-Syrian groups, resulting in one fatality.[14]

PERPETRATING ORGANIZATIONS. By the end of 1986 it became clear that most of the suicide attacks were carried out by secular, non-Shi'ite groups. Of the thirty-one incidents, only seven were perpetrated by fundamentalist Shi'ites (six by the self-styled Islamic Jihad, actually a cover name for Hizballah, and one by al-Dawa). Two additional suicidal car-bombing attacks were carried out by Amal, a Shi'ite organization motivated by secular rather than religious causes.

Most of the attacks were committed by members of various pro-Syrian groups. Ten were carried out by the Syrian Social Nationalist party (SSNP), seven by members of the Ba'ath party, two by the Socialist Nasserite Organization, two by members of the Lebanese Communist party, and one by a Palestinian whose organizational affiliation has not been ascertained. In fact, it seeems that the exact group identification is relatively unimportant, because the suicidal attacks were prepared from start to finish by Syrian intelligence officers, who recruited the suicide drivers

[14] The statistics presented in this section cover the 1981–6 period (inclusive). The data are based on information collected by the Project on Terrorism at the Jaffee Center for Strategic Studies at Tel Aviv University.

from any of several organizations strongly influenced by Syria, provided them with rigged cars, and instructed them about the operation. On several occasions the last messages of the perpetrators were shown on Syrian and on Lebanese television. Typically, President Assad's picture and a large Syrian flag were portrayed on the wall behind the terrorists. In fact, Syria has not tried to conceal its role in organizing these attacks. On the contrary: President Assad himself, in a Ba'ath (the ruling Syrian party) convention in March 1986, paid tribute to the suicide car bombers by reciting their names one by one, and he declared that many more like them would be trained by Syria.

The distribution of the perpetrators of suicidal attacks just presented leads to the unavoidable conclusion that this brand of terrorism is not the exclusive domain of religious fanaticism in general, nor is it a characteristic of Shi'ite self-sacrificial zealots in particular. In most cases the perpetrators sacrificed themselves in the name of a nationalistic rather than a religious idea, and the majority of them were Sunnis rather than Shi'ites.

SEX. Thirty-six persons were involved as suicide perpetrators in the thirty-one incidents, thirty males and six females. Undoubtedly, the great majority of the members in the groups under consideration are males. However, because the distribution of members by sex in these groups is unknown, it is impossible to assess "gender proneness" to suicidal terrorism in this sample.

AGE. Information about age was available for twenty of the thirty-six suicides. Ages ranged between sixteen and twenty-eight, with a mean of 21.3. No systematic difference was found between males and females in this regard. It should be noted that these data are a better representation of the pro-Syrian groups than of the fundamentalist Shi'ites, because the latter have maintained the anonymity of their suicides as a matter of policy. Thus, the ages of only three of the seven fundamentalist suicides are known. These, however, fall within the range just mentioned.

GEOGRAPHICAL LOCATION. All but two of the suicidal car bombings took place in Lebanon; the remaining attacks occurred in Kuwait. Why did the terrorist groups refrain from carrying out suicidal attacks in their main enemies' countries, that is, Israel or the United States? It may be argued that it is much easier to get a car bomb in Lebanon than anywhere else. Still, an effective suicide attack can be carried out by other means—hand grenades, for example. A plausible explanation for the fact that suicidal terrorist attacks have been practically limited to the Lebanese arena lies in the process of recruiting suicidal terrorists. A leader has to sift through a large population to find suitable candidates. Furthermore, it is reasonable to assume that volunteers for such missions have to be used rapidly lest they change their mind, an eventuality that becomes more likely the greater the distance in time and place from their launching point.

Conclusion

The fact that the early suicidal car-bombing incidents were committed by Shi'ite fundamentalists drove many observers to the hasty conclusion that religious fanaticism was a key factor in this phenomenon. As early as January 1984, however, Merari and Braunstein wrote:

The recent phenomenon of Shi'ite suicide terrorism is no exception to what we have known hitherto. It has acquired much publicity as a result of three elements, none of them new in itself: the use of suicides, the use of car bombs, and the use of very large quantities of explosives. Of these three the most worrisome is the last, since it reflects state patronage.

Contrary to the impression that the Iranians and Syrians are trying to create—with the gullible complicity of some media elements—the stock of Shi'ite zealots willing to commit suicide is quite limited. . . . It is not unreasonable to assume that the so-called "Islamic Jihad" would have made more abundant use of the impressive and effective suicide car-bombing technique had it the option to do so. Presumably, then, the operations' organizers simply ran out of volunteers to die.[15]

Half a decade after these words were written, these conclusions still seem plausible.

Suicidal terrorist attacks are very rare. During the period under consideration, thousands of terrorist attacks took place in the Middle East. Suicidal events constituted a small fraction of them.

Culture in general and religion in particular seem to be relatively unimportant in the phenomenon of terrorist suicide. Terrorist suicide, like any other suicide, is basically an individual rather than a group phenomenon: it is done by people who wish to die for personal reasons. The terrorist framework simply offers the excuse (rather than the real drive) for doing it and the legitimation for carrying it out in a violent way.

[15] A. Merari and Y. Braunstein, *Shi'ite Terrorism* (Tel Aviv: Jaffee Center for Strategic Studies Special Report, January 1984).

There is no evidence to support the notion that the influence of a charismatic political or religious leader is in itself sufficient to drive an otherwise nonsuicidal person to wish to commit terrorist suicide. However, such influence may conceivably serve as an ancillary factor, boosting an already existing suicidal tendency and channeling it to a certain modus operandi, time, and place. The influence of a charismatic leader is probably short term and grows weaker as a function of the distance from the original habitat.

Practically all known cases of suicidal terrorist attacks as defined in this chapter have been committed individually. Nevertheless, the use of intragroup commitment for inducing chain or concurrent multiple suicidal attacks cannot be ruled out in the future.

Personality factors seem to play a critical role in suicidal terrorism. Although the available information does not permit any generalizations concerning personality patterns, it seems that a broken family background is an important constituent.

Part IV

Responding to terrorism:
Decision making and the pressures on leadership

11

Hostage taking, the presidency, and stress

MARGARET G. HERMANN AND CHARLES F. HERMANN

Hostage-taking events caused major crises for both Jimmy Carter and Ronald Reagan. During each presidency, hostage taking became a central focus of U.S. foreign policy and an obsession of the president, and it affected domestic as well as international politics. Both presidents found themselves caught in a "damned if I do and damned if I don't" predicament, experiencing the symptoms of personal stress so often associated with decisional conflicts that are consequential for both leader and country. In this chapter we explore why hostage-taking situations have the potential for being stressful for presidents, the constraining effects that this stress can have on decision making, and some ways to help limit the impact of stress in the future.

Why hostage taking produces stress

Hostage taking has been called "smart" terrorism, because the terrorists involved maintain control over the situation, gain media attention for their cause over a sustained period of time, and force governments to recognize them in the course of any negotiations to free the hostages. In effect, the leadership of the terrorist group taking the hostages becomes the puppet master, pulling the strings—some might say jerking the strings—of the government whose people are taken hostage. The aims of the terrorist organization are to gain maximum press and television coverage for their cause and themselves and to increase their bargaining power for the next round.

Hostage taking puts a leader such as the American president in an awkward situation, presenting him with a problem over which he has

211

little control. He is confronted with the unexpected and must cope with adversaries perceived as irrational. The dilemma for the president becomes how to get the hostages released without giving in to the demands of the terrorists or having any of the hostages killed—and how to do so in a timely fashion, without making his administration look as if it is weak or overreacting.

In effect, the president has more than the terrorists to deal with in a hostage-taking event. The media bombard him with questions about what he is going to do about the hostages and broadcast up-to-the-minute reports on their condition, giving the terrorists an opportunity to air their complaints, demands, and the nature of their cause. Neither aspect of the media coverage falls on deaf ears as the attentive, and television-oriented, public becomes involved in what is happening. Moreover, the American people identify with hostages, often wondering what they would do if they were in their shoes. And they urge the president—through their responses to polls, letters to the White House or Congress, and discussions with opinion leaders—to do something quickly to free the hostages. As the situation wears on, public support is put on the line; the president's popularity fluctuates with the public's perception of how well or poorly he is doing in seeking the release of the hostages. Congressional leaders who see the hostage crisis as a possible election issue also put pressure on the president to act. And the families of the hostages write, call, and visit with the president as well as the media. They plead with the president to get their loved ones back for them.

At the core of the problem for the public, for many policymakers, and probably for the president himself is the significant discrepancy between their image of the nation's capabilities and the harsh reality imposed by the terrorists' successful act of taking and holding hostages. The U.S. public and government alike view the nation as the strongest military power in the free world—one of the globe's two superpowers and an undisputed leader in science and technology. How is it possible, they ask, that such a mighty nation appears incapable of protecting its people, or at least of securing their prompt and safe release, from a handful of seemingly poorly equipped men and women usually associated with an impoverished nation or group? This sense of impotence can contribute to an enormous feeling of frustration and even anger. The frustration is particularly acute for a people who pride themselves on their military and technological dominance.

Coupled with the terrorists' demands and ultimatums, the calls for action on the part of those to whom the president is accountable can lead the president to turn what is a foreign policy crisis for the country into a personally stressful event. His administration and job are on the line; his "domestic authority and international prestige," as well as his "image and reputation," are at stake.[1] How the president handles the situation has implications for his reelection, if he is eligible for it, as well as for the interpretation of his tenure in office by history. He can become understandably concerned, anxious, apprehensive, frustrated, uncertain, angry, tentative; that is, he can experience stress. When this happens, the president, in effect, has internalized the event. He has made it a personal issue; his sense of self is under attack. No longer is it the government's problem, it is the president's problem.

Hostage taking exacerbates this tendency to personalize the issue because the terrorists, press, and hostage families act to give the victims a real and immediate identity. The hostages do not remain faceless suffering masses; they are named individuals who may plead their own case over television and whose attractive, anguished wives and children often meet with the president. The predisposition to personalize the issue is reinforced as the president becomes, in a sense, a senior member of each victim's family.

A second reinforcing factor is the usual "innocence" or "patriotism" of the hostages themselves. They typically have done nothing personally to trigger the hostile behavior directed at them except to be in the wrong place at the wrong time. And in some cases they may be dedicated employees of the government simply fulfilling their assigned duties. As a compassionate human being, the president is moved to accept their plight on his own shoulders.

Moreover, as we have learned in the Iran and Lebanese hostage-taking situations, the process of gaining release for the hostages with whom the president has personally identified may stretch over a long period of time. The pressure on the president thus continues to build, as first one tactic and then another is tried to get the hostages freed. With each failure comes a greater sense of futility and more uncertainty over future steps. If early attempts have involved negotiation, there is often the cry from the public and from some on the president's staff to escalate to a military response. And the media begin to suggest that the administration is weak and soft, that the terrorists are winning the battle.

[1] Martha Crenshaw, "The Psychology of Political Terrorism," in *Political Psychology*, edited by Margaret G. Hermann (San Francisco: Jossey-Bass, 1986), 400.

Signs that both presidents Carter and Reagan personalized the hostage events in their tenures and experienced stress are found in the biographies and statements of participants in these situations. From Carter's memoir we compiled the following widely scattered comments:

The safety and well-being of the American hostages became a constant concern for me, no matter what other duties I was performing as President. . . . I was worrying about the hostages. . . . In spite of many other responsibilities, the hostages were always in my mind . . . my most pressing duty still was to secure the release of the hostages. . . . From this remark, some news reporters claimed that I now thought the hostage situation was manageable. If anyone knew how difficult it was to manage, I did. . . . Our hopes had been shattered so many times that I approached this new development with some skepticism. . . . More than anything else, it was still Iran and our hostages that gnawed away at me. . . . The release of the American hostages had almost become an obsession with me. Of course, their lives, safety, and freedom were the paramount considerations, but there was more to it. I wanted to have my decisions vindicated.[2]

Gary Sick, who was responsible for Iranian affairs in President Carter's National Security Council, has observed:

The crisis was highly personalized. To Washington policy makers, the hostages were not abstractions; in many cases they were friends. . . . When President Carter said, as he did on many different occasions both publicly and privately, that the fate of the hostages was on his mind at every waking moment, he was not posturing for political effect. Rather, he was expressing what was a daily reality for almost all of us who were caught up in the crisis.[3]

The Tower Commission Report suggests that Reagan had similar feelings about the American hostages held in Lebanon:

The President was clearly quite concerned about the hostages. Mr. McFarlane told the Board that the President inquired almost daily about the welfare of the hostages. Chief of Staff Regan is reported to have told reporters on November 14, 1986, that "the President brings up the hostages at about 90 percent of his briefings." Mr. Regan is reported to have said that each morning at the daily intelligence briefing, the President asked VADM Poindexter: "John, anything new on the hostages?" . . . By his own account, as evidenced in his diary notes, and as conveyed to the Board by his principal advisors, President Reagan was deeply committed to securing the release of the hostages. It was this intense compassion for the hostages that appeared to motivate his steadfast support of the Iran initiative, even in the face of opposition from his Secretaries of State and Defense [George Shultz and Caspar Weinberger]. . . . The President's expressed concern for the safety of both the hostages and the Iranians who could have been at risk

[2] Jimmy Carter, *Keeping Faith* (New York: Bantam Books, 1982), 459, 460, 470, 480, 496, 525, 558, 580, 594.
[3] Gary Sick, *All Fall Down* (New York: Penguin Books, 1986), 262.

may have been conveyed in a manner so as to inhibit the full functioning of the system.[4]

Several observers of President Reagan have also noted his personal commitment to the freeing of the hostages in Lebanon. "The Iran arms-dealing affair is the mistake of a President whose judgment was warped by his personal anguish at the plight of American citizens in captivity."[5] "You have to know the President to know how strongly he feels about the release of the hostages."[6] "The President was personally driven by that compassion for the hostages from beginning to end."[7] Perhaps the most vivid image the American public had of Reagan's frustration over the hostages was mirrored in his face and voice when he was asked, after the freeing of an American reporter from a Soviet prison, "What about the hostages in Lebanon?" His testy answer was that he was doing everything possible to get them released; it was very important to him.

Effects of stress on decision making

What happens when a president or anyone else experiences personal stress? What is significant for understanding hostage-taking events is the effect this personal stress can have on decision making. A variety of studies in both laboratory and natural settings have found a similar general relationship between the intensity of individual stress and performance on a task.[8] Those situations in which some stress occurs lead to better performance than situations in which the persons performing the task are emotionally detached. In other words, when stress is relatively mild, performance generally improves. The person becomes motivated to act. As the intensity of individual stress increases, however, the rate of improvement

[4] John Tower, Edmund Muskie, and Brent Scowcroft, *The Tower Commission Report* (New York: Bantam Books and Times Books, 1987), 36, 79.
[5] William Safire, "Ten Myths About the Reagan Debacle," *New York Times Magazine*, 22 March 1987, p. 24.
[6] George Bush, "An Interview with the Vice-President," *Time*, 8 December 1986, p. 42.
[7] Edmund Muskie, "Press Interview on Report of Tower Commission Report," *Time*, 9 March 1987, p. 24.
[8] See Richard S. Lazarus, *Psychological Stress and the Coping Process* (New York: McGraw-Hill, 1966); Charles F. Hermann, *International Crises: Insights from Behavioral Research* (New York: Free Press, 1972); George V. Coelho, David A. Hamburg, and John E. Adams, *Coping and Adaptation* (New York: Basic Books, 1974); Irving L. Janis and Leon Mann, *Decision Making: A Psychological Analysis of Conflict, Choice, and Commitment* (New York: Free Press, 1977); and Alexander L. George, *Presidential Decision Making in Foreign Policy: The Effective Use of Information and Advice* (Boulder, Colo.: Westview Press, 1980).

in performance begins to slow and then to stop altogether. If the amount of stress a person experiences continues to increase, performance begins to plummet, and at some point the performance can become much worse than when there was no stress at all. Of course, the amount of stress that a person can absorb before it becomes dysfunctional varies from one person to another and with other factors,[9] but in general the relationship holds.

Most of the research providing the bases for this pattern involves a stress stimulus of fairly limited duration. We know that hostage-taking episodes can last for weeks, months, and even years. It is interesting to speculate about how the general effect on performance might be influenced by situations of long duration in which other demands and activities (some of which may be pleasant and tension-reducing) are interspersed in the life of a person relentlessly exposed to a major source of stress. Rather than the steady, smooth decline in performance suggested in the generalized pattern, the prolonged episode with other intervening events might have a more stair-stepped decline. As the individual is momentarily diverted from the stress-inducing experience, there may be a leveling-off or plateau in the detrimental performance consequences, perhaps even some recovery if the diversion produces relaxation and satisfaction. But as the stress-inducing situation continues unresolved, performance gradually declines. Of course, diverting events of a demanding and unpleasant nature may simply compound the stress a person experiences, in which case performance of all kinds may decline more precipitously.

When does stress become so extreme as seriously to inhibit the quality of decision making and related tasks required of a president? Although it is difficult to predict how much stress a particular person can tolerate before his or her decision making begins to deteriorate, it is possible to describe various symptoms that a person under stress may display and the effects of such stress responses on decision making. In the following sections we suggest some of these symptoms and their effects on decision making, particularly as it applies to presidential behavior in gaining the release of hostages. Having established that presidents Carter and Reagan were experiencing rather strong stress in coping with the Iranian and Lebanese hostage-taking events, we use these presidents where feasible to illustrate our points.

[9] Margaret G. Hermann, "Indicators of Stress in Policy Makers During Foreign Policy Crises," *Political Psychology* 1 (1979): 27–46.

Ways of coping with stress

How do people cope with stress? The research literature suggests that people have three general ways of responding to the negative feelings they are experiencing:[10] they can withdraw from the situation, "take the situation on," or panic.

By withdrawing from the situation people can psychologically distance themselves from the anxiety and other painful feelings they are having by denying any involvement in the event or by restructuring the event. Janis and Mann have described three strategies for avoiding or withdrawing from the situation:[11] people can simply deny that the event is occurring; they can shift responsibility ("pass the buck"); or they can rationalize that the situation is not so bad as it might seem at first glance and claim that there are positive aspects in what is happening. These authors argue that this way of coping with stress—what they call "defensive avoidance"—is more likely when the few alternative ways of dealing with the situation all have negative overtones and there is pressure to act.

To "take the situation on" means that the person becomes involved in coping with the problem, confronting what is happening and trying to deal with it. Confronting the situation may include increased problem-oriented activity. But it also can mean increasingly volatile actions (ranging from aggression to gratitude) toward others who are trying to help cope with the problem, increased rigidity in the proposals for action, or increased intentional deception. Jumping into the fray is generally easier when there are some options for action that show promise of ending the stressful situation and the policymaker perceives there is enough time to put the plan into motion before something else happens.

One way of taking the situation on involves hypervigilance—a state in which there is "indiscriminate openness to all information."[12] People perceive that there ought to be a way out of the dilemma in which they find themselves and frantically search for cues to this solution. And they tenaciously pursue feasible solutions, sometimes without careful attention to their likelihood of success, the costs that may be incurred, or the

---

[10] See, for example, Lazarus, *Psychological Stress;* Janis and Mann, *Decision Making;* M. Hermann, "Indicators of Stress"; and Alexander George, "Adaptation to Stress in Political Decision-Making: The Individual, Small Group and Organizational Contexts," in *Coping and Adaptation,* edited by George V. Coelho, David A. Hamburg, and John E. Adams (New York: Basic Books, 1974).

[11] Janis and Mann, *Decision Making.*

[12] Ibid., 205.

direct or indirect consequences that may result from their success or failure.

Some observers might detect traces of panic, a third possible response to stress, in the previous two categories. As used here, however, panic refers to a nearly complete immobilization of one's cognitive, and often physical, systems. Normal reasoning processes become adversely affected. The same ideas may be repeated over and over again or thoughts may be incomplete. In the face of physical danger, the person who is in a state of panic may be incapable of calling for help or even running away. Acute breakdowns of this sort are in some sense less of a problem in public decision making, because associates typically recognize the person's inability to function and relieve that person of the responsibility of making a decision, even if such action is not publicly acknowledged.

People often have characteristic ways of dealing with stress. Some generally deny that anything is wrong, others consistently pass the buck, and still others bolster their own position when under stress. One way to gain information about a policymaker's typical coping behavior is to learn about the person's usual decision style. Stress accentuates a person's decision style.[13] A policymaker who has a general tendency to delegate may, under stress, tend to shift responsibility; a policymaker whose decision making is guided by an ideology may, under stress, tend to enhance the importance of the ideology; a policymaker who takes pride in always tackling problems head-on, under stress, may insist on solving the problem personally, often to the exclusion of other, more pressing tasks.

Each means of coping with stress discussed here has implications for how a policymaker such as the president will search for information and engage his staff and advisers in the decision-making process. Because there is evidence to suggest that President Carter was hypervigilant in dealing with the Iranian hostage crisis and that President Reagan shifted responsibility in attempting to free the Americans held captive in Lebanon, we illustrate the relationship between coping behavior, information search, and the decision-making process for these two ways of dealing with stress.

HYPERVIGILANT INVOLVEMENT IN THE SITUATION. A policymaker who copes with increasing stress by becoming hypervigilant becomes very sensitive to contextual information but loses his ability to discriminate among the cues being received. The negative feelings the policymaker experi-

[13] M. Hermann, "Indicators of Stress," 27–46.

ences drive him to try all alternatives, "relevant or irrelevant, reliable or unreliable, supportive or nonsupportive."[14] It is important to be doing something, because in the process he is likely to stumble onto the most viable alternative and, in any case, he feels better when he has taken some action—disaster is put off for the moment. This thrashing around can lead the policymaker to try hastily contrived solutions that are as apt to fail as succeed in addressing the problem because their applicability has been poorly evaluated. Everyone gets into the act as the policymaker enlists the help of experts and nonexperts alike—anyone with an idea, new angle, or new piece of information. As a consequence of the focus on present information, the policymaker's time perspective becomes collapsed and he tends to neglect consideration of the future consequences of any action.[15] The immediate danger is so intense, the future seems almost irrelevant. Moreover, while an approach is showing some success, the policymaker develops a fixation on it to the exclusion of other options. But the policymaker is quick to engage in undoing, moving rapidly to change his approach when a decision appears to be going sour. As a result, the policymaker may appear to the public as if he has no firm policy and is indecisive and weak. To rationalize the need for change in tactics and strategy, the policymaker simplifies the adversary and, more important, the limitations on the adversary. Such behavior means that the ability to control events lies with that adversary.

Sick has described Carter's hypervigilance during the Iranian hostage crisis: "One of the consequences of this intense personal commitment [to free the hostages] was a strong impulse to do something, almost as if action was a necessary end in itself."[16] During the course of the 444 days that the hostages were held, Carter tried a "battery of policy initiatives"; when one was perceived to have failed, he moved to try something else. Each failure was blamed on Khomeini for once more failing to give his support. As Carter noted in his diary, "Every time one of the Iranian government officials shows any sign of rationality, he is immediately incompatible with Khomeini and is replaced."[17]

Carter's general decision style, in which he took a personal interest in being a part of the policy-making process by educating himself in the

[14] Janis and Mann, *Decision Making*, 205.
[15] See Charles F. Hermann, *Crises in Foreign Policy: A Simulation Analysis* (Indianapolis: Bobbs-Merrill, 1969); and Ole R. Holsti, *Crisis, Escalation, War* (Canada: McGill-Queen's University Press, 1972).
[16] Sick, *All Fall Down*, 260.
[17] Carter, *Keeping Faith*, 467.

details of the problem under consideration and processing the information needed for analysis and decision, became accentuated in the Iranian hostage affair. As Carter notes, "There were so many conflicting questions and ideas during this time that we took extra steps to insure maximum harmony among the many agencies involved. At least once a day my top advisers . . . met in the Situation Room at the White House to discuss Iran. When I did not meet with them, they prepared written minutes almost immediately after they adjourned. Any questions of policy were referred to me. . . ."[18] He and his staff gave credence to the adage, "Our job is to take a ten percent chance of success, try to turn it into a twenty percent chance, and hope for a break," as they tried "dozens if not hundreds of channels" during the course of the crisis.[19] In one period that spanned several months, they even relied on "two adventurers" as Carter dubbed them,[20] a French lawyer and an Argentine businessman. Each channel and option was pursued until it became clear failure was in sight, then another was chosen. With each change in action came domestic pressure for even more severe actions. The dilemma became, "To what extent should a great nation be prepared to accept short-term humiliation in the interest of long-term strategic objectives that are themselves uncertain? At what point does such humiliation itself begin to produce strategic consequences?"[21]

When a president becomes hypervigilant and immerses himself totally in the decision process, he may well accept advisers as colleagues and set the stage for "groupthink."[22] People who join him in the inner circle become partners in the search for a solution. In the process, such advisers often show the symptoms of excessive concurrence seeking that are characteristics of groupthink. Among these symptoms are a strong sense of vulnerability that requires members to stick together and support one another; a fixation on only one reasonable way of dealing with the situation at any point in time; selective perception and attention to information that validates the chosen option; a high sense that what is being done is right; a stereotyped view of the adversary as irrational; and pressure on all members to go along with the consensus. Groupthink becomes more likely if the task must be performed in the utmost secrecy, because those involved remain even more insulated from sources of in-

[18] Ibid., 462.
[19] Sick, All Fall Down, 297, 313.
[20] Carter, Keeping Faith, 485.
[21] Sick, All Fall Down, 355–6.
[22] See Irving L. Janis, Victims of Groupthink (Boston: Houghton-Mifflin, 1972).

formation outside the group. Descriptions of the decision-making process during both the negotiation and military-rescue phases of the Iranian hostage situation show evidence of this dysfunctional process.[23]

DEFENSIVE AVOIDANCE: SHIFTING RESPONSIBILITY. Janis and Mann use a cartoon to depict the defensive avoidance of a stressful situation they call shifting responsibility. An exhausted woman surrounded by children says to her friend, "Lou makes all the big decisions . . . like should we have a trade agreement with China, should we set up a space station on the moon. He leaves all the little decisions to me . . . like where we should live, where we should send the kids to school."[24] Unlike Harry Truman, whose desk carried the sign, "The buck stops here," the policymaker who shifts responsibility under stress delegates difficult decisions to someone else. Often the person wishing to shift responsibility gives it to people who promise that they can resolve the situation with benefits for all—"outside agents of dubious reputation who promise a less painful solution than the genuine experts, who insist that the person himself must take responsibility."[25] In effect, the policymaker reduces his own stress by leaving the field, putting the stressful situation into someone else's hands—someone who knows what the policymaker wants and insists that he or she can resolve the problem.

If the policymaker cannot escape responsibility completely, he will tend to minimize his personal accountability by blaming what is happening on the situation, on luck or fate, on the manipulations of an adversary, or on the constraints inherent in his job. More than ever, successes are viewed as one's own doing; failures are attributable to outside forces.[26] As Alexander George has observed, it is in the nature of the presidential role "that there will be many occasions on which one simply cannot make a good decision without some sacrifice to one's own interests or those of some significant others."[27] The role, not oneself, is to blame for any failure. In the hostage-taking situation, the terrorists also become a target for attribution of blame. They are forcing the policymaker to take countermeasures. This declining sense of responsibility makes aggressive and

[23] Carter, *Keeping Faith;* and Sick, *All Fall Down.*
[24] Janis and Mann, *Decision Making,* 5.
[25] Ibid., 58.
[26] See Susan T. Fiske and S. F. Taylor, *Social Cognition* (Reading, Mass.: Addison-Wesley, 1984); and Donald R. Kinder and Susan T. Fiske, "Presidents in the Public Mind," in *Political Psychology,* edited by Margaret G. Hermann (San Francisco: Jossey-Bass, 1986).
[27] George, "Adaptation to Stress," 186.

hostile behaviors toward the terrorists more feasible, because the policymaker cannot be held accountable for the consequences.

When a policymaker shifts responsibility, the individual or group (the latter is more likely in a major crisis) to whom the task is delegated must, nonetheless, develop a working relationship with the policymaker. Basic management procedures specify the initiation of practices that are widely accepted as necessary if the organization is to be expected to cope effectively with the problem. The objectives of the delegated task must be clear and agreed-upon between the policymaker and the task group. If trade-offs become necessary among the objectives, a shared sense of priorities must exist. Some consensus on what constitutes success—and, even more critically, failure—must be established, along with deadlines for reporting progress. The entire operation depends on careful monitoring, with balanced reporting to the policymaker or his representative, who remains detached from the operation and able to assess its performance and ask critical questions.

When a policymaker elects to deal with stress by distancing himself from the problem, however, these necessary elements may not be created and maintained. Potential indicators of failure tend to intensify the policymaker's experience of stress, which he is trying to reduce. Even periodic monitoring reengages him with the problem, foiling the self-imposed stress-reduction technique of shifting responsibility. Under these conditions, perhaps more than normally, the temptation for his staff to tell the policymaker what he wants to hear is extremely strong. But denying subordinates the chance to discuss the problem candidly with him and to obtain his judgment on the appropriateness of a particular path greatly increases stress and the possibility of group pathology.

Once again the Tower Commission Report is revealing about how President Reagan dealt with the stress he experienced in considering the release of the American hostages in Lebanon. In a section titled "Failure of Responsibility," the report concludes:

In his obvious commitment [to freeing the hostages], the President appears to have proceeded with a concept of the initiative that was not accurately reflected in the reality of the operation. The President did not seem to be aware of the way in which the operation was implemented and the full consequences of U.S. participation. The President's expressed concern for the safety of both the hostages and the Iranians who could have been at risk may have been conveyed in a manner so as to inhibit the full functioning of the system.

The President's management style is to put the principal responsibility for policy review and implementation on the shoulders of his advisors. Nevertheless, with such a complex, high-risk operation and so much at stake, the President should have ensured that the NSC system did not fail him. He did not force his policy to undergo the most critical review. ... At no time did he insist upon accountability and performance review. ... The Board found a strong consensus among NSC participants that the President's priority in the Iran initiative was the release of the U.S. hostages. But setting priorities is not enough when it comes to sensitive and risky initiatives that directly affect U.S. national security. He must ensure that the content and tactics of an initiative match his priorities and objectives. He must insist on accountability. For it is the President who must take responsibility for the NSC system and deal with the consequences.[28]

President Reagan shifted responsibility; he magnified his usual decision style of delegating authority during the Iran-contra affair by transferring authority. And in the process he unleashed what Apple has called the "reckless cowboys, off on their own on a wild ride."[29] The National Security Council staff believed they were given authority to get the hostages released and acted on that authority. They formed a cohesive unit and worked to keep people who disagreed with what they were doing, such as Shultz and Weinberger, out of the process.[30] Given the need for the utmost secrecy, this group led a covert operation that "functioned largely outside the orbit of the U.S. government"[31] and thus was never challenged by the normal checks and balances of bureaucratic politics.

Strategies for reducing stress in hostage-taking events

Are there strategies that can help American presidents cope with hostage-taking situations more effectively? Can we reduce the dysfunctional and disruptive effects of stress on presidents' behavior? Considering that terrorism, particularly the taking of hostages, is unlikely to cease in the near future, can we strengthen our government's hand by diminishing the stress on those who have to make a response? We believe there are at least five strategies that could limit the effects of stress during hostage-taking situations: (1) humanizing the enemy, (2) depersonalizing the situation for the president, (3) "emotionally inoculating" the people involved in the decision process, (4) encouraging dissent among the president's advisers, and (5) continuing the study of how presidents manage stress.

HUMANIZING THE ENEMY. Just as terrorists tend to see all people and governments as either for or against them, government leaders faced with dealing with terrorists often do the same. As Holsti has observed, one of

[28] Tower, Muskie, and Scowcroft, *Tower Report,* 79–80.
[29] R. W. Apple, Jr., "Introduction," in ibid., xv.
[30] Ibid., 81.   [31] Ibid., xv.

the casualties of high stress is the ability to enter into the frames of reference of others.[32] Instead, people experiencing stress tend to dehumanize the enemy, enabling them to deal with the enemy without any sense of remorse. The enemy is irrational—he deserves what he gets.

Studies of terrorists, however, suggest that terrorism does not appear to be the result of mental pathologies.[33] "A general psychiatric explanation of terrorism is impossible. To define all terrorists as mentally ill would be an easy way to solve the problem, simply by invoking evil spirits in order to exclude from normality those from whom we want to be as different as possible."[34] People who join terrorist groups have needs, beliefs, and grievances not utterly unlike those of other people; people who lead terrorist groups are motivated by drives for survival and image-maintenance similar to those that motivate governments. To deal effectively with people who take hostages, we need to be able to put ourselves in their shoes, to understand what they want, and to consider what it would take to help them save face and release the hostages.

But putting ourselves in the shoes of the terrorists cannot mean simply assuming that they have the same values or motives as we do. As Crenshaw notes:

Appropriate countermeasures must be tailored to accurate assessment of terrorist behavior. How terrorists perceive the threat of government coercion may determine whether or not policies of deterrence will work. How terrorists interpret success and failure may be critical to policy effectiveness, since what the government regards as a threat of punishment may be considered by the terrorist as a reward. Policies intended to inhibit terrorism may instead lead to its escalation.[35]

During hostage-taking situations presidents need people on their decision-making team who are acquainted with the groups who have taken the hostages. Although it would be better if such persons could remain on assignment with the president throughout the emergency, periodic consultation with these experts would be preferable to none at all.

[32]Holsti, *Crisis, Escalation, War*, 199.
[33]See, for example, Crenshaw, "Political Terrorism"; R. R. Corrado, "A Critique of the Mental Disorder Perspective of Political Terrorism," *International Journal of Law and Psychiatry* 4 (1981): 293–310; K. Heskin, *Northern Ireland: A Psychological Analysis* (New York: Columbia University Press, 1980); H. Jäger, G. Schmidtchen, and L. Süllwold, *Analysen zum Terrorismus* (Opladen: Westdeutscher Verlag, 1981), vol. 2, *Lebenslauf-Analysen;* and W. Rasch, "Psychological Dimensions of Political Terrorism in the Federal Republic of Germany," *International Journal of Law and Psychiatry* 2 (1979): 79–85.
[34]Franco Ferracuti and F. Bruno, "Psychiatric Aspects of Terrorism in Italy," in *The Mad, the Bad and the Different: Essays in Honor of Simon Dinitz*, edited by I. L. Barak-Galantz and C. R. Hurt (Lexington, Mass.: Heath, 1981), 206.
[35]Crenshaw, "Political Terrorism," 408.

Such a need suggests it is important to have within the intelligence community people who are knowledgeable about various terrorist groups and a roster of people around the world who have dealt with or studied particular terrorist organizations. And in the event of a terrorist incident, the president and his top advisers should have ready access to these specialists.

DEPERSONALIZING THE SITUATION FOR THE PRESIDENT. As noted at the beginning of this chapter, hostage-taking events abroad that involve American citizens have all the ingredients for producing stress in presidents. They, in effect, become domestic as well as foreign policy crises as the media, the families of the hostages, the public, and Congress seek action and criticize how the president behaves. Such situations threaten the president's self-image as well as the reputation and image of his administration. Presidents appear to personalize the event—to take it on as a personal problem, not just as a foreign policy problem that the government must solve. The issue becomes how to reverse this trend and help presidents keep the problem at the policy level rather than making it personal. How can we help the president depersonalize hostage-taking situations?

Several possibilities exist. The first involves educating the media concerning the role they play in making hostage-taking events stressful for the president; a second is to keep the hostages' families at a distance from the president; and a third involves setting up a standard operating procedure for dealing with such events that would include the president but not consume him. Each of these proposals enhances the potential for helping the president keep the situation at arm's length—of depersonalizing the event.

The media are a critical part of any hostage-taking situation, particularly on the international scene. Rubin and Friedland have used the analogy to theater in describing how terrorists use the media when they have hostages. The media enable the terrorists to "make all the world a stage"— "to attract an audience and deliver a message."[36] And the action involved in the kidnapping of hostages makes good copy. The question is, do members of the media understand the difficult position they put the president in when they dwell on the sufferings of the hostages and their loved ones, or when they ask repeatedly what the president is going to

[36] Jeffrey Z. Rubin and Nehemia Friedland, "Theater of Terror," *Psychology Today* (March 1986): 22.

do and when he is going to act? "The media are important to terrorists because they not only relay information but, like good drama critics, interpret it as well. The slant they give—by deciding which events to report and which to ignore, by intentionally or unintentionally expressing approval or disapproval—can create a climate of public support, apathy, or anger."[37] The media need to continue their recent considerations of what the responsibilities of a free press are in covering hostage episodes, including the distinction between reporting new developments and rekindling a story that for the moment has not changed. Some guidelines, even if unevenly applied, might heighten their sensitivity to the role they can play in enhancing the stress of the president.

Probably the greatest push for personalization of the crisis comes from the families of the hostages who, understandably, put pressure on the government to get their loved ones freed. Interacting with the families and receiving letters from the families provide great image-making events for the president. But they also increase the identification of the president with the victim—the victim becomes more real and the pressure to do something grows more intense. We need mechanisms to keep the victims and their families at a distance from the president. In some sense they need to remain just another constituent who needs some help—not the next-door neighbor or part of his extended family. The more agencies outside the president's staff that can deal with the hostages' families and control the information the president receives, the less likely the president is to personalize the situation. In effect, the president needs to be helped to dehumanize the victims.

One last proposal to depersonalize the situation involves the further development of standard operating procedures for dealing with the terrorist kidnapping of American citizens abroad. In his examination of the American search for a policy on terrorism, Lynch observes that there is a proliferation of agencies with counterterrorism responsibilities:

The proliferation of agencies . . . is due in part to greater awareness of the growing terrorist threat. However, this raises the danger that bureaucratic complexities will encourage less than complete cooperation among the agencies. The lines of authority will be vague, responsibilities uncertain, and accountability impossible. Additionally, strategies to deal with terrorism may never be fully developed because decision makers will respond to each new crisis on an ad hoc basis, as a discrete event, unrelated to those which have gone before.[38]

[37] Ibid., 24.
[38] Edward A. Lynch, "International Terrorism: The Search for a Policy," *Terrorism: An International Journal* 9 (1987): 3.

To the extent this characterization is accurate, it suggests the existence currently of ad hoc coordinating mechanisms for dealing with hostage-taking events that necessarily increase the involvement of the president. In the absence of an established interagency group with strong authority and leadership, the president is the logical person to coordinate policy or set up a coordinating group. Thus, he is more likely to become personally caught up in what is happening because nothing will get done unless he sets it in motion. Were stronger standard operating procedures for such situations in place, the president would have less of himself on the line. Moreover, the situation might not automatically assume crisis proportions, because persons with expertise and previous experience would be available to help the president, and there would be proven working procedures.

"EMOTIONALLY INOCULATING" THE PEOPLE INVOLVED IN THE DECISION PROCESS. Janis and Mann describe a technique to help decision makers deal with the buildup of stress in situations in which a sequence of decisions are being made. They call the procedure emotional inoculation—something analogous to the increase of antibodies in the body in reaction to an injection of a small amount of a virus or bacteria. If the policymaker considers not only the positive consequences of his decision but also thinks about the negative things that may happen, he is better able to deal with the negative results if they do happen. In effect, the policymaker prepares himself for setbacks and thus is less overwhelmed if they occur. The individual has "an opportunity to anticipate the loss, to start working through the anxiety or grief, and to make plans that might enable him to cope more effectively with the subsequent crisis."[39]

The research that Janis and Mann muster to support the notion of emotional inoculation suggests that the resulting reduction in the buildup of stress is worth the investment of time and effort. Consideration of how our policy might fail (as well as succeed), and what happens if it fails, encourages forward planning and the assignment of people to think about next steps. Having some ideas about next steps in the face of setbacks, in turn, helps to limit the stress that is experienced. Here is where a catalogue of previous dealings with international hostage-taking situations becomes important. If we were to plot the chronology of events in previous hostage-taking episodes, which types of decisions would we find to

[39] Janis and Mann, *Decision Making*, 389.

have been followed by failure, and which by success? Are there any patterns in the reactions to the decisions that might provide us with information to use in an inoculation procedure for the next time? Because we are dealing with people's lives in a hostage-taking event, there is a need for policies to succeed. But experience tells us that there are often many failures before a success. Can we prepare policymakers to deal with failure through an inoculation procedure?

ENCOURAGING DISSENT AMONG ADVISERS. When we are ready to act, dissent is the last thing we want to hear. We have discussed enough; it is time to do something. Yet as George, C. Hermann, and Janis have observed, this tendency to cut off or limit debate on an issue to only those in favor has serious repercussions for the effectiveness of the resulting decision.[40] When policymakers are under stress, this tendency often leads to premature closure or fixation on only one reasonable option and increased concurrence seeking or groupthink. As C. Hermann has shown, generally the exclusion of alternatives and challenges from the decision-making process prompts policymakers to engage in more extreme behavior than would have been the case if the process had not been disrupted.[41] The Tower Commission Report suggests that the isolation of dissent in the Iran-contra affair permitted the NSC staff members to conduct the operation without oversight and caution.[42]

Many techniques for encouraging the expression of dissent have been proposed in the literature, ranging from the appointment of a devil's advocate and the institutionalization of multiple advocacy[43] to systematic use of a balance sheet[44] to the training of a member of the president's staff in stress management.[45] As important as adopting some technique for assuring dissent is the need for openness to other options and to es-

[40] George, *Presidential Decision Making;* Janis, *Victims of Groupthink;* and C. Hermann, *International Crises,* and "Decision Structure and Process Influences on Foreign Policy," in *Why Nations Act,* edited by Maurice A. East, Stephen A. Salmore, and Charles F. Hermann (Beverly Hills: Sage, 1978).

[41] Charles F. Hermann, "The Effects of Decision Structures and Processes on Foreign Policy Behavior," paper presented at the International Society of Political Psychology meeting, Washington, D.C., 24–26 May 1979.

[42] Tower, Muskie, and Scowcroft, *Tower Report.*

[43] George, *Presidential Decision Making.*

[44] Janis and Mann, *Decision Making.*

[45] Margaret G. Hermann and Charles F. Hermann, "Maintaining the Quality of Decision Making in Foreign Policy Crises: A Proposal," in *Towards More Soundly Based Foreign Policy: Making Better Use of Information,* edited by Alexander L. George, Report to the Commission on the Organization of Government for the Conduct of Foreign Policy (Washington, D.C.: U.S. Government Printing Office, 1975), Appendix D.

timates and evaluations of consequences. Moreover, dissent is a two-way street; if people who feel differently decide it is inappropriate to express their opinions, they are as guilty as the leadership when premature closure and groupthink occur. As the Tower Commission Report observes about Shultz and Weinberger, who both distanced themselves and were excluded from decision making on the Iran-contra affair: "Their obligation was to give the President their full support and continued advice with respect to the program or, if they could not in good conscience do that, to so inform the President. . . . They were not energetic in attempting to protect the President from the consequences of his personal commitment to freeing the hostages."[46]

CONTINUING STUDY OF THE EFFECTS OF HOSTAGE TAKING ON THE PRESIDENCY. A survey of research on terrorism reveals that there has been little examination of the pressures such events put on those government authorities who must cope with them. Yet this piece of the puzzle is crucial to understanding policy in dealing with a terrorist situation. It is as if we were interested in learning about only one side of the issue—the terrorists and what they do. But as this essay suggests repeatedly, terrorist events create problems that affect the policymakers who confront them and who, in turn, affect the outcome of the crises. To deal effectively with the phenomenon of terrorism, policymakers must understand their own reactions and how these reactions affect their decision making. Only then will they be equipped to deal adequately with the hostage-taking event.

[46] Tower, Muskie, and Scowcroft, *Tower Report*, 82.

12

Taking vows:
The domestication of policy-making
in hostage incidents

GARY SICK

Every story of Presidential decision-making is really two stories: an outer one in which a rational man calculates and an inner one in which an emotional man feels. The two are forever connected.

James David Barber[1]

The holding of the American hostages had cast a pall over my own life and over the American people since November 4, 1979. Although I was acting in an official capacity as President, I also had deep private feelings that were almost overwhelming. The hostages sometimes seemed like part of my own family. I knew them by name, was familiar with their careers, had read their personal letters written from within their prisons in Iran. I knew and had grown to love some of the members of their families, and had visited with them in Washington and even in their hometowns around the country. More than anything else, I wanted those American prisoners to be free.

Jimmy Carter[2]

[Secretary of State Cyrus Vance] clearly was motivated by a personal sense of responsibility for his imprisoned colleagues, and his compassionate feelings were stirred by meetings with their families. The President was similarly moved. (I deliberately decided to avoid such meetings in order not to be swayed by emotions.)

Zbigniew Brzezinski[3]

The president [Reagan] is a man of compassion. He's sitting there—you have Peggy Say [sister of hostage Terry A. Anderson], you have all the families saying "Please, you've got to do something."

Donald T. Regan[4]

[1] James David Barber, *The Presidential Character: Predicting Performance in the White House* (Englewood Cliffs, N.J.: Prentice Hall, 1972), 7.
[2] Jimmy Carter, *Keeping Faith: Memoirs of a President* (New York: Bantam Books, 1982), 4.
[3] Zbigniew Brzezinski, *Power and Principle: Memoirs of the National Security Adviser, 1977–1981* (New York: Farrar, Strauss, Giroux, 1983), 481.
[4] White House Chief of Staff Donald T. Regan describing the reasons for President Ronald

When the U.S. embassy in Tehran was attacked on 4 November 1979 and all its occupants were taken hostage, the event was regarded as an aberration in international political experience. To be sure, in antiquity it was not uncommon to hold hostage a family member or valued associate of another ruler as a guarantee of good faith. Kidnapping for extortion also occurred periodically in nearly every society, and criminals and terrorist bands occasionally took hostages to shield themselves from police retaliation. Officials of the U.S. embassy in Tehran had, in fact, nine months earlier been taken captive briefly by a band of revolutionaries in the immediate aftermath of the overthrow of the shah.[5] Nevertheless, the active and prolonged acquiescence by a government in the kidnapping and incarceration of diplomats and private citizens on its soil for political purposes was regarded as an anomaly.

Although the circumstances of the Iranian hostage taking have not recurred in the eight years since that time, the act of hostage taking for political purposes has become distressingly familiar, largely because of the actions of radical *Shi'i* groups operating in the political chaos of Lebanon. As this chapter was being written in 1987, twenty-six hostages from nine countries were being held by various political factions in Lebanon,[6] and the second consecutive president of the United States was embroiled in a severely damaging political crisis because of his handling of a hostage situation.

Hostage episodes can no longer be regarded as anomalous. They have become an insidious feature of the contemporary international political landscape. Recent history has shown that no government or political system is immune from this phenomenon, and none has any entirely satisfactory answers about how to deal with it. The United States, in two successive and quite different administrations, has shown itself to be particularly vulnerable to this special form of terrorism.

Because the problem apparently will not vanish, there is some virtue in trying to think about it more systematically. What special conditions distinguish a hostage episode from other kinds of terrorist incidents? Are there distinctive psychological pressures associated with hostage inci-

Reagan's decision to sell arms to Iran in 1985–6, quoted in the *Washington Post,* 16 November 1986.

[5] This attack on Valentine's Day, 14 February 1979, is recounted in William H. Sullivan, *Mission to Iran* (New York: W. W. Norton, 1981), 257–64. It terminated, as is typical of such outbursts, when the government intervened, and it resulted in an apology from one of the leading personalities in the new Iranian regime, which was only three days old at the time.

[6] *The Economist,* 31 January 1987, p. 32.

dents that affect the behavior of decision makers? How do these pressures affect policy?

The following observations are based on my experience as a participant in the Tehran hostage crisis from the vantage point of the National Security Council. I have had the opportunity to ponder that experience and, as an outsider, to follow the policy twists and turns of several subsequent crises. I can offer no easy or authoritative answers to the questions posed above. There are, I believe, no easy answers. But these collected impressions may shed some light on the phenomenon and provide some cautionary tales in the likely event that we go through the experience yet again.

The impersonal versus the personal in foreign policy

Bureaucracy is an instrument designed to introduce order and efficiency to the management of complex human tasks. Bureaucratic systems separate a problem into its component elements, create offices ("bureaus") to deal with each of those elements, develop job descriptions for the performance of each subtask, and train staff to perform those functions in an efficient and reliable fashion.

A bureaucratic organization chart is the equivalent of a computer program. It defines a logical series of steps to process a problem (e.g., how to determine which persons will be authorized to operate motor vehicles) from beginning (application) to end (issuance of a license). Like a computer, the instructions at each stage consist of "if . . . then" statements (if the applicant has the necessary documentation, then proceed to the written test). Unlike a computer, these successive hurdles or thresholds are administered by human bureaucrats who can be correctly regarded as impersonal cogs in a large machine.

The impersonal nature of bureaucracy, which has earned it its unenviable reputation, is in reality its greatest and most enduring strength.[7] A bureaucracy subjects each applicant (or issue) to a relentless series of tests without regard to personality or human charity ("If you do not have proof of birth, I cannot process your application"), with the sole objective of certifying a proper outcome. Making exceptions to the rules for

---

[7] Max Weber says simply that bureaucratic administrative organization "is superior to any other form in precision, in stability, in the stringency of its discipline, and in its reliability." Weber, *The Theory of Social and Economic Organization* (New York: Free Press, 1964), 337.

personal reasons or accepting inducements to bypass one or more steps in the process is regarded as unprofessional, immoral, or even illegal. Bureaucrats are indoctrinated to value and maintain the objectivity of the process as their first priority, otherwise the "machine" breaks down. The system may be "heartless," but it ensures consistent standards.

Much of the standard literature analyzing international politics and decision making in foreign policy may be viewed as an effort to "solve" the foreign policy problem by breaking it down into its component elements and by devising mechanisms for ensuring more consistent and effective outcomes. The notion of the "balance of power," which is the traditional organizing principle for the analysis of international relations, attempts to define interactions among nations in quasi-physical terms in order to draw some generalizations and rules out of an otherwise bewildering array of activity.

The concept of the "national interest," which is essential to such analysis, was devised as an effort to define the fundamental needs and goals of a state in an objective form that would permit more rigorous, impersonal analysis. At least in theory, if the national interest is defined accurately and if the power relationships with other key states are properly understood, foreign policy decisions can be undertaken more systematically, with higher confidence of predictable outcomes.

It need not concern us here that the considerable literature that has evolved from these and other analytical constructs has thus far failed to produce a scientific method of foreign policy analysis and decision making. Rather, these remarks are intended only to draw attention to the impulse of foreign policy observers and practitioners to develop a general model of foreign policy behavior, thereby reducing the problem to manageable proportions and deducing rules and procedures that would at least in principle be susceptible to bureaucratic organization and management.

In fact, the absence of a reliable working theory of international relations has not inhibited the establishment of U.S. government structures for dealing with foreign policy issues that look, sound, and act like true bureaucracies. These include the Department of State, the National Security Council staff, the Central Intelligence Agency, and substantial portions of the Department of Defense as well as many other agencies. In good bureaucratic fashion, these agencies conduct the foreign policy business of the country in their own vocabulary of impartial and impersonal analysis. They prize their objectivity and sometimes operate as if interests, policy relationships, and options were susceptible to the kind of deliberately structured decision-making process represented in the lines and boxes of a bureaucratic organization chart.

Alas, we know (and they know) that reality is otherwise. Although the Department of State and other foreign policy institutions have adopted the protective coloration of bureaucratic forms, their functions are far more formless and indeterminate than Weber's ideal type. In fact, the closer one gets to the top of the organizational chart and the making of "high policy," the less bureaucratic it becomes.[8] The considerable literature on "bureaucratic politics," which concerns itself largely with high-level decision making in foreign policy and national security matters, is not so much about bureaucracy as about court politics in a quasi-bureaucratic setting.[9]

There is nothing very interesting about bureaucratic decision making—it is largely preordained and routine. The discovery of "bureaucratic politics" was, in fact, the discovery that the national security apparatus, which had all the characteristics of a bureaucracy, did not behave like a bureaucracy at all. When Morton Halperin outlined alternative strategies for "Involving the President" (Getting to the President: Through Channels, Going Alone, Going Through the White House Staff; Securing a Presidential Decision: Building a Consensus, Persuasion, Compromise, etc.),[10] he was describing the timeless occupation of the courtier. The situations and maneuvers he educed would have been immediately recognizable to Cardinal Richelieu and Machiavelli. They could better be fit under Weber's description of "traditional authority," in which the following features of bureaucratic administration are absent:[11]

1. "A clearly defined sphere of competence subject to impersonal rules" (Dean Rusk once remarked, "The real organization of government at higher echelons is not what you find in textbooks or organization charts. It is how confidence flows down from the President.")
2. "A rational ordering of relations of superiority and inferiority" (Does primary

---

[8] This phenomenon was recognized by Weber, who noted in passing that "at the top of a bureaucratic organization, there is necessarily an element which is at least not purely bureaucratic." Ibid., 335.

[9] Seminal studies include Richard E. Neustadt, *Presidential Power: The Politics of Leadership:* (New York: Wiley, 1960); Graham Allison, *Essence of Decision: Explaining the Cuban Missile Crisis* (Boston: Little, Brown, 1971); I. M. Destler, *Presidents, Bureaucrats, and Foreign Policy* (Princeton, N.J.: Princeton University Press, 1972); and Morton H. Halperin, *Bureaucratic Politics and Foreign Policy* (Washington, D.C.: Brookings Institution, 1974).

[10] Halperin, *Bureaucratic Politics and Foreign Policy,* chapter 11.

[11] Ibid., 343.

responsibility for foreign policy reside with the secretary of state or with the national security adviser?)
3. "A regular system of appointment and promotion on the basis of free contract" (Is policy formulation to be left to the professionals who staff the bureaucracy from one administration to the next, or to political appointees who reflect the ideological views of the incumbent?)

All this is by way of preface to the assertion that decision making in foreign policy at or near the presidential level is almost never a tidy operation conducted according to impersonal rules. On the contrary, it is a highly personal process whose outcomes are influenced by the personalities of individuals at or near the pinnacle of power and by the character and style of the president himself. As James David Barber noted in his classic study *The Presidential Character,* the president is not "some abstract embodiment of civic virtue, some scorecard of issue stands, or some reflection of a faction, but . . . a human being like the rest of us, a person trying to cope with a difficult environment." [12] The reflections that follow will suggest that decision making in a hostage crisis, and particularly presidential decision making, is subject to those special conditions—only more so.

The human dimension of hostage incidents

The fundamental characteristic that distinguishes a hostage incident from other, more conventional, foreign policy problems is the constant and unyielding awareness that the lives and welfare of individual, identifiable human beings are at stake. They are not abstractions. They have names. They have families. In some cases, they are friends and colleagues.

Recalling the long first morning of the Iranian hostage crisis, when open telephone lines connected the small group in the Operations Center of the State Department to the staff under siege in Tehran, I later wrote:

Each telephone line was connected to a small speaker on the long table, and the voices were familiar to all of us as friends, colleagues, acquaintances. Elizabeth Ann Swift, who was reporting on an open line from the embassy, had been in my office only a few weeks earlier. Her voice from Tehran had the same unhurried professionalism and edge of determination that had impressed me during our earlier conversation when she was assessing the difficulties for a woman reporting on political developments in a revolutionary Islamic society.

There was an easy familiarity in the conversations being conducted from points halfway around the world that gave the scene an intimacy and immediacy not unlike members of a family discussing a mutual problem. Each of us in the room

[12] Ibid., 4.

bore some measure of responsibility for the circumstances these familiar voices were now describing, and in those long morning hours, as one telephone line after another abruptly went silent, each of us had to ask ourselves the questions that would trouble many Americans in the long months ahead: Why had we let it happen? Could it have been prevented?[13]

For their own psychological protection, people who bear responsibility for the conduct of foreign policy attempt to insulate themselves from the gravity of their decisions by depersonalizing the process. Virtually every decision of any consequence has implications for the lives and welfare of many thousands of private individuals. A decision maker who agonized over the fate of each of them would presumably be paralyzed. Instead, every policymaker, regardless of his or her own humane instincts, mentally and rhetorically transforms these "objects" of policy into impersonal, abstract categories.

This is not necessarily evil, nor is it the peculiar fate of high-level foreign policy officials. We all do it. Sociologists deal with classes and interest groups, not named individuals. Political scientists discuss political movements and structures without undue attention to the human beings who populate them. The philosophical concept of the "general good" is an attempt to reconcile and justify the inevitable truth that, in any decision of moment, some will benefit and others will be hurt. Such an approach is essential to any analysis that attempts to draw general rules from the particulars of experience or to maintain a "value neutral" posture.

It is also psychologically reassuring. The statesman who has just made a difficult decision that may result in personal anguish for a large number of people will sleep better in the conviction that it was taken as the result of an "objective" analysis of the "national interest" in the context of the existing "balance of power" (or "correlation of forces") in the pursuit of "regional stability."

Moreover, there is a dominant presumption that a decision taken on the basis of an objective appraisal of the available facts will produce better policy than a decision taken primarily for idiosyncratic or personal reasons. I am sufficiently a product of my educational and professional background to share that presumption, but I am also enough of a product of the modern age to recognize that terrible decisions can result from the implacable application of abstract principles. We have witnessed great

---

[13] Gary Sick, *All Fall Down: America's Tragic Encounter with Iran* (New York: Random House, 1985), 176.

crimes committed in the name of "scientific principles." An assassination is still an assassination, although it may be labeled, as it was in Vietnam, "termination with extreme prejudice." The vocabulary of objectivity may shade into euphemism, and the insulation it provides to the decision maker, while comforting, may simply mask, rather than prevent, excesses of personal psychological aberration.

No such comfort was available to the people dealing with the Iran hostage crisis. There were some who were prepared to argue that the hostages should be regarded as symbolic troops in an undeclared war whose lives were expendable in the higher interests of national honor. One of my colleagues proposed that we should officially declare them dead and then proceed to deal with Iran accordingly. But despite the universal awareness of the potential pitfalls of policy-making in a highly personalized environment, so far as I am aware none of these suggestions or others like them were ever seriously considered. For better or worse, the lives of the hostages were present as a palpable reality in the minds of key decision makers at every stage of the crisis. Concern over their welfare affected every major policy decision.

The highly personalized decision making of the hostage crisis was not necessarily right. It was simply a reality. As I wrote in my account:

When President Carter said, as he did on many different occasions both publicly and privately, that the fate of the hostages was on his mind at every waking moment, he was not posturing for political effect. Rather, he was expressing what was a daily reality for almost all of us who were caught up in the crisis.

I remember discussing the crisis with my family shortly after the hostages were seized and telling them that until the hostages were freed, their welfare would take precedence over everything else in my life. It was almost like taking religious vows.[14]

We have since observed the same intense preoccupation on the part of President Reagan and members of his administration in dealing with the TWA hijacking in June 1985 and the attempts to free a group of U.S. hostages in Lebanon. The evidence suggests that this reaction is instinctive, powerfully human, and—perhaps—unavoidable in situations of this kind.

The hostages' families

The public and private activities of the hostages' families played a key policy role in every U.S. hostage incident. Their constant presence—through

[14] Ibid., 221.

the media or in person—ensured that even the most hardened politician would find it difficult to resist the personalization of the crisis. The relatives of the hostages were constant reminders to the public and to the policymaker that the imprisoned individuals were flesh and blood, with parents, spouses, children, and friends.

Many family members are conscious of the danger to their loved ones if they should be forgotten or transformed into abstract symbols, and it is impressive to observe the sophistication and responsibility that a number of grieving family members have displayed in representing the rights and interests of the hostages. Several years ago, I found myself appearing on the same television program with the wife of a man who was then being held hostage. The host attempted to play on her emotions, but she clearly had decided on the message she wished to convey and she delivered it with exactly the right mixture of concern and restraint. Her performance would have been the envy of any assistant secretary of state.

The families' role in the Iranian hostage crisis was probably unique in any U.S. foreign policy situation, past or future. Almost immediately after the hostage situation began, family members joined State Department staff in a large room immediately adjacent to the Operations Center, where they manned telephones and provided continuing contact with the many hostage family members scattered across the country. This arrangement was quickly institutionalized, and, five months after the crisis began, the family members organized themselves as the Family Liaison Action Group (FLAG), which played a crucial role in public and government perceptions throughout the crisis.[15] The daily presence of family members in a room just outside the Operations Center was a constant reminder to the members of the Iran Task Force, if any were needed, that the lives of real people were at stake.

Zbigniew Brzezinski, as indicated in the quotation at the beginning of this chapter, deliberately avoided meetings with the hostage families in order to distance himself from purely personal considerations. But Brzezinski was an appointee, not a politician. Both Presidents Carter and

---

[15] The best description of the family operations in the Iran hostage crisis is found in the chapters by Harold Saunders in Warren Christopher et al., *American Hostages in Iran: The Conduct of a Crisis* (New Haven, Conn.: Yale University Press, 1985), 61, 136–40, 291. The president of FLAG was Katherine Keough, wife of one of the two nonofficial hostages. Louisa Kennedy, the spokeswoman for the organization, explained the acronym as follows: "The fifty stars represented the fifty hostages held at the American Embassy compound; the three colors in the flag represented the three hostages held at the Foreign Ministry; and the thirteen stripes represented the thirteen released [in November 1979] hostages."

Reagan met with family members of the hostages, and both were strongly affected by these encounters. President Carter first met with the assembled families less than a week after the embassy was taken in Tehran. He described the meeting as follows:

On November 9, I went to the State Department to meet with the hostages' families. Although the building was only a few hundred yards from the White House, the trip seemed long to me. There was no way for me to know how the families would react, but when we finally met, it was obvious that they and I shared the same feelings of grief and alarm. . . . The conversation was emotional for all of us, and afterwards I was pleased when the families issued a statement of support for me and called on the nation to remain calm. This meeting was the beginning of a close relationship between us, which never faltered during the succeeding months.[16]

In this passage, Carter betrayed the same emotion and uncertainty that any of us might feel in paying a call on a family that had lost a close relative. What is going through their minds? What can I possibly say? Members of FLAG later told me that they encountered this same funereal reaction from the many heads of state and high government officials with whom they met.

What Carter did not mention in his memoir was that, in the course of the meeting, he promised the families he would take no action that would endanger the lives of the hostages. Although that decision was entirely characteristic of Carter, the meeting came at a moment when he was being pressed by his national security adviser to take a different tack. Just that morning, Brzezinski had argued to Carter that "your greater responsibility is to protect the honor and dignity of our country and its foreign policy interests. At some point, that greater responsibility could become more important than the safety of our diplomats."[17] Vance had responded by arguing for restraint and caution.

After the meeting with the families, the president told his chief of staff: "You know, I've been worried all week about the hostages as a problem for the country and as a political problem for me. But it wasn't until I saw the grief and hope on the faces of their wives and mothers and fathers that I felt the personal responsibility for their lives. It's an awesome burden."[18]

The meeting with the families effectively resolved for the moment the tension in Carter's own mind between Brzezinski's emphasis on national honor and Vance's stress on the hostages' safety. Primary concern for the

---

[16] Carter, *Keeping Faith*, 460.

[17] Hamilton Jordan, *Crisis: The Last Year of the Carter Presidency* (New York: Putnam, 1982), 44.

[18] Ibid., 54.

lives of the hostages remained the keystone of U.S. policy for at least the following five months.

Evidence about President Reagan's reaction to meetings with hostage relatives is necessarily more fragmentary. However, the statements of his own chief of staff cited at the beginning of this chapter suggest that his meetings with family members were a significant factor in Reagan's decision to provide arms to Tehran in return for Iranian assistance in freeing the U.S. hostages in Lebanon.

Presidents are politicians, and they are human beings. As president, it is relatively uncommon to have direct contact on a personal and private level with an aggrieved constituent, particularly on an issue related to foreign policy. But the normal barriers between a president and individual citizens are removed during hostage crises, and the president finds himself almost in the position of a neighborhood politician, dealing with the specific problems of his constituents on a personal basis. The evidence suggests that these contacts have exerted a powerful influence on two successive presidents. That phenomenon is less likely to be shared or even understood by the president's professional advisers, who may not have been present, who may not experience the same sense of personal responsibility, and who are not, in most cases, elected politicians.

Walter Lippmann once complained about U.S. presidents, "They announce, they proclaim, they disclaim, they exhort, they appeal and they argue. But they do not unbend and tell the story, and say why they did what they did, and what they think about it."[19] At least in the case of Jimmy Carter, and to some degree in the case of Ronald Reagan as well, we have been told quite a lot about why they did what they did in dealing with two different hostage incidents. What we have learned is that they did not act in some impersonal manner on the basis of general principles, but, rather, that their responses were not very different from the way many of us might have responded in dealing with a domestic or family problem.

The media and U.S. domestic politics

The political dimension of a hostage incident makes itself felt most intensely in the interplay of domestic and foreign policy.[20] Presidents un-

[19] *New York Herald Tribune*, 29 January 1942. Cited in Simon Serfaty, "Lost Illusions," *Foreign Policy* 66 (Spring 1987): 18.
[20] Some of the remarks in this section were adapted from an earlier article by the author,

derstand that the actions of terrorists place in jeopardy not only their immediate political agenda but, more important, their image and their very legitimacy. The picture of President Carter trapped in the White House and rendered politically helpless by the actions of a handful of radical students and their supporters in Iran is indelibly etched on the consciousness of present and prospective political leaders.

Hostage incidents may or may not have an effect on U.S. political and security interests abroad. They always have an effect on U.S. public perceptions about the nature of presidential leadership. A president faced with a situation in which the lives of innocent civilians are at stake faces an agonizing public dilemma. If he orders military action to terminate the crisis quickly, he risks causing civilian deaths. If he does not act, he risks appearing impotent or indecisive.

The media play a crucial role in this process. Their minute-by-minute accounts, often accompanied by live coverage of events, move the problem out of the closed atmosphere of the White House situation room and into the living rooms of American families. Coverage of the TWA hijacking was so vivid and controversial that there were widespread calls for the imposition of restraints. Although these criticisms prompted several television networks to conduct a review of their procedures, there is little reason to expect that future coverage of such events will be substantially different. Hostage takings, like kidnappings, are human dramas of universal fascination. They are "big" stories by any estimation (the case of the kidnapping and murder of the Lindbergh infant in 1932 is still remembered as one of the most sensational in the history of American journalism), and it would be unrealistic to expect the media to treat them otherwise.

What effect does this have on government decision makers? There is no question that officials' lives are made more difficult during a crisis by intensive news scrutiny. The media's on-the-spot coverage creates a constant sense of immediacy and pressure, while background interviews with family members and others personalize the victims by taking the viewer into their homes and neighborhoods. All this generates public sympathy and increases pressure on the government to do something, when the wisest course may be to play for time.

But the case should not be overdrawn. Some of the official criticism of the media is simply the result of the classic Washington inclination to

"Terrorism: Its Political Uses and Abuses," *SAIS Review* 7, no. 1 (Winter-Spring 1987): 11–26.

"shoot the messenger" when faced with embarrassing or frustrating circumstances. The impression has sometimes been created that if it were not for the availability of the media, terrorists would have no audience and hence no incentive for their political theater. That was not true, however, in either of the two most prominent recent cases. Despite all the publicity the Iranian hostage crisis received, its origin and eventual resolution were the products of domestic Iranian revolutionary politics, not media coverage. In the case of trading arms for the hostages in Lebanon, the U.S. hostages in Lebanon had virtually disappeared from public consciousness and their captors had shown little interest in publicity during the period that the U.S.-Iranian negotiations were under way. It was President Reagan, not the media or the public, who was obsessed with getting the hostages freed.

Occasionally the media play a pernicious role. For example, NBC reported in the early days of the Iran hostage crisis that two U.S. emissaries were being dispatched to Iran. The report was broadcast despite government objections, and shortly thereafter Ayatollah Khomeini announced that the emissaries would not be received in Tehran. On occasion, the media have skirted perilously close to the role of negotiator, as when TV anchorman David Hartman asked Amal leader Nabih Berri during a live ABC interview at the time of the TWA hijacking, "Do you have any final words to President Reagan this morning?"

Because of the efficiency of the media, the public often has essentially the same information as the president at about the same time, so every viewer is free to "play the game" by imagining how he or she would handle it. Standard presidential techniques for buying time—"confer, defer, refer"—are not credible, and the public quickly develops a finely honed expertise about the minutiae of the circumstances that will not be satisfied by generalities. Everyone waits to see what the president will do, and to second-guess him as soon as he does it.

The most important effects of media attention, however, are its amplification and personalization of the crisis. The media contribute to the process of transforming an international issue into a domestic political crisis for the president. There is perhaps no other type of situation that subjects the president to such intense public scrutiny, and the president is aware that his image as a decisive and effective leader is constantly at risk. Inevitably, that recognition raises the stakes of the crisis, and it may lead to a degree of personal commitment and self-examination on the part of the president that is unusual in foreign policy issues.

Public image and self-image

This brief analysis has suggested that hostage incidents are generically different from other types of decision making in foreign policy. When dealing with most major foreign policy issues, whether it is nuclear deterrence or alliance relations or trade policy, the decision maker can take refuge in the vocabulary of grand strategy. In making decisions on such matters, even when the human consequences are immense, the president or other decision maker is able to maintain a certain psychological distance in the belief that the decision was justified by an objective analysis of available information and the application of an impersonal set of rules or general principles.

Hostage incidents do not permit even the facade of impersonality. The hostages are known, their families are a constant presence, and the responsibility for their welfare and safety seems to reside in the person of the president rather than the office of the presidency. If it is true that decision making in foreign policy is by its nature nonbureaucratic, then decision making in a hostage situation is the antithesis of the bureaucratic ideal of impersonal rules unemotionally applied.

The admittedly limited evidence of three cases over eight years provides reason to suspect that presidents—as politicians, as human beings, as symbolic representatives of the state, and as leaders—feel an exceptionally heavy personal weight of responsibility in these incidents. They are likely to identify with the victims and their families more than some of their advisers, and, as leaders of the most powerful nation on Earth, their frustration at being unable to resolve the problem is intense.

There is some evidence to suggest that hostage takings are not just foreign policy or national crises, but that they are in a special sense personal crises for the presidents who must deal with them. In some respects, the issue may be less a matter of public image than the self-image of the leader himself. Certainly the Iran hostage incident dominated the life and thoughts of President Carter beyond the point that could be explained by the gravity of the issues involved. Similarly, in the Iran arms-sales affair, President Reagan apparently adopted the cause of the U.S. hostages in Lebanon almost as a personal crusade, despite the fact that they were receiving little media or public attention.

Perhaps because of their personal identification with the issue, both Presidents Carter and Reagan appeared to believe that their own political fortunes were closely associated with the fate of the hostages. In Carter's case that was a defensible proposition, because the hostage crisis was undoubtedly an important political liability as election day approached. Even if the hostages had been released in the final month before the November 1980 election, however, their release might have had much less effect on the election than many would have expected. The damage to Carter's image had already been done by the months of futile waiting, and I suspect that a last-minute release would not have reversed it. The time for desperate measures was months earlier, when negotiations collapsed. In that sense, the attempted rescue mission in April was perfectly timed. If it had succeeded, it might well have affected Carter's fortunes (though it would not have overcome the economic problems that many people believe were the ultimate reason for his defeat). A resolution of the hostage crisis at the eleventh hour, in my view, would have had only marginal political effect.

It is more difficult to explain President Reagan's almost frantic efforts to secure the release of the U.S. hostages in Lebanon just before the congressional elections in 1986. One hostage was released two days prior to the election and promptly appeared in a blaze of publicity at the White House. Americans were pleased, but the election results provide no evidence that many of them changed their votes because of the event. Did President Reagan believe they would? On the basis of subsequent revelations about the origins of the arms deal with Iran, there is reason to suspect that President Reagan was so personally engaged in the fate of the hostages—that is, his own self-image was so involved—that he might indeed have overestimated the political impact of even a limited resolution of the hostage situation.

Ultimately, we cannot really know. An essay such as this can describe the peculiar psychological conditions and stresses that affect a president in dealing with a hostage situation, but it cannot answer the questions that all of us would like to ask. We cannot replay the historical tape to see whether the decisions taken in any given hostage situation would have been different under other circumstances. And, despite a flood of memoirs and reflections, we can never really know what goes on inside a president's mind in balancing one set of considerations against another.

Perhaps Walter Lippmann was right after all. Even when presidents do appear to "unbend and tell the story," they know—and we suspect— that there is more to the story than we are being told. For their own good reasons, presidents are going to tell us only as much as they want us to know. The rest is speculation.

Part V

The psychology of terrorism:
What can we know? What must we learn?

13

Questions to be answered, research to be done, knowledge to be applied

MARTHA CRENSHAW

At the conference during which early drafts of most of the essays in this volume were presented, the U.S. State Department's ambassador-at-large for counterterrorism, L. Paul Bremer, remarked that once the action starts, officials cease to worry about the "why" of terrorism and, lacking the "leisure" for theory, revert to intuitive guidelines. The problem with this dismissal of the practical uses of theory is that the policymaker's "intuition" depends on implicit sets of values and assumptions about the causes and processes of terrorism. Information about terrorism, however fragmentary, is routinely interpreted and "converted" into usable form by intelligence analysts, and the government's demand for relevant information peaks during crises. Furthermore, the State Department admits, paradoxically, that expertise on terrorism is called into play only during the management of crises. In other words, officials may deny that theory is relevant, but they rely on it constantly, at no time more than during a crisis, when they think they have escaped its influence.

It is difficult to understand terrorism without psychological theory, because explaining terrorism must begin with analyzing the intentions of the terrorist actor and the emotional reactions of audiences. The task assigned for this chapter is to identify those questions about terrorism that psychological research might be most helpful in answering. My goal is not to suggest specific psychological theories or methods or to review the literature but to propose research questions that are both interesting for students of terrorism and appropriate for psychological approaches.

Several problems are evident at the outset. Because terrorism is what we are trying to explain, the most obvious question concerns what it is.

247

Do researchers agree on a definition of the dependent variable that is sufficiently precise and bounded to be useful? Terrorism is often presented as an undifferentiated phenomenon, yet its conduct takes a variety of complex forms. Terrorism differs in level of violence, innovativeness, and choice of targets. The actors who use it are different. Its effectiveness varies. Are different theories necessary to explain different types of terrorism, if such types can be identified?

Related to this question is another problem of definition, this time with regard to the independent variable: What is meant by psychological approaches? The conference participants believed that claims to clinical diagnosis are misleading. Even the metaphorical use of clinical terms was rejected as dangerously inappropriate. What, then, are the appropriate scope and focus of psychological analysis?

Another problem in linking psychological theory to research on terrorism concerns purpose. What do we hope to achieve? Is prediction possible? And, more important, should the behavioral sciences contribute to policy recommendations? Academic researchers frequently fear misinterpretation or misuse of their findings. They suspect that embryonic ideas and incomplete evidence are appropriated and "converted" to misleadingly definitive conclusions by the government. Yet the generalizations and recommendations that psychological study produces should be directed toward concrete political issues rather than narrow disciplinary concerns. Psychological approaches to terrorism should avoid obscurity as well as utopianism.

If these impediments to inquiry can be overcome, another question arises: Should future research focus only on those questions that appear to be answerable? That is, should the selection of questions for the psychology research agenda depend on their feasibility? It is not always easy to assess the practicality of research questions in advance, but certainly in the field of terrorism studies, testing ideas against reality is particularly difficult. Data are frequently inaccessible, both because extremists in the underground are reluctant to talk freely to researchers and because governments have an interest in protecting information that has national security implications. Interviewing terrorists after the fact is unlikely to result in an accurate reconstruction of original motive. Still, if research on terrorism is to go beyond description, posing the right questions is as important as finding answers. For the same reason, identifying the puzzles to be solved should precede selection of methodologies and data.

If research is to be both theoretically imaginative and politically prac-

Topic	Level of analysis		
	Individual	Group	Society
Causation/prevention Conduct/management Consequences/control			

Figure 13.1. Framework for a psychological analysis of terrorism.

tical, two sets of criteria for inclusion must be joined. The first is the government's and society's interest in acquiring knowledge about terrorism. The interests of these defenders against terrorism (opposition groups that use terrorism against the state are usually treated as the initiators of conflict, although they do not necessarily perceive themselves as such) are based first on the *prevention* of violence. Preventing terrorism can be seen as a form of conflict resolution. It requires dealing with the conditions that cause terrorism as well as responding in a way that brings campaigns of terrorism, once launched, to an end. If prevention fails, the government must try to minimize the destructiveness of terrorism. The government must thus be concerned with the *management* of specific terrorist incidents or campaigns with the intention of affecting immediate outcomes. Last, government has a responsibility to *control* the harmful political and social effects of terrorism. Policymakers must contain psychological damage in the aftermath of terrorism. In general, most government effort appears to center on crisis management rather than prevention or control. Questions for psychology could be organized in terms of these three categories.

A theoretical orientation toward the subject, however, suggests a second classification framework, different in purpose but compatible with policy interests. Theoretical inquiry might center on, respectively, the *causes, conduct,* and *consequences* of terrorism. This set of conceptual categories must be considered in terms of appropriate levels of analysis, one framework for which is suggested in Figure 13.1. We can analyze terrorism at the level of the individual practitioner or the collective actor, the terrorist group. In turn, both actors, individual and group, must be seen in relation to society as a whole. Similarly, terrorism alters the behavior of individuals, collective actors such as the terrorist organization or the government, and societies.

The integration of these levels of analysis is a significant problem for research on terrorism. Certainly the subject of individual motivation for participation is critical to constructing a theory of the causes of terrorism. Terrorism is not a direct result of social conditions but of individual perceptions of those conditions. Terrorism is not, however, the act of an individual. Acts of terrorism are committed by groups who reach collective decisions based on commonly held beliefs, although the level of individual commitment to the group and its beliefs varies. It is a political act performed by individuals acting together and collectively trying to justify their behavior. These justifications reflect prevailing social values, and so neither individual nor group behavior can be isolated from its environment. These factors must also be related to explanation of the outcomes of terrorism, a topic that is often neglected. Propositions about the effects of terrorism are widely assumed but rarely demonstrated. We should investigate the psychological consequences of terrorism for the terrorists themselves, for society, for victims, and for government.

Questions of individual motivation

One of the major tasks for research on the causes of terrorism is identifying the psychological benefits to the individual of participating in an organization that employs terrorism. Analysts have suggested a variety of possible incentives; risk, stress, excitement, power, identity, belonging, and social approval are representative examples. Do these incentives change from individual to individual or from group to group? Are they unique to terrorism? What is the difference, for example, between the terrorist and the soldier? Does each person have a different need that terrorism fills? Do nationalist organizations in divided societies provide psychological rewards that revolutionary groups in cohesive populations do not? Do the incentives offered by right-wing groups differ from the attractions of the left? Is it possible that entrance into the underground is not deliberate but coincidental—a result of the chance life encounters that Albert Bandura describes elsewhere in this volume?

Analysis of the biographical profiles of terrorists can reveal patterns in individual experiences and backgrounds. Do social and economic categories tell us anything about the psychological incentives for terrorism? For example, does the participation of women in terrorism require a specific psychological explanation?

Even if most terrorists come from identifiable categories (the young, children from broken homes, the underprivileged, middle-class rebels, etc.), most of the people in the given social category do not participate in terrorism. How, then, do we explain the behavior of the few that do? One way of finding the point at which the barrier to terrorism is crossed and ideas are translated into action is to compare political radicals or extremists who reject terrorism with its adherents. Studies of violent protest and political activism could provide a baseline for comparison. Is the difference in levels of participation attributable to personality, to socialization, or to opportunity? It would be useful to compare the sympathizer, who assists but does not personally participate, with the militant activist.

The solution, in turn, may depend on the answer to a question that was suggested earlier: How are people recruited into groups that use terrorism? It is essential to analyze the dynamics of the entry process. In Chapter 5 of this volume, Ehud Sprinzak suggests that there are stages of radicalization. Rather than a sudden conversion, is the process of becoming a terrorist usually one of gradual commitment? Is terrorism the result of personal disappointment with nonviolent modes of political expression? Are potential terrorists people who hold fixed ideological beliefs, or do people acquire extremist views as a result of participating in the group? If moral inhibitions exist, how are they overcome? Does political conviction precede action or does participation in terrorism lead to a search for rationalization?

The group and the resort to terrorism

The group may be more important than the individual to the initiation and conduct of campaigns of terrorism. The comfort of belonging to a community of the like-minded may be the dominant psychological incentive for many members. As the group is formed, a collective mind-set emerges. The collectivity is bound together not only by a common commitment to shared political goals but by psychological interdependencies, which should be identified and analyzed.

Historically, the existence of the group frequently precedes the move to terrorism. The decision often provokes factionalism—sometimes to the point of dissolution of the original group and its replacement by a smaller, more homogeneous, cohesive, and extremist core. The views of group members who reject the shift to terrorism deserve study as a point of comparison.

Questions can also be raised about relationships between leaders and followers and between occupants of different roles in the organizational structure of the group. The sources of authority in violent opposition groups are incompletely understood. Is charismatic leadership the norm? Do narcissistic personalities emerge as dominant? What power resources do leaders possess? Which roles within the organization are considered as elite? How are women regarded? What roles do they occupy? Terrorist groups are organized differently; some are rigid hierarchies, others are extremely decentralized. These factors may determine or be determined by psychological interactions. Ideological differences may also affect authority patterns; right-wing extremists would be expected to be hierarchical, for example.

The content and structure of the collective belief system as well as the way it is formed are important elements in the process of terrorism. Are these beliefs complex or simple, flexible or rigid? Even when interviews are not possible, statements and literature can be evaluated in terms of dominant beliefs, symbols, myths, ideological references, scripts, metaphors, views of history, and images. Given that many of the organizations we study are long-lived, we can analyze changes in expressed beliefs over time. While recognizing that the relationship between genuinely felt beliefs and public expression of convictions is difficult to measure, we must also ask whether public rhetoric is internalized or articulated as a rationalization. Most important is the question of whether the beliefs of the users of terrorism differ in any appreciable way from the beliefs of political actors who do not use terrorism.

If there is confirmation for the hypothesis that a distinctive collective belief system exists, to what extent do these attitudes depart from objective standards of rationality or strategic behavior? What detaches the group, and with it the individual, from reality? Is it true that the longer a group exists, the less its members appreciate alternatives and consequences? Which groups are likely to entertain the fantastical conceptions of warfare with the state that Franco Ferracuti has noted among Italian left-wing groups?

Important ingredients of collective attitudes are the perception of the government and the expectation of government response to terrorism. For example, do terrorists expect and even need hostility? Is terrorism fundamentally a provocative act? Or, from the terrorists' viewpoint, is terrorism a defensive response to perceived injustice?

A related question concerns the contagion effects of terrorism. To what extent is terrorism imitative? If terrorists act not in response to their own circumstances but to the example set by others, we must identify the relevant external reference groups. For example, terrorist groups in Western democracies frequently model themselves after third-world revolutionaries.

Society and the causes of terrorism

Few analysts hold the view that terrorism is structurally produced. Theories of collective political violence that attribute it exclusively to the environment—to class structure, economic disparities, or patterns of discrimination—do not seem immediately applicable to terrorism, which is not mass action. Few of the people exposed to the same situation react with terrorism.

Nevertheless, without assigning undue causal significance to social forces, it is still important to trace the links between background conditions and the incidence of terrorism. Do terrorists reflect society or deviate from the norm? What are the class backgrounds of terrorists? Do patterns of leadership and authority within terrorist organizations mirror those found in the wider society? Processes of socialization affect susceptibility to the attractions of terrorism, ability to overcome moral restraint or fear of the costs, and collective beliefs. In nationalist or separatist groups in particular, the influence of history and family traditions may be decisive. The role of political culture is significant in bringing meaningful symbols and narratives to the individual's attention. Whether people rebel in an effort to seek social approval or to reject the establishment, their rebellion still reflects prevailing values.

Furthermore, sustained terrorism is not possible without a certain level of popular support. What are the environmental sources of support for terrorism? When is support withdrawn?

Government actions can be seen as part of the conflict relationship between challenger and regime or as part of the environment for terrorism. Certainly research should not ignore the possibility that governments provoke oppositional terrorism, or that they may initiate terrorist methods themselves.

Determinants of the process of terrorism

Many of the same factors that contribute to the initiation of terrorism also affect the forms it takes. Here, however, we are concerned with the operations of terrorist organizations (rather than with the inception of the strategy) and with how terrorist actions unfold. Some groups, for example, choose to act on the international level rather than restricting their violence to the domestic context. Some (the Popular Front for the Liberation of Palestine—the PFLP—for example) hijack airliners, whereas others (the Irish Republican Army—IRA) rarely engage in hostage taking or international operations. Some groups are more innovative or more brutal than others. The question is often raised as to why some groups seem more willing to sacrifice their members while others avoid risk. (Merari, in Chapter 10 of this volume, suggests that "suicidal" acts are rare.) Although some organizations have made seizing hostages or attacking civilians into a routine, others focus on military attacks that resemble conventional warfare. How can these differences be explained?

A starting point might be to examine the personality traits of leaders. During hostage seizures, the attitudes and predispositions of the captors may become critical determinants of outcomes. Much attention has been devoted to what has been called the Stockholm syndrome, a relationship of intimacy between captor and victim first observed during a bank robbery in Sweden. This theory predicts that the terrorist will become favorably disposed to a hostage over time and that the victim will come to identify with the aggressor. The applicability of this theory to hostage-taking episodes in which the perpetrators are politically motivated and intend in advance to take hostages is questionable. An alternative view of hostage seizures suggests that stress, fatigue, and the pressures of time often push hostage takers to erratic and violent behavior. Does the general pattern of relationship between hostage and captor depend on particular circumstances (e.g., length of the incident, nature of government communications, personality of the negotiator) or on the characteristics of the individual terrorists and victims and their relationships with each other?

Collective beliefs based on ideology or political culture also affect choice of method. For example, the IRA has a rigid self-image based on perceptions of history and society and the role of Irish republicanism in more than a century of political conflict. The IRA does not normally take hostages and rarely acts outside the borders of the United Kingdom and the Republic of Ireland. The organization has generally abandoned the practice of civilian bombings in favor of selective assassinations of military and police personnel. Is this apparent self-restraint based on considerations of self-image? Or is it due to a strategic calculation of the likely consequences of taking hostages or mounting operations abroad?

Terrorist organizations vary in terms of their stability (or degree of internal unity) and longevity. Many groups are torn by factionalism and disputes. Internecine rivalries may lead to the escalation of violence, as competing factions strive to outdo one another in order to gain ascendancy over a movement or a constituency. Are there psychological explanations for divisiveness? In Italy, for example, disagreements between imprisoned former leaders, who clung to their roles as authority figures, and the operational leadership on the outside provoked acrimony and division.

Another phenomenon that deserves study is brutalization as a result of participation in violence. With the passage of time does terrorism become more violent because moral restraints are eroded? Is a loss of moral inhibition more likely in certain groups or with certain types of persons? Are such persons then exploited by leaders? Alternatively, some members of terrorist organizations may become disgusted with excessive cruelty and abandon the group. Under what circumstances does moral disapproval lead to exit from the group? Are IRA apologies for "accidental" victims, for example, directed at the public or at IRA members?

Yet another question concerns how the terrorists perceive the government, an issue directly related to problems of crisis management. The conflict between the government and its challengers is a determinant of the process of terrorism. The relationship between government initiatives, whether forceful or conciliatory, and terrorist response should be studied in detail. For example, it is widely believed that giving in to terrorists' demands encourages them to continue their activities, but evidence for this proposition is weak. Nevertheless, American policymakers appear to derive satisfaction from maintaining a no-concessions stance. Is the motive for rejecting concessions actually deterrence of future terrorism? Why are hostage seizures so troubling to American officials?

A larger issue for the research agenda involves social learning. To what extent do terrorists learn from their experiences? How and why do groups adapt to changing circumstances—changes in government policy or public reactions? How do governments learn about terrorism? How do they define the threat?

The consequences of terrorism

The preceding discussion of the process of terrorism partially considered the effects of terrorism on its practitioners, at individual and group levels.

To what extent does the use of violence promote its continuation or escalation? Do the attitudes of people who use terrorism change as a result of their use of violence? Under what conditions are people either encouraged or disillusioned by their own actions? Does participation in violence lead to brutalization through the disengagement of moral restraints, and thus to continuation or escalation, or does involvement lead to disillusionment and sometimes an end to violence?

Related questions concern the effects on terrorists of the responses of government and society. What government policies produce what effects on the perceptions and actions of the groups they wish to defeat? Are concessions to terrorism incitements to further violence? Do hostile responses provide psychological rewards? Are underground groups sensitive to the effects of their actions on public opinion? Does a negative public reaction discourage terrorism? Can social rejection be attributed to the indiscriminacy of terrorist methods, to government education of the public, to the length of time that violence is experienced, to numbers of casualties, or to identities of victims?

It is often suggested that high levels of violence in a society may become self-perpetuating. If children are socialized into patterns of violence (as in Northern Ireland or Lebanon), such destructive behaviors become part of the social fabric. They are passed down from generation to generation through families, schools, and religion. Attacks on civilians may become routinized and habitual. Does this reaction, in fact, occur?

Here a distinction should be introduced between the general reaction of "society" and the responses of different segments of the populace. The difference between direct and indirect audiences is pertinent. Direct audiences are those people who identify with the physical victims of terrorism. Their vulnerability to the threat suggests likely reactions of fear and anxiety, possibly even the classic reaction of terror. Are such extreme reactions actually common? Are populations ever sufficiently intimidated by terrorism that they accede to the terrorists' demands? Or is terrorism more likely to result in a hostile backlash, as it did in West Germany, Israel, and Italy? How does terrorism produce a polarization of attitudes? Does it usually create cohesion in the direct audience? Does it result in the stereotyping of all dissenters or even all members of "out" groups as terrorists?

In contrast, indirect audiences are spectators who do not experience personal vulnerability. They may sympathize with victims, terrorists, or neither, but often they are removed from the immediate threat by physical distance as well as by virtue of their identity. To them, terrorism is drama. Feelings of curiosity, distress, or vicarious satisfaction of desires for vengeance may dominate their attitudes. Interest in terrorism may stem from the same roots as curiosity about natural disasters or violent crime. Terrorists may take on the characteristics of a mythical enemy. Is fear of terrorism related to the level of actual threat? Is it related to attitudes toward risk? Moreover, because terrorism may stimulate enthusiasm and support in some audiences, we should not forget its mobilizing potential.

We cannot study popular reactions to terrorism without analyzing the media, because in this era of instantaneous mass communications and transnational violence almost all public information about terrorism is communicated via commercial news networks. The entertainment value of terrorism as real-life drama—furnishing both suspense and pathos—is undeniable. The use of highly emotional language and references to symbols can intensify public reactions. Critics often charge that television promotes terrorism by portraying it as heroic and glamorous. Other observers deplore television's focus on the suffering of victims, which may spread panic and alarm. Despite widespread concern in the United States with the effect of televised violence on behavior, especially that of children and adolescents, there are few empirical studies of the actual role of media coverage of terrorism.

Without this context, the specific issue of how populations react to hostage seizures should be addressed. Public pressures on governments to give in to the demands of hostage takers are often thought to be irresistible. Public opinion is supposed to compel policymakers to concede to terrorist demands. Is there evidence for this proposition? Are publics in democracies preoccupied with hostages? Are the news media to blame for exploiting the issue? Are policymakers, as the products of a vulnerable society and culture, emotionally distressed by the plight of hostages, a situation the hostages' families remind them of constantly? To what extent does the personality of the policymaker determine his or her sensitivity to the sufferings of hostages?

A fundamental dilemma seems to be involved in the formulation of counterterrorism policies: How are governments to deal with adversaries that they do not see as rational? Although it might be wise to treat terrorism as only one among the many crises that the government confronts, in reality it seems that policymakers and the public regard the terrorist crisis as novel and unprecedented. There is a serious contradiction between (1) the belief that terrorists are calculating actors who will be deterred by the threat of punishment and who are engaged in the familiar occupation of "warfare" and (2) the belief that terrorists are "fanatics"—mysterious, alien, and unpredictable. These inconsistencies may make the response to terrorism susceptible to emotional judgments, misperceptions, and oversimplification. Is the issue of terrorism unusual in this regard?

A first problem, then, is to identify the beliefs about terrorism held by policymakers. What determines these beliefs and how do they, in turn, influence perceptions and actions? For example, do American policymakers seek a conceptual understanding of terrorism and its causes, or do they use analogical reasoning, comparing terrorism with familiar past cases while denying that such comparisons are valid? Do stereotypes predominate, and if so, which stereotypes? Is there a consensus of views among policymakers?

In dealing with terrorism, policymakers may easily become trapped by their own rhetoric. Leaders may use emotional symbols and metaphors in their public explanations in order to elicit popular support for policies. They then find themselves either believing their own interpretations, originally designed purely for public consumption, or unable to avoid acting as though they believed them. If acting in terms of beliefs reinforces them, then each subsequent action or policy statement increases political conviction. Circumstances and deadlines force policymakers into actions that they subsequently justify and rationalize in terms of popular and simple beliefs, such as the assumption that an aggressive Soviet Union is the sponsor of worldwide terrorism. They may then be forced into deception and subterfuge in order to disguise these policy contradictions.

Another possibility for error in policy-making may result from the propensity of decision makers to exaggerate the causal importance of their own actions, when in reality little is known about how terrorism diminishes or subsides. Government actions are only one factor in a complicated process. The temptation to regard all terrorism as directed against the United States (and as a consequence to ignore or exclude violence that is not anti-American) may be part of this psychological syndrome. By explaining terrorism exclusively as a reaction to U.S. policies and actions, policymakers overlook significant indigenous causes. As they exaggerate the importance of the threat to U.S. interests, official communications increase public apprehensions. In haste, policymakers may also discount the costs and liabilities of counterterrorist policies.

A further question concerns the direct psychological effect of terrorism on physical victims of terrorism, both former hostages and survivors of bombings or attacks. The available evidence indicates that terrorism has long-term and highly traumatic effects on many victims. In 1986, recognizing that terrorism produces extreme suffering, Congress passed legislation providing medical benefits to U.S. government employees who have been held hostage as well as to their families. In this respect, comparison of responses to terrorism with reactions to natural disaster or crime could be instructive.

In practical terms, governments and business are concerned with instructing personnel in appropriate coping mechanisms if taken hostage. What sort of advice can psychological researchers offer to people likely to be taken hostage? Is it reasonable, for example, to recommend that hostages develop a personal rapport with their captors? Or should the hostages avoid calling attention to themselves?

Conclusions

The scope of the research agenda for psychological inquiry into terrorism is broad, because psychologically based models of politics are concerned (even if implicitly) with motivation, that is, the sources of behavior and attitudes—a subject that is at the center of explanations of terrorism. At the same time, psychological variables must be integrated with environmental factors in order to reach a comprehensive theory. What is the weight of psychological mechanisms in the decision-making process for both governments and opposition groups?

Applying psychological analysis to terrorism is not a dismissal of terrorism as irrational or an insistence that emotions predominate in political behavior. Even the most extreme of political actors are capable of thinking rationally at least some of the time. Studies of criminal, cult, and gang behavior offer interesting comparisons. Cognitive psychology and the use of information-processing frameworks can provide rich insights into political behavior, including terrorism. A psychological approach need not deny that political commitment is a strong motivation or that terrorist calculations can be logical.

In general, there is a need for more comparative research, and for more cumulative research patterns. Too few researchers in the field of terrorism build on the work of others. The quest for theoretical generalization should be balanced with attention to detail. Access to data will always be a problem, but not to the extent of curtailing inquiry.

Last, researchers should recognize that terrorism is not an abstract intellectual problem, interesting only to a small community of scholars. It is a sensational current event, which means that as the opportunities for obtaining funding for scholarly research increase, so also do the discomforts associated with being at the center of a noisy, sometimes irresponsibly conducted, controversy. Unfortunately, if serious researchers ignore the public debate, the field will be left to simplistic rhetoric and confused assumptions. The knowledge that can be gained through research can clarify popular conceptions and educate policymakers. Demystification of terrorism is one of the most important public contributions the psychological approach could make.

14

Understanding terrorist behavior:
The limits and opportunities of
psychological inquiry

WALTER REICH

Several aspects of terrorism seem susceptible to psychological inquiry—the effects of terrorism on its victims, for example, and the behaviors of both terrorists and authorities during hostage negotiations. But the aspect of terrorism that seems most susceptible of all to such inquiry—that, for better or worse, almost begs for it—is the psychology of the terrorists themselves: their developments, motivations, personalities, decision-making patterns, behaviors in groups, and, some would argue, psychopathologies. Certainly, the public has turned to psychiatrists and psychologists regularly, particularly after witnessing especially violent terrorist acts, to explain this aspect of terrorist behavior; and psychiatrists and psychologists, just as regularly, have rushed to give explanations, sometimes without even being asked.

But susceptible as terrorists' motivations and personalities may be, in principle, to psychological inquiry, such inquiry, in practice, is regularly beset by problems that, in devious but powerful ways, limit, undermine, or even vitiate it—problems that, in the main, stem from too exclusive a focus on psychology itself or too narrow a definition of it. This chapter focuses on some of those problems and, when possible, suggests ways in which they can be avoided or overcome.

Overgeneralization

Persons and groups have carried out terrorist acts for at least two thousand years. During that considerable span of human experience, such acts have been carried out by an enormously varied range of persons with an enormously varied range of beliefs in order to achieve an enormously varied range of ends—including, in the case of at least one terrorist group, as I note later, no end at all. Even if we are careful to include in our historical catalogue of terrorist acts only those that satisfy one contemporary, restrictive definition of the term—let's choose, for our purposes here, the State Department's definition, which, in recent years, has been "premeditated, politically-motivated violence perpetrated against noncombatant targets by subnational groups or clandestine state agents, normally intended to influence an audience"—the list we can produce is breathtaking in its variety and scope. Given this variety and scope, it would be foolish to believe that many psychological principles can be adduced that apply to and explain all of the entries on the list.

To be sure, terrorism is not nearly so broad and universal a phenomenon as, say, violence or war—phenomena that occur under such astonishingly varied circumstances and for such astonishingly varied reasons that few would even dream of offering a single, overarching psychological theory to explain them all. Still, terrorism is so varied and complex a phenomenon that it should give pause to anyone whose aim it is to understand it—or, to be more precise, whose aim it is to understand the many different terrorisms that the deceptively singular term covers.

Yet psychological accounts of terrorism are replete with explanations that ignore or blur the variety and the complexity.[1] Blanket statements, some of which will be cited later, tend to be made that attribute certain characteristics to "terrorists" with the implication that all terrorists, of whatever variety, possess them. In part, it is a problem of semantics: It is always hard for writers to remind readers that only one particular group of terrorists is being discussed and not all of them through recorded history. But that is probably too generous an explanation for this penchant for psychological overgeneralization about terrorism. Too often overgeneralization is a product of loose and weak thinking, a disregard for the need for evidence, and the habit, unfortunately endemic in so many areas of psychological discourse, of having a single idea and applying it to everything.

Even the briefest review of the history of terrorism reveals how varied and complex a phenomenon it is, and therefore how futile it is to at-

---

[1] See H. H. A. Cooper, "What Is a Terrorist: A Psychological Perspective," *Legal Medical Quarterly* 1 (1977): 16–32; H. H. A. Cooper, "Psychopath as Terrorist: A Psychological Perspective," *Legal Medical Quarterly* 2 (1978): 188–97.

tribute simple, global, and general psychological characteristics to all terrorists and all terrorisms.

Some of the earliest terrorist campaigns were carried out in an arena that has seen so many of them in recent years, the zone now known as the Middle East. Perhaps the most striking of these campaigns was the one carried out by two Jewish groups during the first century A.D., the Zealots and the Sicarii. Their primary goal was to inspire popular insurrection among Judea's Jews against its Roman occupiers, an insurrection that would result not in a compromise with the occupiers but in total rebellion. A second purpose, perhaps no less assiduously pursued, was to cleanse Jewish religious institutions and society of persons too closely aligned with Roman and Hellenistic ways. The method used by the Sicarii, or daggermen, was assassination. As Josephus describes it:

The Sicarii committed murders in broad daylight in the heart of Jerusalem. The holy days were their special seasons when they would mingle with the crowd carrying short daggers concealed under their clothing with which they stabbed their enemies. Thus, when they fell, the murderers joined in cries of indignation, and through this plausible behavior, were never discovered. The first assassinated was Jonathan, the high-priest. After his death there were numerous daily murders. The panic created was more alarming than the calamity itself; nearly everyone, as on the battlefield, hourly expected death. Men kept watch at a distance on their enemies and would not trust even their friends when they approached.[2]

The goals of the Zealots and of the Sicarii were clearly political—they wanted an end to Roman subjugation—and depended on the belief that extraordinary actions were necessary in order to rouse a passive or corrupted populace. But their goals were also religious, and depended on the belief that such actions not only were justified on religious grounds but would even bring on divine intervention.

Another early terrorist movement in the Middle East, that of the Assassins, also had political goals, but these were ultimately designed to serve primarily religious ends. Active from the eleventh through the thirteenth century A.D., the Assassins, whose origins were in Shia Islam, believed that Islam had been corrupted; and, also using daggers, they assassinated Muslim leaders who, they believed, represented and propa-

---

[2] Josephus, *The Jewish War*, in *Works* (London: Heinemann [Loeb Classical Library], 1926), quoted in David C. Rapoport, "Fear and Trembling: Terrorism in Three Religious Traditions," *American Political Science Review* 78, no. 2 (1984): 658–77. On the Zealots and Sicarii, see also S. J. D. Cohn, *Josephus in Galilee and Rome* (Leiden: Brill, 1979); David C. Rapoport, "Introduction: Religious Terror," in *The Morality of Terrorism: Religious and Secular Justification,* edited by David C. Rapoport and Yonah Alexander (New York: Pergamon, 1982); and M. Smith, "Zealots and Sicarii: Their Origins and Relations," *Harvard Theological Review* 64 (1971): 1–19.

gated that corruption. They sought not only the death of their enemies but also the publicity that the assassinations excited—publicity that, they hoped, would result in attention to their cause, recognition that it was just, and the bringing about of a new, cleansed, and revitalized theological and social order.[3]

The era of modern terrorism is usually said to have begun in the nineteenth century with the rise, in Russia, of the *Narodnaya Volya* (People's Will). In 1879, that party's program spoke of "destructive and terroristic activity," and its methods, which involved assassination of Tsarist officials in the hope of provoking Russian society into revolution, were opposed by later Russian revolutionaries, particularly the Bolsheviks, who believed that revolution could be attained successfully not by "individual terror" carried out by a small elite of intellectuals but by class struggle carried out by the masses. Such individual terror came to be called "propaganda by the deed"[4]—that is, the method, using extreme acts, by which the masses would be stirred not only to understand the depth of their subjugation but also the vulnerability of the authorities. As Peter Kropotkin puts it:

By actions which compel general attention, the new idea seeps into people's minds and wins converts. One such act may, in a few days, make more propaganda than thousands of pamphlets. Above all, it awakens the spirit of revolt; it breeds daring. . . . Soon it becomes apparent that the established order does not have the strength often supposed. One courageous act has sufficed to upset in a few days the entire governmental machinery, to make the colossus tremble. . . . The people observe that the monster is not so terrible as they thought . . . hope is born in their hearts.[5]

But repression, such a terrorist hopes, is born in the hearts of the authorities. They react fiercely, Kropotkin predicts; the masses suffer terribly, become enraged, and respond with revolution.

For many anarchists, terror itself was an end; indeed, one anarchist group in Russia during the revolution of 1905–7 advocated *bezmotivniy terror* (unmotivated terror).[6] For anarchists, the invention of dynamite introduced an era of exciting destructive possibilities in which individuals

---

[3] See Rapoport, "Fear and Trembling," 658–77. See also Bernard Lewis, *The Assassins: A Radical Sect in Islam* (London: Weidenfeld and Nicholson, 1967).
[4] This term was probably first used in the declaration of the Italian Federation of the Anarchist International of 3 December 1876. See Ze'ev Iviansky, "Individual Terror: Concept and Typology," *Journal of Contemporary History* 12 (1977): 43–63.
[5] Peter Kropotkin, "The Spirit of Revolt," in *Revolutionary Pamphlets* (New York, 1968), 35–43, quoted in Iviansky, "Individual Terror," 43–63.
[6] See Walter Reich, "Serbsky and Czarist Dissidents," *Archives of General Psychiatry* 40 (1983): 697–8.

could be, in their actions, as powerful as governments. Some anarchists advocated violence aimed not just at authorities but also at the general public, particularly those parts of it, such as the bourgeoisie, who could be identified as supporting the existing order merely because they profited from it. "There are no innocents," Emile Henry, the young French anarchist, said at his trial for throwing a bomb into the Café Terminus.

For the early Russian revolutionaries who advocated terror, however, it was to be carried out with discrimination and with clear purposes in mind. Authorities were the targets, not ordinary citizens. But even then the method had to be justified. And the justification was that the authorities' monopoly on power gave the revolutionaries no other choice, and that, in overturning mass tyranny, which was responsible for mass deaths, assassinations were actually life-saving and moral. Such terrorists, usually intellectuals, spent a great deal of time worrying about, and seeking justifications for, the moral dilemmas provoked by the method they had adopted.

During the early part of this century, as revolutionary, ideological terrorism grew strong, so did terrorism aimed at nationalist ends. Such terrorism developed great prominence in Ireland, but it was also evident in the Balkans, Armenia, and elsewhere. Between the wars, especially in the 1920s, right-wing terrorism, particularly by the Nazis and the Italian Fascists, was used to intimidate enemies and create publicity; a number of right-wing groups in Eastern Europe devolved into little more than criminal gangs.

After World War II, guerrilla warfare related to decolonization predominated, although terrorism occurred in a number of areas; for example, it was used by the Irgun and the Stern Gang in mandate Palestine. But in the 1960s and 1970s terrorism of several varieties once again became a frequent occurrence in a number of geographic zones. In Western Europe and Latin America it was, and remains, heavily left wing; one 1986 communiqué by a Belgian left-wing terrorist group, the Fighting Communist Cells, restated, for the thousandth time, and in the same apocalyptic, incendiary language used in previous ideological iterations, such terrorism's goal: the resumption of combat so that "the spark sets the plain ablaze, so that the class struggle burns down history."[7] Elsewhere, nationalist-separatist terrorism was prominent among the Palestinians, Basques, Armenians, Croatians, Sikhs, Tamils, and others. And

---

[7] James M. Markham, "Terrorists Put Benign Belgium Under Mental Siege," *New York Times*, 6 February 1986, p. A-2.

the IRA continued its campaign against the British, now the oldest terrorist campaign in the world. Recently, in the 1980s, terrorism in the
name of another cause, religion, reemerged with particular force and ardor in the Middle East, primarily in Lebanon and Iran, with its special
characteristics and justifications, thus bringing the history of terrorism
full circle to its beginnings in that convulsed corner of the world.

Certainly, a number of themes and characteristics are shared by many
of the terrorist groups and movements mentioned in this short history;
the goals of achieving terror and publicity for the cause are shared by
nearly all of them. But one searches with difficulty, and probably in vain,
for psychological qualities that are shared by all or nearly all of the terrorists and terrorist groups mentioned here. The constellation of psychological qualities that may characterize West European terrorists, such as
the Red Army Faction of West Germany, Direct Action of France, and
the Red Brigades of Italy, is probably quite different from the ones that
characterize or characterized, say, the followers of Abu Nidal or the
members of the Palestinian Front for the Liberation of Palestine, the Armenian ASALA, the Basque ETA, the Shi'ite groups, the Croats, or even
the leftist terrorists in Latin America, such as the Tupamaros of Uruguay,
the Shining Path of Peru, the Montoneros of Argentina, or the M-19 of
Colombia. Indeed, even within the United States, the qualities that may
have characterized the Weatherman group were no doubt different from
the ones that characterized the black members of the Symbionese Liberation Army. And regarding fundamental attitudes toward one of the central facets of terrorism—violence—different terrorist groups, even those
that have shared the "left wing" designation, have, across the decades,
varied enormously. Thus, the *Narodnaya Volya* tortured themselves about
the snuffing out of any life, even that of a hated government official,
whereas modern-day leftist terrorists, as well as most others both now
and in the past, have managed to justify easily almost any killings, even
of the most indubitably innocent souls.

Moreover, the terrorist groups themselves shift in character. Some terrorist groups that were once on the right have ended up on the left, and
vice versa; and most are, in fact, mixtures of types, such as leftist nationalists, rightist nationalists, religious nationalists, and so on. In terrorism,
there are many mixed and borderline conditions.[8]

---

[8] For an extended and rich discussion of the many varieties of terrorism and of the ways in
   which various terrorist movements have undergone radical changes over time, see Walter
   Laqueur, *The Age of Terrorism* (Boston: Little, Brown, 1987).

The lesson that the psychological researcher must draw from the long history of the terrorist enterprise, and especially from its variety and complexity, applies not only to the study of individual terrorists but also to the study of the terrorist groups themselves. Like individual terrorists, the groups to which they belong, and ultimately the communities from which those groups arise, are not necessarily alike in their psychological characteristics, even if they share certain goals or orientations.

Religiously oriented or nationalist terrorists, for example, are driven by forces and shaped by circumstances that are usually specific to particular religious or nationalist experiences—experiences that lend powerfully determining characteristics to those particular groups. Why else have some nationalities with deep feelings of having been wronged by history or by other nationalities, such as the Palestinians, Basques, Armenians, and Croatians, given rise to groups that carry out terrorism in order to right those wrongs, whereas other nationalities that have been wronged, such as the Germans who were displaced from Eastern Europe after World War II and many other nationalities that lost parts of their homeland or were never permitted a homeland, have not? And why have some terrorist movements persisted in their efforts for decades whereas others have not?

Clearly, differences in the political circumstances surrounding those groups, as well as in the responses given to their grievances and actions, have played important roles in determining the nature, momentum, and success of their terrorist efforts. But no less important have been the particular characteristics of terrorist groups themselves. However similar such groups may be, they are usually, in significant ways, also very different; and, as in the cases of individual terrorists, the differences are probably at least as telling as the similarities.

Reductionism

Closely related to the problem of overgeneralization is the problem of reductionism: Just as it is easy, and usually unjustified, to attribute specific characteristics to a wide range of terrorists and terrorist groups, so it is easy, and usually unjustified, to attribute all or much of terrorist behavior to one or another specific cause. Yet this has often been done, and occasionally it still is.

In the 1870s, as terrorism was gaining strength not only in Russia but also in Italy, Cesare Lombroso, who believed that criminality in general was a congenital condition, attributed terrorist behavior, and in particular bomb throwing, to pellagra and other vitamin deficiencies. At the same time, other authorities examined the connection between terrorism and barometric pressure, moon phases, alcoholism, droughts, and cranial measurements.[9]

A century later, some authors have returned to biological causes to explain terrorist violence. David G. Hubbard, a psychiatrist, has suggested that there may be a connection between inner-ear vestibular function and terrorism.[10] He has also suggested that terrorism may be partly a result of the levels of certain chemicals in the brains of terrorists, specifically norepinephrine, acetylcholine, and endorphins.[11] Paul Mandel, a biochemist at the Center for Neurochemistry in Strasbourg, having studied the inhibitory effects of gamma-aminobutyric acid (GABA) and serotonin on violence in rats, extrapolated his findings to terrorism. He suggested recently, in a newspaper interview, that emotional self-stimulation can lower brain serotonin levels so as to promote the violence associated with religious fanaticism, and that the Ayatollah Khomeini "suppressed his GABA and serotonin levels through religious excitation . . . and now there's no inhibition." According to the newspaper, Mandel believes that the ayatollah would have benefited from drug treatment.[12]

Presumably, not only would the ayatollah have benefited if he had taken drugs, but so would Iraq, Kuwait, the whole Persian Gulf, the thousands of Iranian Revolutionary Guards reportedly blown up while holding their plastic keys to Paradise, and, not least, the Western hos-

[9] Cesare Lombroso and R. Laschi, *Le Crime Politique et les Révolutions* (Paris, 1982), passim. The ideas of Lombroso regarding the physical causes of terrorism, as well as those of others, are discussed in Laqueur, *Age of Terrorism*, 151.

[10] David G. Hubbard, "Terrorism and Protest," *Legal Medical Quarterly* 2 (1978): 188–97.

[11] David G. Hubbard, "The Psychodynamics of Terrorism," in *International Violence*, edited by Y. Alexander and T. Adeniran (New York: Praeger, 1983), 45–53. For research on the relationship between dopamine, norepinephrine, acetylcholine, and aggression in animals, see Louis J. West, "Studies of Aggression in Animals and Man," *Psychopharmacology Bulletin* 13 (1977): 14–25.

[12] Quoted in Jon Franklin, "Criminality Is Linked to Brain Chemistry Imbalances," *Baltimore Evening Sun*, 30 July 1984. For both animal and human studies on the relationship between GABA, serotonin, and aggression in both animals and human beings, see Gerald L. Brown and Frederick K. Goodwin, "Human Aggression—A Biological Perspective," in *Unmasking the Psychopath*, edited by W. H. Reid et al. (New York: W. W. Norton, 1986); Gerald L. Brown, Frederick K. Goodwin, and William E. Bunney, Jr., "Human Aggression and Suicide: Their Relationship to Neuropsychiatric Diagnosis and Serotonin Metabolism," in *Serotonin in Biological Psychiatry*, edited by B. T. Ho et al. (New York: Raven Press, 1982), 287–307.

tages who fell into the hands of the Iranian-inspired Hizballah in Lebanon.

Less reductionistic but still problematic efforts have been made to attribute much of terrorism to mental illness—efforts reviewed by Corrado.[13] Two authors, for example, have expressed the view that terrorists are psychopaths.[14] Certainly, terrorist groups reside at the fringes of the societies they inhabit, and it stands to reason that those groups might preferentially attract persons with various mental illnesses so that the proportion of their membership that is made up of the mentally ill might be higher than that proportion in the general population. It seems clear, however, that the proportion is not strikingly high, and that terrorists do not, in general, suffer from mental illnesses either of a psychotic or other type.[15] To be sure, Ferracuti and Bruno, in studying the prevalence of mental illness among Italian terrorists during the 1970s, found more among members of right-wing groups than among members of left-wing groups;[16] but even among those terrorists, psychopathology does not appear to be the primary source of terrorist motivation or activity.

Nor does that constellation of characteristics long sought but still not found, the "terrorist personality," appear to account for terrorist behavior; indeed, it almost certainly does not exist. The most exhaustive interview studies of terrorists ever carried out, sponsored by the West German Ministry of the Interior and involving 227 left-wing West German terrorists and 23 right-wing extremists, revealed a number of patterns in the personal histories of the subjects that seemed significantly more common among them than among other West Germans of their age—patterns such as the loss, at an early age, of one or both parents, severe conflicts with authorities, and frequent episodes of school and work failures.[17] But other

---

[13] R. R. Corrado, "A Critique of the Mental Disorder Perspective of Political Terrorism," *International Journal of Law and Psychiatry* 4 (1981): 293–310. Heskin has come to this conclusion also regarding IRA terrorists; see K. Heskin, *Northern Ireland: A Psychological Analysis* (New York: Columbia University Press, 1980).

[14] See Cooper, "What Is a Terrorist," 16–32, and K. I. Pearce, "Police Negotiations," *Canadian Psychiatric Association Journal* 22 (1977): 171–4.

[15] W. Rasch, "Psychological Dimensions of Political Terrorism in the Federal Republic of Germany," *International Journal of Law and Psychiatry* 2 (1979): 79–85.

[16] F. Ferracuti and F. Bruno, "Italy: A Systems Perspective," in *Aggression in Global Perspective*, edited by A. P. Goldstein and M. H. Segall (Elmsford, N.Y.: Pergamon, 1983).

[17] G. Schmidtchen, "Terroristische Karrieren: Soziologische Analyse anhand von Fahndungsunterlagen und Prozessakten" ["Terrorist Careers: Sociological Analysis Based on Investigation and Trial Documents"], in *Analysen zum Terrorismus [Analysis of Terrorism]*, edited by H. Jäger, G. Schmidtchen, and L. Süllwold (Opladen: Westdeutscher Verlag, 1981), vol. 2, *Lebenslauf-Analysen [Biographical Analysis]*.

patterns—in particular, two personality constellations, one consisting of extreme dependence on the terrorist group, extroversion, a parasitic life-style, and stimulus seeking and the other consisting of hostility, suspiciousness, aggressiveness, and self-defensiveness—also are described in the study[18] and are difficult to compare with the patterns for other persons of the same age who live at society's edge.

In any case, these patterns of individual history or personality, even if they could be demonstrated to be characteristic of these particular kinds of terrorists—a demonstration that has not been accomplished—are unlikely to be characteristic of other terrorists from other groups. The paths to a life of terrorism appear to be quite different in different societies and different types of groups. If any "terrorist personality" reliably could be found among West German leftists, it probably would be very different from the typical personalities (if such typical personalities were in fact to exist) of Middle Eastern terrorists of the nationalist or religious sort, and even different from leftist terrorists in Latin America.

Other attempts at attributing terrorist behaviors, in some blanket way, to particular psychological mechanisms, processes, or characteristics also seem to be without foundation. It is unlikely, for example, as Corrado has noted, that "narcissism" explains the terrorism of even a small number of ideologically radical groups,[19] or that the death wish does, either.[20]

Even attempts to explain, on the basis of one or another motivation, certain very stylized, specific terrorist acts by specific populations in specific places—in particular, suicide car bombings by Shi'ites against Israelis in southern Lebanon—ultimately have been shown to be wrong, or only partly true. To be sure, some of those bombers probably were quite ready to blow themselves up in a holy act of explosive, Paradise-seeking martyrdom. But in the case of at least one such about-to-be suicide car bomber, a sixteen-year-old Shi'ite from Beirut's southern suburbs who was apprehended by the Israelis just before he was about to drive the lethal car that had been prepared for him, the motivation was not religious. Rather, he was coerced by officials of the Shi'ite militia, who used threats against his family. The last thing the secular boy wanted to do, it

[18] Süllwold, "Stationen in der Entwicklung von Terroristen: Psychologische Aspekte Biographischer Daten" [Stages in the Development of Terrorists: Psychological Aspects of Biographical Data], in Analysen zum Terrorismus, edited by Jäger, Schmidtchen, and Süllwold, vol. 2.

[19] See Christopher Lasch, The Culture of Narcissism (New York: W. W. Norton, 1979), 154, and Gustave Morf, Terror in Quebec: Case Studies of the F.L.Q. (Toronto: Clarke, Irwin, 1970), 107, quoted in R. R. Corrado, "A Critique," 293–310.

[20] See Cooper, "What Is a Terrorist," 16–32, and "Psychopath as Terrorist," 253–62.

turns out, was to kill himself—either for Allah or for anyone or anything else.[21]

Inadequate appreciation of the palpable and psychic rewards of belonging to terrorist groups

Just as there is a psychology of needs, so there is a psychology of rewards. Certainly, a life of terrorism can satisfy needs such as support and approval from other members of the terrorist group, opportunities for violence, lashing out against the world of one's parents, and many others of which most of us would not be proud.

But there are other things that a life of terrorism can provide that, although they may also be things of which most of us would not be proud, may play a significant role in the decision of some terrorists to join terrorist groups—things such as power, prestige, privilege, and even wealth. These things, described pungently in an essay by Conor Cruise O'Brien,[22] are attractive to young people from impoverished backgrounds—backgrounds of the sort that are common in many zones of terrorist conflict, such as the Middle East and Northern Ireland—and together serve as a powerful impetus for many of these people to join terrorist groups. They are especially accessible to terrorists in cultures that have a long and persistent revolutionary tradition—cultures in which terrorist traditions have popular roots.

And the rewards of joining can be enormously satisfying. In some groups, terrorism can provide a route for advancement, an opportunity for glamour and excitement, a chance at world renown, a way of demonstrating one's courage, and even a way of accumulating wealth.[23] No

[21] Thomas J. Friedman, "Boy Says Lebanese Recruited Him as Car Bomber," *New York Times*, 14 April 1985, p. 1. For a general discussion of the motivations of suicide bombers, see Chapter 10 in this volume.

[22] Conor Cruise O'Brien, "Thinking About Terrorism," *Atlantic Monthly* (June 1986), 62–6.

[23] The annual budgets of a number of terrorist organizations now exceed the budgets of some small states. According to Laqueur (*The Age of Terrorism*, 102), in 1975 the annual budget of Fatah was $150 million to $200 million (in 1980 dollars), with other Palestinian factions gathering their own millions; the IRA's budget was, in the same year, $1 million to $3 million; and the budgets of each of several South American groups, raised from the sales of illicit drugs, were $50 million to $150 million in 1985. With such sums changing hands in clandestine ways, significant amounts are bound to reach the pockets of people at least as interested in comforts as in selfless causes. Even George Ibrahim Abdullah, the Christian Lebanese terrorist for whose release from a French prison his friends and relatives engineered a wave of Paris bombings in September 1986, devolved, according to his neighbors in the Lebanese village of Qobayat, from a nationalist idealist into a fighter not for a cause but for wealth. Referring to Abdullah's group, one

small advantages, these, and almost totally unstudied by researchers seeking to understand why terrorists become terrorists, and why they continue to do what they do.

Psychologizing motivations that are understandable enough when discussed in everyday language

"Hatred," "revulsion," "revenge"—these terms characterize precisely the feelings and motivations of many terrorists. Somehow, they seem too human for psychiatrists and psychologists to use in scientific discourse. But used they should be. Using them brings us closer to the psychological states of many terrorists, and to what they want, than using the milder terms with which we may feel more comfortable, such as "anger" or "frustration"—terms that convey a lesser sense of some terrorists' moods and convictions.[24]

These nonprofessional but accurate descriptive terms should be used

neighbor told a reporter, "They were once idealists and now they do it all for money." See Nora Boustany, "The Christian Village That Spawned the Paris Bombers," *Washington Post*, 26 October 1986. On the tendency that develops among some terrorists to accumulate precisely the material goods whose accumulation they despise in others, see Michael Baumann, *Terror or Love: Bommi Baumann's Own Story of His Life as a West German Urban Guerrilla* (New York: Grove Press, 1979), p. 104.

[24] For examples of what appear to be hatred, revulsion, and revenge as the primary goals of various terrorist groups and acts, see Thomas L. Friedman, "Armed and Dangerous: A Mideast Consumed by the Politics of Revenge," *New York Times*, 5 January 1986, sec. 4, p. 1, about Abu Nidal and some other Palestinian groups.

In the case of Abu Nidal and his organization, Jerrold Post's thesis that "the cause is not the cause" seems apt. (See Chapter 2 in this volume.) According to this thesis, the official, political goals of the organization, as publicized as they may be, are less important than the goal of maintaining the existence of the terrorist organization itself. Post's thesis is strengthened, I think, by an appreciation of the central roles that such feelings as hatred and revenge have come to play in the ethos of some terrorist groups—roles that have displaced, and even rendered irrelevant, most of the original nationalist ones. However, whereas Abu Nidal might not stop terrorism even if the Palestinians were to achieve a state that displaced not only all of Israel but also every other country in the Middle East, most terrorist groups probably ultimately could be satisfied enough by the achievement of their goals to stop their terrorism, despite their current feelings of hatred and vengefulness—although what they might consider satisfactory achievements may require from their adversaries comprises that, for them, would add up to nothing less than political or national suicide. Thus, feelings of hatred and desire for revenge are shared by many terrorists, and these feelings probably increase the difficulty the terrorists may have, for other reasons, in stopping their terrorism. For a small percentage of these terrorists, however, those feelings probably constitute the residue of the nationalist and idealist goals for which they adopted a life of terrorism in the first place.

For a specific example of terrorist actions that appeared to observers to be explicable only in terms of a logic of hatred, revenge, and the need to commit violence, see Don Podesta, "Terror for Terror's Sake: Motive Missing in Egyptair Hijacking," *Washington Post*, 1 December 1985, p. A-1.

in psychiatric discourse because they are true, and because they can help explain, in some cases, the continuation of terrorism even after significant demands have been satisfied. Terrorists' frustration may be lessened by such achievements, but the hatred, the revulsion, and especially the desire for revenge may not. Therefore, these motivations may continue to spur the terrorist enterprise even after many demands have been satisfied.

Even psychiatrists and psychologists accustomed to professional language should, in this very human arena, use the most powerfully human terms. The words we use in discussing a subject affect the way in which we think about it. If we use words like "hatred," "revulsion," and "revenge" rather than "anger," "opposition," and "desire for political change," we may better understand the kinds of responses that need to be constructed to contend with the impulse and reality of terrorism.

Our own impulses—the preference for compromise, say, and for reason—may produce pallid rejoinders to demands that are, in many cases, apocalyptic. The language we use in discussing and examining terrorist groups should reflect with fidelity the reality of their members' inner lives and provide us with a realistic sense of which responses, in which cases, might be effective in reducing terrorism, and which might not.

Ignoring rational reasons for choosing a terrorist strategy

Many terrorist groups routinely offer strategic, logical reasons to explain their use of terrorism; and many people who study terrorism just as routinely prefer to believe that those reasons are only covers for the real reasons, which must derive solely or primarily from deep needs. Sometimes they do—but rarely solely, and sometimes not even primarily.

Numerous declarations and memoirs by terrorists going back to the nineteenth century provide rationales for the adoption of terrorist strategies, such as the assertion that terrorism is an efficient revolutionary method, and perhaps the only one, that can be used by a weak force against a powerful regime.[25] Many of these rationales are summarized

[25] See, for example, the following documents and works: Peter Kropotkin, "Programma Ispolnitel'novo Komiteta" [Program of the Executive Committee], in *Literatura Sotsial'no Revolutsionnoi Partii 'Narodnoi Voli'* [*Literature of "The People's Will" Social Revolutionary Party*] (Paris, 1905); Nikolai Morozov, *Terroristicheskaya Bor'ba* [*The Terrorist Struggle*] (London, 1880); Michel Confino, *Violence dans la Violence* (Paris: F. Maspero, 1973); Carlos Marighella, *Mini Manual of the Urban Guerilla* (London, 1971); Menachem Begin, *The Revolt* (Los Angeles: Nash, 1972); Leila Kadi, *Basic Political Documents of the Armed Palestinian Resistance Movement* (Beirut: Palestine Liberation Or-

by Martha Crenshaw in Chapter 1 of this volume and elsewhere.[26] In general, it should be remembered that, although these rationales are the rationales of terrorists, and although what they often rationalize is acts of indiscriminate murder, the rationales may make strategic sense. To the extent that they do, psychological research should not ignore them. Strategic logic can spur actions no less powerfully than emotional logic.

Inaccessibility to direct research on terrorists

Many terrorists believe, for good reason, that any attempt to explain their motivations in psychological terms diminishes the validity of their ideas, their actions, and their beings. If they are serious in their commitment to their causes and have no illusions that they can convert to their views the researcher who asks to meet with them—a researcher who is likely to be seen as a representative of the government, society, or class against which they have organized their actions—they are likely to refuse to meet with that researcher, even if they are languishing in prison with nothing else to do. Agreement to meet with a psychiatrist or psychologist is more likely to occur when the terrorists have already begun to have doubts about their decision to adopt a terrorist career; and, in such cases, the information provided, as rich as it may be, is inevitably affected by the change in psychological orientation.

Ignoring state terrorism and the destructive acts of Western governments

Critics, especially critics on the political left, object to terrorist studies in part on the grounds that they tend to ignore (for reasons of ideological convenience, they often argue) the kind of terrorism that has produced more destruction than any other: the terrorism carried out by states against their own people. These critics often argue that terrorism researchers have insufficient sympathies for the sources of most modern terrorist movements—the aspirations of the poor and the oppressed to shake off the yoke of colonial or capitalist rule or to end the occupation of their homelands by nations or peoples or governments that are supported by Western colonial interests.

ganization Research Center, 1969); and Charles Foley (ed.), *Memoirs of General Grivas* (London: Longman's, 1964).

[26] See Martha Crenshaw, "The Logic of Terrorism," Chapter 1 of this volume, and "The Strategic Development of Terrorism," a paper prepared for delivery at the 1985 annual meeting of the American Political Science Association, New Orleans.

As a result of this lack of sympathy, those critics argue, terrorism specialists tend to see terrorism in purely negative terms. In addition, the critics argue, because the terrorism researchers are generally members of Western societies, they are inclined to support the regimes and types of polities—namely, liberal democracies—that are the targets of so many terrorist groups, and fail to see the ways in which those regimes oppress certain minorities, classes, or national groups or support other countries that do so. Such oppression, the critics argue, constitutes a form of terrorism, a terrorism that is often far worse in its effects, scope, and ruthlessness than the acts of the substate terrorists.[27]

These arguments cannot be dismissed outright. State terrorism has certainly been the most potent and destructive form of terrorism the world has seen: Nazi Germany and the Soviet Union, to name the two regimes that have engaged in it most egregiously, have indeed amassed deaths that a near eternity of conventional substate terrorist actions could not hope to accomplish. Whether substate terrorist actions have become the focus of terrorism specialists because of an ideological preference for Western values and interests and whether such a preference distorts the effort to understand terrorism in psychological terms are, however, different matters.

For some terrorism specialists, including some who concern themselves with the psychology of terrorism, Western interests and concerns probably *are* paramount. This may be due, in part, to the fact that most of these specialists are Westerners themselves, as well as to the fact that they are well acquainted with the ravages that substate terrorism has caused. In addition, some of these specialists have been employed by their governments in the military, the police, or the foreign-affairs bureaucracies, or have worked as consultants to these organizations. In those roles they have had, as their primary responsibility, the theoretical or operational task of combating terrorist activities—a responsibility whose exercise is not promoted by the readiness to feel empathy for terrorist aspirations, whether of the revolutionary or the third-world variety.

Many researchers interested in the psychology of terrorism, however, appear to be genuinely interested in terrorism as a human activity—as a product of individual and group motivation, thinking, and interaction. Although capable of recognizing, and even having empathy for, terrorist

---

[27] A vigorously argued formulation of much of this position is contained in a 1977 review of eleven books on terrorism by Anthony Arblaster, "Terrorism: Myths, Meaning and Morals," *Political Studies* 25, no. 3 (1977): 413–24.

needs and feelings, most of them also recognize the human toll exacted by those needs and feelings as they are expressed through terrorist behavior. They are accustomed to working with individuals and groups, and so find it natural to work with substate terrorists. But they tend to feel unprepared—as a result of a lack of theory and experience, rather than ideological bias—to deal with the psychologies of leaders and nations that carry out terrorism against their own or other peoples or that are accused by one or another terrorist group, or by people sympathetic to those groups, of doing so.

In the main, the kinds of actions carried out by terrorist individuals and groups differ in character, strategy, scope, and motivation from the kinds of actions carried out by states against persons or populations who oppose, or are considered undesirable by, those states. The nature of terrorist behavior, and perhaps also the nature of the moral and psychological questions raised by that behavior, differs in the cases of state and substate terrorism and requires different methods of analysis.

The complaint that terrorism specialists, including those who study the psychology of terrorism, have a selective preference for studying one kind of terrorism rather than another is not utterly without merit. But that criticism does not necessarily render impossible the valid study of the one, and it does not facilitate the successful study of the other.

Suggestions for research

In the light of these problems, as well as the evolving nature of terrorism in our time, what should researchers do who wish to study the psychology of terrorism? Which issues should they keep clearly in mind, and which questions should they ask? A few suggestions come to mind:

1. Certainly, researchers should remember that terrorism is varied and complex and that terrorists should not be discussed as if they all have the same motivations, aims, and forms of behavior. It is precisely because it is so easy to overgeneralize and to engage in psychological reductionism that researchers should take special care to identify the individuals and groups whose behaviors they are studying, limit their explanations to those individuals and groups, define the circumstances under which those explanations are valid, and not suggest that their explanations explain more than they do.

2. A strong acquaintance with the history of terrorism seems especially important for researchers in this field; it is important for them to appre-

ciate not only the great breadth of terrorist experience but also the analogues of modern attitudes that existed in previous times. The power of history to teach by analogy has been well demonstrated by two researchers at the Rand Corporation who examined the fascination that terrorists of a hundred years ago had for the new and powerful material called dynamite, the advantages they saw in it, the ways in which they rationalized its use, and the ways in which they did, in fact, use it.[28] These researchers' goal was to consider whether terrorists' experience with dynamite, which was a superexplosive a hundred years ago, might teach us anything about the ways in which terrorists today might seek to use contemporary superexplosives—that is, nuclear ones—or other means of mass killings, such as chemical and biological weapons. They concluded that we do, in fact, have something to learn from history in this case and that millenarian terrorists consumed by a desire for revenge are probably the ones who would be most likely to use nuclear devices if they could obtain them. The study was a good and judicious use of history as a tool of analysis; more such studies are worth doing.

3. Studying the rewards of the terrorist life would add an important perspective to our understanding of terrorist motivations. The achievement of status and comfort is an attractive goal in all sectors of society, both in the West and in the East, and both in industrialized and in third-world societies. This also seems to provide powerful motivation in terrorist groups, and it deserves deeper examination.

4. Direct research on terrorists is difficult but valuable. Whenever it is possible, it should be attempted. When it is not possible, and certainly in historical cases, attention should be paid to the words that terrorists issue—memoirs, pronouncements, rationales. Although these words may be self-serving, that does not mean that they are not also, in some significant way, revealing.

5. The psychology of state terrorists is worth examining no less than is the psychology of substate terrorists. If knowledge of the latter is sketchy, knowledge of the former is even more so. People who carry out state terrorism tend to be even less available to direct study than people who carry out substate terrorism. Still, enough is available in the form of documents and witnesses to offer a substantial basis for fruitful research.

6. In any study of group psychology, it is important to consider the

---

[28] David Ronfeldt and William Sater, "The Mindsets of High-Technology Terrorists: Future Implications Form an Historical Analog," *Rand Note N-1610-SL*, prepared for Sandia Laboratories (Santa Monica, Calif.: Rand Corporation, March 1981).

nature of the group and the connections between it and the larger community of sympathy from which it arises; it makes a difference if that community is large and supports the terrorist enterprise or if it is small and unrepresentative of the larger population in whose name the terrorists claim to struggle—a population that, in fact, rejects both the terrorists and their struggle.

7. One of the chief dangers of terrorism is the destructive potential of the responses it may precipitate. In nineteenth-century terrorist writings, provocation was identified as a goal of revolutionary terrorist acts: Provoke the government to institute repressions and the population will see just how repressive and worthy of removal that government is. In this age of international terrorism, in which the United States, a superpower with nuclear weapons, is frequently targeted by groups supported by various states, some of which may, in turn, be supported by the Soviet Union, the dangers of escalation and, ultimately, large-scale death are, if remote, nevertheless serious. It may be of some value to examine just how rationally terrorists and their state sponsors think about the international consequences of their actions, and just how rationally the leaders of large countries that are the targets of terrorist actions think about the consequences of their countermeasures.

8. Why do some radical oppositionist groups become terrorist while others, under the same or similar circumstances, continue to pursue essentially peaceful means to achieve their goals? To be sure, political and strategic arguments can be adduced that show why terrorism is an effective strategy. But it is rarely the only strategy that can be pursued. What circumstances in the environment of oppositionist, not-yet-terrorist groups, or within the groups themselves, give the members of such groups the sense, at some point, that terrorism is the only possible—indeed, the necessary—choice? What role, if any, do governments play in provoking or promoting that sense? If they do play such a role, is there anything they can or should do to act in some other way so that the initial, fateful step from radical opposition to terrorism—a step examined by Ehud Sprinzak in Chapter 5 of this volume—is not taken?

9. Finally, what induces terrorists to discard their terrorist careers, if not the ideologies that spawned and sustained those careers? The experience of the Italian "penitents," described by Franco Ferracuti in Chapter 4 of this volume, is instructive; but too little is understood about this phenomenon, and more study of it would be well justified.

Being alert to these issues and asking these questions would lead to a better psychological understanding of terrorist behavior. Most important for psychological researchers is the need to remember that terrorism is a complicated, diverse, and multidetermined phenomenon that resists simple definition, undermines all efforts at objectivity, forces upon all researchers moral riddles of confounding complexity, and is as challenging to our intellectual efforts to understand it as it is to our collective efforts to control it. It is an example and product of human interaction gone awry and is worth studying and understanding in the human terms that befit it: as conflict, struggle, passion, drama, myth, history, reality, and, not least, psychology.

About the editor and contributors

ALBERT BANDURA is the David Starr Jordan Professor of Social Science in Psychology at Stanford University and the author of many works in social psychology, including *The Social Foundations of Thought and Action: A Social Cognitive Theory; Social Learning Theory; Aggression: A Social Learning Analysis; Psychological Modeling: Conflicting Theories; Principles of Behavior Modification; Social Learning and Personality Development;* and *Adolescent Aggression.* Professor Bandura, who received the Distinguished Scientist Award from the American Psychological Association and the Distinguished Contribution Award from the International Society for Research on Aggression, is a member of the American Academy of Arts and Sciences. He has been a Guggenheim fellow and a member of the editorial boards of many scientific journals, and has served as president of the American Psychological Association.

MARTHA CRENSHAW is professor of government at Wesleyan University, where she has taught international politics and foreign policy since 1974. She is the author of *Revolutionary Terrorism: The FLN in Algeria, 1954–1962* and the editor of *Terrorism, Legitimacy and Power: The Consequences of Political Violence.* Her most recent research has been on the psychology of terrorism, the internal politics of terrorist organizations, the development of terrorist strategies, and the effects of terrorism. Professor Crenshaw has held fellowships from the National Endowment for the Humanities, the Russell Sage Foundation, and the Harry Frank Guggenheim Foundation and has been a consultant for the U.S. Department of State and the U.S. Department of Defense.

FRANCO FERRACUTI is a faculty member at the University of Rome, where he is professor of criminological medicine and of forensic psychiatry, professor in the postgraduate training schools, professor of penal law, forensic medicine, and medical psychiatry, and director of the Postgraduate Training School in Clinical Criminology and Forensic Psychiatry. During 1978–81, Dr. Ferracuti was a consultant to the Italian Ministry of the Interior, which he served as an adviser on antiterrorism. He is the author of nearly two hundred publications, including many on terrorism and political violence.

TED ROBERT GURR is professor of government and politics at the University of Maryland, College Park. His dozen books and monographs on political conflict, governmental performance, and criminal justice include *Violence in America: Historical and Comparative Perspectives* (with Hugh Davis Graham), *Why Men Rebel* (winner of the Woodrow Wilson Prize as best book in political science of 1970), and *Rogues, Rebels and Reform: A Political History of Urban Crime and Conflict.* His current work is concerned with the role of the state in conflict processes and with trends in internal conflict, especially in highly stratified and segmented societies.

CHARLES F. HERMANN is the director of the Mershon Center and Mershon Professor of Political Science at the Ohio State University. He is the author of *Crisis in Foreign Policy: A Simulation Analysis,* editor of *International Crises: Insights from Behavioral Research,* and coeditor of *Why Nations Act.*

MARGARET G. HERMANN is a research scientist at the Mershon Center at the Ohio State University. She is the editor of *A Psychological Examination of Political Leaders* and *Political Psychology: Contemporary Issues and Problems,* and a coeditor of *Describing Foreign Policy Behavior.* She has been president of the International Society of Political Psychology and vice president of the International Studies Association.

KONRAD KELLEN studied law at the Universities of Heidelberg and Munich. After emigrating to the United States, he served in the U.S. Army during World War II in Europe. He served as chief of the Information Department of Radio Free Europe for eleven years, and in 1964 he joined the Rand Corporation, where he worked on problems related to national security as well as terrorism. Dr. Kellen is the author of a political biography of Khrushchev, a study of psychological warfare, and a book on the fall of Vietnam. His articles have appeared in *Foreign Affairs,* the *Yale Review,* the *New York Times Magazine,* and other publications.

MARTIN KRAMER is associate director of the Dayan Center for Middle Eastern and African Studies at Tel Aviv University. He is the author of

Islam Assembled: The Advent of the Muslim Congresses and the editor of *Protest and Revolution in Shi'i Islam* and *Shi'ism, Resistance and Revolution*, and has published many articles on Islam and, particularly, Shi'ism.

WALTER LAQUEUR is the author of *Guerrilla* and *Terrorism* as well as the *Guerrilla Reader* and *The Terrorism Reader* and the *Dawn of Armageddon*. He is cochair of the International Research Council of the Center for Strategic and International Studies and was concurrently director of the Institute of Contemporary History and the Wiener Library in London. He has been, since 1966, editor with George Mosse of the *Journal of Contemporary History*. His last academic position was that of university professor at Georgetown University. He has also taught at Harvard University, the University of Chicago, Brandeis University, Tel Aviv University, and Johns Hopkins University.

ARIEL MERARI, a psychologist, is a senior fellow and director of the Project on Terrorism at the Jaffee Center for Strategic Studies at Tel Aviv University. Dr. Merari is the author of *Shi'ite Terrorism* and is the editor of *On Terrorism and Combatting Terrorism*. He serves as a consultant to the Office of the Prime Minister of Israel and has also held positions at the University of California at Berkeley and at Stanford and Harvard universities.

JERROLD M. POST is professor of psychiatry, political psychology, and international affairs at the George Washington University. After obtaining his B.A. and M.D. degrees from Yale University, Dr. Post received his postgraduate training in psychiatry from the Harvard Medical School and the National Institute of Mental Health. Dr. Post has devoted his career to the field of political psychology, spending most of it as a research psychiatrist with the U.S. government, for which he founded and directed the Political Psychology Center. A founding member of the International Society of Political Psychology, he has been elected to its governing council and is a member of the editorial boards of the journals *Political Psychology* and *Terrorism*. Dr. Post is the author of many articles on the psychology of terrorism and of leadership.

DAVID C. RAPOPORT is professor of political science at the University of California, Los Angeles. He is the author of *Assassination and Terrorism* (the first book-length study of the two phenomena) and editor of *The Morality of Terrorism: Religious and Secular Justifications* and *The Rationalization of Terrorism*, and he has written many articles on the history of terrorism, on the relationship between terrorism and religion, on the self-perceptions of terrorists, and on military history. Professor Rapoport, who obtained his Ph.D. degree from UCLA with a dissertation that introduced the concept of "praetorianism," taught at Barnard College before joining the faculty of UCLA.

WALTER REICH, M.D., is a Senior Scholar at the Woodrow Wilson International Center for Scholars. He is former director of the United States Holocaust Memorial Museum and was Senior Research Psychiatrist at the National Institute of Mental Health. In addition to his clinical and research work in psychiatry, Reich has focused on problems in international affairs, particularly in relation to the Soviet Union and the Middle East, and is the author of *A Stranger in My House: Jews and Arabs in the West Bank.* Reich is also a contributing editor of the *Wilson Quarterly* and publishes frequently in scholarly journals as well as newspapers and magazines. He has been a fellow in the Kennan Institute for Advanced Russian Studies of the Woodrow Wilson Center, a Lustman fellow at Yale University, and the David J. Fish Memorial Lecturer at Brown University.

GARY SICK is adjunct professor of Middle East politics and visiting scholar at the Research Institute on International Change at Columbia University. He is the author of *All Fall Down: America's Tragic Encounter with Iran* and, as a Navy captain, he was on the staff of the National Security Council from 1976 to 1981, serving as the principal White House aide for Iranian affairs during the Iranian Revolution and the subsequent hostage crisis. Professor Sick writes frequently on Middle Eastern affairs, particularly about Iran, for newspapers and magazines as well as scholarly journals.

EHUD SPRINZAK is senior lecturer in political science at the Hebrew University of Jerusalem. He is the author of *Neither Law nor Order: Illegalism in Israeli Political Culture,* as well as many articles on extremism, violence, and terrorism in Israel and their effects on the condition of that country's democratic institutions. During 1985–6 Dr. Sprinzak was a fellow at the Woodrow Wilson Center. He received his B.A. and M.A. degrees from the Hebrew University and his Ph.D. degree from Yale.

Index

Abdel-Rahmen, Omar, 116
Adams, Charles J., 105
Al-Jihad
   and *The Neglected Duty*, 104–6
   objectives and activities of, 108–17
al-Amin, Ibrahim, 138, 142, 149, 151
Anarchic-ideologues
  group dynamics of, 32–3
  social origins and psychosocial dynamics of, 29–31
Anderson, Terry A., 154, 230
Arafat, Yasir, 37
Armenian Secret Army for the Liberation of Armenia (ASALA), 29–30
Armstrong, Karleton Lewis, 96
Assassinations in Egypt, 124–7, 129
Avrich, Paul, 15

Baader, Andreas, 55–6, 196
Baader-Meinhof group, 55–6, 94
Backlash, 94–7, 102
Baeyer-Kaette, W., 33
Barber, James David, 230, 235
Basque separatists, 29, 37, 38, 59, 61
Baumann, Michael, 53–4
Beckurts, Kurt, 44
Ben Barka, Mehdi, 152
Ben Bella, Ahmed, 152
Berri, Nabih, 138, 242
Bion, W., 31–2
Black Panthers, 77
Black September organization, 17–18
Blackmail, terrorist bargaining as, 21
Bollinger, L., 29
Braunmuehl, Gerold von, 44, 57
Braunstein, Y., 206
Bremer, L. Paul, 247
Bruno, F., 60–1, 269
Brzezinski, Zbigniew, 230, 238–40
Bureaucracy, nature of, 232–4

Calvert, Gregory, 75
Canadian separatism, 98–9. *See also*
   Front de Liberation du Québec
Carmichael, D. J. C., 167
Carter, Jimmy
  hostage-taking crisis under, 211, 214, 216, 218–20, 230, 237
  hostages' families and, 230, 238–40
Central Intelligence Agency, 233
Clark, R., 29, 61
Conflict of legitimacy, 81–2
Corrado, R. R., 269
Counterterrorist measures, 169
  moral justification of, 165–7
Crenshaw, Martha, 24, 26, 92, 224
Crisis
  of confidence, 80–1
  of legitimacy, 82–3
Cultural factors, suicidal terrorism and, 196–9

Defense avoidance as stress-coping mechanism, 221–3
Dehumanization, 180–2
Department of Defense, 233
Department of State, 233, 234, 262
Depersonalization in hostage-taking events, 225–7
Deterrence, 99–101
Disengagement. *See* Moral-disengagement mechanism(s)
Dissent among advisers in hostage-taking events, 228–9
Dodge, David, 149
Dohrn, Bernardine, 70

Eban, Abba, 18
Egyptian terrorists. See *Al Jihad; Nizari*
Eisenhower, Dwight D., 72
Ejercito Revolutionario del Pueblo (ERP), 23

285